Education in the Technological Society

The Vocational-Liberal Studies
Controversy in the Early
Twentieth Century

Education in the Technological Society

The Vocational-Liberal Studies Controversy in the Early Twentieth Century

ARTHUR G. WIRTH

Graduate Institute of Education
Washington University

INTEXT EDUCATIONAL PUBLISHERS
College Division of Intext
Scranton / San Francisco / Toronto / London

The Intext *Series in*

FOUNDATIONS OF EDUCATION

Consulting Editor

HERBERT M. KLIEBARD
The University of Wisconsin

ISBN 0–7002–2414–9 (cloth)
ISBN 0–7002–2398–3 (paper)

COPYRIGHT ©, 1972, BY INTERNATIONAL TEXTBOOK COMPANY

Library of Congress Catalog Card Number: 78–177303

To Marian

Foreword

In a technological society education becomes the link between every individual and his chance for a significant role in that society. What kind of education is necessary is debated today as it has been since the beginning of the industrial revolution.

"Academic or vocational," "comprehensive or dual," and "general or specialized" are still the conflict positions that attract more devotees than cool analysis. Because of the dehumanizing tendencies of technology which threaten the democratic dream and the growing pressures for people with technical skills, the debate is more important today than in the past. How can cultural renewal be accomplished within a technological society? How can individual differences be developed while learning the skills required in the system? How can the variety of aptitudes among our citizens be developed most effectively for the individual and the society? How can we integrate skill development and liberal study? Can the educational system change enough to meet the challenge of serving every person while also serving us all?

The long standing arguments of John Dewey and the vocational philosophers during the period of 1900 to 1917 have greater cogency today than at the turn of the century. The author has done an excellent job in clarifying the way in which these philosophical positions about education have truly derived from the interaction of education with society—primarily the scientific-technological explosion.

Too few educators and public policy makers are aware of the possibility of liberalizing education, increasing individual freedom and improving human values through a marriage of academic and vocational education. Can it be that the greatest change agent available to improve education lies in this union? Can we continue to believe that simply doing more efficiently what we already do in schools will be adequate? Can we imagine that simply applying technology to the methods of instruction will be an answer?

The problem as to how this nation must change its educational system to prepare individuals to control and to live more effectively in a technological society is the overriding question. Every educator who wishes to help solve this problem must understand the arguments which have been made and the societal forces which implement or kill such proposals.

Education in the Technological Society is a book which delineates the positions of the past and clarifies the arguments we face today. This book gives the backdrop of the evolving contest for the mind and heart of American education not only by the educational philosophers but by the crunching demands of pressure in a technological society. The author clearly delineates the group pressures generated in the twentieth century, the response of educators, and the philosophical issues which arise in redesigning the curriculum of American schools.

Any educator or public official who helps develop policy or programs dealing with the education of educators, or the education of our children, must understand the controversy of vocational versus liberal studies. The author states it well when he writes: "The compelling question of our time remains whether it will be possible to humanize life under technological conditions: whether democratic traditions of responsible participation can be revitalized, and whether individuals can attain a sense of personal meaning under conditions of the urban-industrial society."

It is a book to read if one is to understand the basic issue to be debated in education for the next ten years.

GRANT VENN
Director
AASA National Academy for School Executives

Washington, D.C.
October, 1971

Preface

It is not strange to find that many groups were demanding changes in the schools as we entered the twentieth century. We had to find out if persons and institutions could cope with the realities of an emerging urban-technological-corporate society.

One of the most dramatic movements for school reform, as an alternative to the literary-classical tradition, was the vocational or industrial education movement. John Dewey in *Democracy and Education* said that the chief philosophical issues in his time centered in the debate over vocational factors in education. Edward Krug in *The Shaping of the American High School* quoted an observer who said that the demand for industrial education was "a mental epidemic, much like the free-silver crusade and the Klondike gold rush."

This study is an effort to understand the responses that Americans made to the question of what kind of education they wanted for their children in the technological era. Many of the questions debated then —over the relation of liberal to vocational studies, and over which kinds of education for different social classes—turned out to be issues we have lived with ever since. An analysis of the value conflicts which surfaced may sharpen our awareness of important choices we confront today.

As I draw this study to a close I am clearly aware of the many persons who made indispensable contributions to the work. The probings of graduate students in seminars, and informal interactions with my colleagues in the Graduate Institute of Education helped to shape and clarify my understanding of the subject. I am indebted to Raymond E. Callahan of Washington University, Robert Mason of Southern Illinois University (Edwardsville), John Gadell of Wright State University, W. Richard Stephens of Indiana University, and George Axtelle of the United States International University who read the manuscript at early stages. My colleague Raymond E. Callahan, in particular, helped me see important value questions through his studies on the efficiency movement, and W. Richard Stephens sharpened my awareness of the influence of industrial education leaders in initiating school guidance programs and in sponsoring the development of junior high schools. John Gadell's doctoral study on Charles Prosser provided insight into the complexities of the vocational education movement. I am grateful to Dr. George Champlin, Director of the Center for Technological Study of San Francisco State College and to Dr. Fred Drewes, Director of the Technology for Children Project in New Jersey for their patience in explaining their own programs and for calling my attention to the reformation in industrial arts education taking place at the Ohio State University and Stout State University (Menomomie, Wisconsin).

My research assistant, Mrs. Andrea Emrich, delights in striving for clarity in English sentences. Her editorial pencil often led me to comprehend a point I was trying to make. Mrs. Hope Lamkin and the secretaries of the Graduate Institute of Education made their talents available in preparing the many revisions of the manuscript. They joined the fray on numerous occasions to help meet some new deadline or crisis.

The research upon which the study is based was made possible by financial support from the Graduate School of Arts and Sciences of Washington University and by a grant from the United States Office of Education. Dr. Laurence Goebel of the United States Office of Education was gracious and encouraging beyond the requirements of his office while I engaged in the research leading to my final Office of Education report: "The Vocational-Liberal Studies Controversy Between John Dewey and Others (1900–1917)." However, the opinions expressed are those of the author alone and do not imply endorsement by Washington University or the U.S.O.E.

My wife Marian, and Vicki, Scott, and Patty put up with my preoccupations and gave me support in times of troubles.

I wish to thank the following publishers for permission to quote passages from copyright materials which have been cited in the text: Holt, Rinehart & Winston, Inc., St. Martin's Press, Inc., The University of Wisconsin Press, E. P. Dutton & Co., Inc., Beacon Press, Saturday Review, Inc. (1968), Chas. A. Bennett Co., Inc., G. P. Putnam's Sons, Random House, Inc., The Macmillan Company, and the Labor and Public Welfare Commission, U.S. Senate.

ARTHUR G. WIRTH

St. Louis, Missouri
October, 1971

Contents

part I

American Education in the Technological Society: Issues and Initial Responses

INTRODUCTION

> The question is whether or not our beautiful libertarian, pluralist and populist experiment is viable in modern conditions.[1]

Looking at the set of forces in contention in the vocational education movement (1900–1917) we can see more than how technology acts as a pressure for institutional change. We can see something about the conflict of the two Americas we have become in the hundred years since the Civil War: the America which defines its aspirations in terms of the blind drive for an increase in material goods, and that other America which Paul Goodman has described as the "libertarian, pluralist and populist experiment."

To be blunt and to oversimplify, the choice then and now is whether schools are to become servants of technocratic efficiency needs, or whether they can act to help men humanize life under technology.

In the liberal-vocational studies debate prior to the Smith-Hughes Act, the technocratic drives of what Paul Goodman calls the Empty Society of mindless productivity showed in the social efficiency philosophy of David Snedden and Charles Prosser. On the other hand, John Dewey tried to define an approach that would combine democratic and humanistic values with science and industry. The value choices at issue in the differences between these two philosophies showed at crucial

---

[1]Paul Goodman, *People or Personnel and Like a Conquered Province* (New York: Vintage Books, 1968), p. 274.

1

points as the American people sought to define the kind of education they wanted for their children in the twentieth century. While we speak at present of "the post-industrial society" there are, in fact, major continuities between our present condition and the America that was emerging at the opening of the century—corporate and urban as well as industrial. It is possible to gain insights about ourselves and our condition by looking at the responses we made in the early round of our struggles.

One cannot pinpoint exactly when a term like "industrial education" first came into use. It was heard more frequently after the Civil War, and it was marked from the beginning with a fuzzy imprecision of meaning. In a loose sense it referred to pressures to replace or supplement classical education with school offerings designed to meet the complex skill needs of an industrial America. In higher education the "vocational" element was manifest in the land-grant universities created to teach "agriculture and the mechanic arts." For the youngest children it was evident in efforts to introduce manual activities into kindergartens and programs for immigrant children. In between, it encompassed a bewildering variety of new classes in commercial education, domestic science, agricultural education, manual training, and trade training.

In a narrower sense one may speak of the industrial or vocational education *movement* in the period 1900–1917 as the coordinated effort to win state and federal support for vocational education which culminated in the passage of the Smith-Hughes Act. Even then it cannot be discussed apart from its effects on general education. As we shall see, industrial education was a powerful factor in the creation of school counseling and guidance programs, and in moves to create junior high schools and comprehensive senior high schools.

It gradually became clear that a technology-based culture is dependent on formal education and skill training for its survival. This realization was accompanied by a growing worry that the transformation of schools to serve technocratic needs might subvert the traditional common school goal of preserving and advancing democratic traditions and values. With issues of such magnitude at stake every move to introduce change into school practice and structure triggered the anxious attention of major interest groups. Questions of pedagogical theory became highly controversial as the connection between educational change and economic and political realities became clear. One cannot view the educational history of the period without being reminded of Jerome Bruner's contention:

> A theory of instruction is a political theory in the proper sense that
> it derives from consensus concerning the distribution of power within

the society—who shall be educated and to fulfill what roles? In the very same sense, pedagogical theory must surely derive from a conception of economics, for where there is division of labor within the society and an exchange of goods and services for wealth and prestige, then *how* people are educated and in what number and with what constraints on the use of resources are all relevant issues. The psychologist or educator who formulates pedagogical theory without regard to the political, economic, and social setting of the educational process courts triviality and merits being ignored in the community and the classroom.[2]

In Part I we examine some of the origins of educational changes related to the industrialization of the society. Next we consider the responses of selected interest groups: business, as represented by the National Association of Manufacturers, the American Federation of Labor, and liberal urban reform forces of the progressive era like the settlement house leaders. We observe gradual and uneasy efforts toward a coalition of these groups, together with farm organizations, resulting in the formation of a typical progressive pressure group—the National Society for the Promotion of Industrial Education, which worked to promote its school reform program at state and national levels. We note the reactions of the NEA, in the face of pressure from NSPIE, and examples of resultant school innovations—guidance programs and the comprehensive junior and senior high schools. In following the industrial education movement to its triumph in the passage of the Smith-Hughes Act in 1917, we learn something too of the strategies generated in the struggle for power and advantage in a society of contending interest groups.

In Part II we examine philosophies of education which articulated the value and policy questions at issue. We consider the philosophy of social efficiency, which made the case for retooling American schools to serve the needs of a technocratic, meritocratic society. We examine the complex analyses of John Dewey, who tried to create a philosophy in which the values of science, technology, and democracy would complement each other—in short, to devise an education for citizens who might be at home in the new technological world. We attempt to understand what Dewey meant by his generally ignored statement in *Democracy and Education:*

At the present time, the conflict of philosophic theories focuses in discussion of the proper place and function of vocational factors in

[2]Jerome Bruner, "Culture, Politics and Pedagogy," *Saturday Review,* May 18, 1968, p. 69.

education. . . . Significant differences in philosophical conceptions find their *chief issue* in connection with this point.[3]

Finally, we point to examples of contemporary educational practice which represent alternatives to narrow technocratic solutions—alternatives that just might be a part of a general effort to reform institutions to serve the needs of persons in the technological era.

It is clear now that people everywhere on earth need to understand the subtle and profound effects of science and technology on human institutions. Samuel P. Hays, in *The Response to Industrialism,* reminds us that it is no longer a matter of parochial interest to study the American experience with industrialism.

> By mid-century . . . other people outside the Western world began to experience the same transformations in their lives which Americans had faced long before. The speed and shock of change were greater, the resistance to innovation often more intense, and the adjustments even more complex and difficult. But beneath these differences lay a common experience that could well serve as a basis for a common understanding among the world's peoples. To the historian, there is no more exciting task than to chart the different ways in which industrialism has affected countries all over the world and the varied manner in which peoples have responded to it. For all of us, there is no better method of enlarging our understanding . . . than to know intimately how we responded to the very forces that millions now face elsewhere.[4]

The American people with their traditional concerns for personal and political freedoms are among the first to confront the question of whether it will be possible to create a social order which combines technological efficiency with democratic values. At the moment we are confused. As Paul Goodman has put it, "We do not know how to cope with the new technology, the economy of surplus, the fact of One World that makes national boundaries obsolete, the unworkability of traditional democracy."[5]

When we are ill and seek help through therapy, we have to know where we have been, and what has happened to us, in order to gain a clearer picture of what we might become. Similarly, social malaise makes it necessary to reflect on history as a means to self-understanding. The material which follows is offered in the hope that it will make a contribution to that end.

[3]John Dewey, *Democracy and Education* (New York: Macmillan, 1916), p. 358. (Italics added.)

[4]Samuel P. Hays, *The Response to Industrialism: 1885–1914* (Chicago: U. of Chicago Press, 1957), pp. 192–193.

[5]Goodman, *op. cit.,* p. 258.

1/ *Industrialization and Education in the Post-Civil War Decades*

American wars have spawned forces with revolutionary consequences for American society. The Civil War was a notable example. It generated the conditions for a new society marked by technology and urbanism. Changes erupted in the last four decades of the nineteenth century which jolted traditions and institutions. Education was no exception. There was, of course, no grand design to guide innovations. Rather, one detects in the post-Civil War period a series of pragmatic responses to the dominating fact of the industrialization of society. In retrospect, we can see that the earliest educational innovations were made at levels designed to train leaders who could handle the complexities of industrialism. A major target of attack was traditional classical education at both the college and secondary levels. Critics demanded a more prominent role for the sciences in the curriculum and a new emphasis on the application of experimental methods to the solution of technical and social problems. Corporate bureaucracies marked by job specializations began to proliferate. Their capacity to function required an upgrading of work skills at all levels. To secure technically trained leaders, professional schools were established; to fill the lower-level job needs of business and industry, practical courses were added to grammar and secondary school programs.

A. THE LAND-GRANT COLLEGES AND PROFESSIONAL ENGINEERING SCHOOLS

The land-grant college movement, launched by the Morrill Act during the Civil War, illustrates several of these new educational emphases. A variety of discontents with the prewar traditional classical colleges had been building before the Morrill Act. The conviction grew that programs based on science, modern languages, and practical applications would be more suited to the demands of a democratic, dynamically growing country. By the 1850's public interest in reform

5

had increased; and a number of organizations, particularly agricultural groups, had begun to press state legislatures for action.

Jonathan Baldwin Turner, of Illinois College, was one of the reform leaders. He made a plan for new colleges designed to help people cope with scientific-technological reality. Throughout the 1850's he repeatedly delivered versions of a speech which proved to have wide appeal: "A Plan for a State University for the Industrial Classes." In this speech Turner outlined his arguments for the need for such an institution, together with ideas for its scope and emphasis.

> All civilized society is, necessarily, divided into two distinct co-operative, not antagonistic, classes: a small class, whose business is to teach the true principles of religion, law, medicine, science, art, and literature; and a much larger class who are engaged in some form of labor in agriculture, commerce, and the arts.[1]

He called the former the professional, the latter the industrial class. Ninety-five out of one hundred persons would be in the second group. This industrial class, he said, would "want and ought to have, the same facilities for understanding the true philosophy—the science and art of their several pursuits, (their life business) and of efficiently applying existing knowledge thereto and widening its domain in their pursuits."[2] He was skeptical of schools which immersed students in books only. "The most natural and effective mental discipline possible for any man arises from setting him to earnest and constant thought about the things he daily does, sees, and handles, and all their connected relations, and interests. The final object to be attained, with the industrial class, is to make them *Thinking Labourers;* while of the professional class we should desire to make *Labourious Thinkers.*"[3]

Turner doubted that the schools needed by industrial men could be grafted onto conventional colleges with their classical traditions. He envisaged schools which would relate closely the study of physical sciences with practical experimentation on farms and orchards. Such schools should expand their offerings eventually to include courses in all the sciences and arts, and in fields such as commerce, mining, transportation and government. They would generate research which would

---

[1]Arthur B. Mays, "The Concept of Vocational Education in the Thinking of the General Educator, 1845–1945," Bureau of Educational Research, Bulletin No. 62 (University of Illinois, 1946), p. 13, citing Jonathan Baldwin Turner, "A Plan for an Industrial University for the State of Illinois" (manuscript, University of Illinois Library), p. 371.

[2]*Ibid.*

[3]*Ibid.,* p. 14.

form the base for an "industrial" literature,[4] and they would produce teachers qualified to teach the new curriculum. The goal, Turner said, was to found schools which would serve the working class in the same way in which traditional colleges had always served the professional classes.

There was a Jacksonian cast to Turner's rhetoric. While he talked about two classes of men, the thrust of his recommendation was toward the creation of an institution that would reduce the separation of the classes. He recognized that the "industrial" classes would need training for their occupations. They would need schools analogous to those which already prepared men for the "learned professions."

The efforts of Turner and like-minded colleagues added momentum to a movement which resulted in the Land Grant College Act signed by Lincoln in 1862. After the passage of the Act, the land-grant college movement wobbled in its early years. There was little recognition of the educational significance of the Morrill Act either by general educators or by the public at large. Carl Becker pointed out that "as late as 1891 the founders of Poole's Index to Periodical Literature could find no more than six articles on the subject that were worth listing."[5] The debates in Congress nearly ignored the educational features of the Act and concentrated instead on differences over distribution of land provisions. Land speculation fever was at its height, and there was bitter struggle among the states over the share of public lands to be granted each under the Act.

It took a while for the educational focus of the land-grant colleges to find its direction. The content of the science of agriculture, for example, had to be created; and the original staffing had to be drawn from professors of traditional colleges who knew little of agricultural practice. Farmers were initially skeptical that professors, from their ivory towers, could teach anything of practical value. For a time there was a drive to eliminate all theoretical study from the new college and to place the workshop at its center. This "popularist" approach was borrowed from the Worcester Massachusetts polytechnical school, which strove to simulate genuine shop conditions and to produce salable arti-

---

[4]One may note in passing the kind of loose usage given the terms "industrial" and "industrial education." At this period the tendency was to use the terms for everything that applied to all vocations other than the "learned professions." The loose use of "industrial" points to a growing recognition of a wide range of needs of the technological society that were spawned by forces different in nature from those of preceding stages. A sure road to madness is to seek consistent use of terminology in the history of "vocational" or "industrial" education.

[5]Carl L. Becker, *Cornell University—Founders and the Founding* (Ithaca, N.Y.: Cornell U. Press, 1943), p. 37.

cles. The idea of making worshops the center of campus studies failed to take hold, however; and by the 1880's the main trend had shifted from narrowly practical programs for the "industrial classes" to a new emphasis on programs for technically competent leaders. This trend was given a boost by the passage of the Hatch Act in 1887, which created agricultural experiment stations as adjuncts to the land-grant colleges. These experiment stations provided avenues for the channeling of practical applications of research to the dirt farmer himself. By this time, as the sciences of agriculture were developing, farmers had become convinced that the magic formula for increased production lay in the union of theory with practice in experimental work. The groundwork was laid for one of the creative achievements of American society, the revolution in agriculture.

The theory-practice model was clearly evident in the kind of leadership Andrew White provided at Cornell University. Ezra Cornell, the philanthropist founder, pictured himself as an honest "mechanic and farmer," another example of the American rags-to-riches success story. When Cornell advocated the introduction of university-connected factories through which poor boys could support themselves, White demurred and persuaded him to accept a different orientation. White had democratic goals, but he insisted that Cornell University should exemplify the union of the liberal with the practical. Precollege instruction might provide training in how to make shoes and chairs; but the task of the university was "to send out into all parts of the State and Nation thoroughly trained graduates, who should develop and improve the main industries of the country, and by their knowledge and example, train up skillful artisans of various sorts and in every locality."[6] Shops and farms could occupy a place on campus, not simply to train a few more farmers or artisans, but to be used as laboratories where the application of science to practical needs might be explored.

A similar development took place in the professionalization of engineering education. As the railroads moved across the country there was a severe shortage of trained engineers, yet engineering schools were slow in appearing. Only a handful of such colleges existed prior to the Civil War, including the original one at West Point. The Land Grant Act created means for rapid expansion in the seventies and eighties. In 1860 there were perhaps only five schools of engineering; by 1880 the number had increased to eighty-five.

This history of Rensselaer Polytechnical Institute illustrates the transition from a crude "school for mechanics" approach to the ideal of

---

[6]Andrew White, *Autobiography* (New York: Century, 1905), Vol. I, p. 371. For a more extensive account of these developments see Berenice M. Fisher, *Industrial Education: American Ideals and Institutions* (Madison: U. of Wisconsin Press, 1967), pp. 59–60.

modern engineering training. The goal of Stephen Van Rensselaer in founding the school in 1824 was "to qualify teachers for instructing the sons and daughters of farmers and mechanics, by lectures or otherwise, in the application of experimental chemistry, philosophy, and natural history, to agriculture, domestic economy, the arts and manufacture."[7] By the 1840's Rensselaer Institute had been reorganized to follow the model of the great French technical schools. The new goal was to produce architects, and civil, mining, and topological engineers "upon an enlarged basis with a liberal development of mental and physical culture."

Francis A. Walker, head of the Massachusetts Institute of Technology in the 1880's, saw the need to professionalize the education of engineers. The program he projected included technical education of high quality, experience in the experimental methods and attitudes of science, and liberal studies designed to imbue engineers with a humane perspective.

Thus the last three decades of the nineteenth century were marked by the founding of schools of engineering, associations for engineers, and the establishment of engineering journals. Engineering became a profession. The times called for such a development, as critics had become increasingly impatient with the mistakes and limitations of "amateur engineers." The era was past when engineers could be trained from mere experiences on the job.

It was from the establishment of engineering schools that the manual training movement in precollegiate education was generated. This movement in turn was to play an important role in the development of vocational education.

B. THE MANUAL TRAINING MOVEMENT

We have noted thus far only the innovations at higher levels of education, which were designed to produce leaders for the new technical order. Precollegiate education, however, could not escape being affected. The manual training movement was, in part, an offshoot of the move to train engineers. Manual training became one of the liveliest subjects of debate at NEA meetings for several decades. The discussions rose to a peak of intensity in the 1880's and early 1890's. William T. Harris, with his methodical mind, made an analysis of subjects discussed at NEA meetings and reported that the topic of manual training was the fourth most popular item during the period from 1858 to 1890.[8] There

---

[7]Berenice M. Fisher, *Industrial Education: American Ideals and Institutions*, p. 61.

[8]Edgar B. Wesley, *NEA: The First Hundred Years* (New York: Harper, 1957), p. 49.

is little doubt that it would have ranked higher at the end of that period.

It is no simple task to evaluate the manual training movement or to make neat generalizations about it. Similar movements which burst into prominence and grip public attention for periods of time are undoubtedly symptomatic of forces that lie deeper than the surface flow of words. We lack as yet a probing study of the manual-training phenomenon which would relate it meaningfully to broader social-intellectual contexts. General accounts of the movement are available elsewhere,[9] and we shall not repeat the narrative account at length. We limit ourselves to noting some relations of manual training to the industrialization of America.

Both of the acknowledged leaders of the manual training movement, John O. Runkle, President of Massachusetts Institute of Technology, and Calvin M. Woodward of Washington University had responsibilities for developing training programs for engineers. They shared the ideal of creating a new breed of engineer who would be both technically competent and sensitive to civic needs. Both were discouraged by evidence that engineering students lacked rudimentary skills in the use of tools and knowledge of basic mechanical processes.

In search for new ideas, Runkle and several of his staff members visited the Philadelphia Centennial Exposition in 1876. There they saw a display on the theory and practice of tool construction, brought to the United States by Victor Della Vos, director of the Imperial Technical School of Moscow. The Russians had devised a system of carefully graded projects for the development of skills in the use of selected tools and materials. Basic mechanical skills and principles were taught in careful separation from the making of actual products. This method was a striking alternative to the American apprenticeship tradition, with its stress on specific skill training.

Runkle recommended the immediate adoption of such a program for students of mechanical engineering. A secondary school, the School of Mechanic Arts, was founded shortly thereafter, as an adjunct and preparatory school attached to M.I.T. While Runkle's first concern was with the rationale for engineer training, he saw almost at once that his ideas had broader implications. He argued that manual training "could help restore the dignity of labor to manual occupations, satisfy the demand for skilled labor, ease the conflict between capital and labor, and aid the development of industries."[10]

Calvin Woodward, Dean of the O'Fallon Polytechnical Institute at Washington University and head of its manual training school, had

[9]See for example Cremin, Krug, Fisher, Barlow. (See Bibliography.)
[10]Fisher, *op. cit.*, p. 67.

problems similar to Runkle's. When students were sent to the early workshop he established, Woodward found that they were inept in shop procedures. Before hearing of Della Vos, Woodward had begun to develop his own series of graded programs to teach basic mechanical principles and use of tools. Then came Runkle's public endorsements of the virtues of the Russian method: Woodward knew that he was on the right track. He created a three-stage program which led to the degree of Dynamic Engineer. Qualified boys at age fifteen would be admitted to the Manual Training School for three years. They were given shop work to get a basic grounding in joinery, founding, and machinery; but they also took demanding courses in mathematics, science, language, literature and drawing. "The aim is to master the range of every tool and to cultivate the habit of analyzing complicated processes into simple elements."[11] The four-year engineering course that followed consisted of two years of general education and literary studies, then two years of specialization in mechanical or civil engineering.

Woodward, like Runkle, became convinced that the manual-training rationale had important implications for the reform of general education. In several decades of campaigning Woodward maintained that the salutary effects of manual training could be helpful to almost everyone at all levels of education. It is fair to say, however, that his argument aimed at the value of manual training for those who were ambitious to advance in the industrial society. The first object of the school, as listed in its catalogue, was "to furnish a broader and more appropriate foundation for higher technical education."[12] Woodward established stiff admission standards, and quality work was demanded in academic subjects as well as in the shops. Some idea of Woodward's expectations is suggested in the comments of a visitor to a school patterned after Woodward's:

> In neatness, in discipline, in perfection of execution, in balancing and blending activities, the school leaves little to be desired. The work is so systematic, its results so definite, *its effect upon the mind, hand,* and *character* so marked, that all objectors will do well to visit this

[11] *Ibid.*, p. 69, quoting Calvin M. Woodward, "The Training of a Dynamic Engineer in Washington University, St. Louis," *Trans.* ASME, Vol. 7 (1885–86), p. 745.

[12] Other purposes listed were: "(2) To serve as a developing school where pupils could discover their inborn capacities and aptitudes, whether in the direction of literature, science, engineering, or the practical arts. (3) To furnish to those who look forward to industrial life opportunity to become familiar with tools, materials, the methods of construction, and exact drawing, as well as with mathematics, elementary science, and ordinary English branches." Calvin M. Woodward, "Manual, Industrial, and Technical Education in the United States," *Report of the U.S. Commissioner of Education* (1903), p. 1019.

institution, and take the time to study its working before making up their verdict.[13]

Woodward's school was designed for future leaders of industry. They would be well served by the qualities of discipline, systematic work, and insight into basic process, which they learned in the manual training programs.

While Woodward believed that manual training would be of great value for working-class boys and would act to counter their tendency to drop out, the truth is that the percentage of lower-class youth attending high school was small. Woodward liked to quote the comment of one visitor to his school which reflected the kind of aspirations he had for his boys: "The difference between the ordinary, stupid, dirty mechanic's apprentice and one of these intelligent, handy, clean, gentlemanly lads is as that between night and day."[14]

The manual training movement caught on in the eighties, and such schools were opened throughout the Midwest and the East. Some of the movement's most avid supporters were leaders of business and industry. Two such enthusiasts were Colonel Augustus Jacobson and Charles H. Ham, both of Chicago, who became converts after visiting Woodward's school. They were active in persuading the Commercial Club of Chicago to establish a manual training school there in 1884.

Jacobson and Ham had sensed the need for the critical middle-level type of industrial personnel and felt that the manual training approach would fill the gap. They were also convinced by Woodward's argument that his method of teaching the arts underlying handicraft skills constituted a valuable but incomplete preparation for any skilled handwork. Chicago employers were needing more skilled workers and they hoped that Woodward's kind of schools would produce them. After visiting the St. Louis school, Colonel Jacobson wrote to a Cleveland newspaper:

> The parent who sees a manual training school in operation sees solved before his eyes the problem of how his boy may be sure to make a good living in the world. . . . To the extent of the number of the graduates of the Manual Training School, the nation is sure of intelligent and valuable citizens. When these boys enter active life they will not need to wait for "something to turn up," because they will be able to turn up something for themselves.[15]

Woodward was fond of quoting the Colonel's statement that "manual training means not fewer, but more ladies and gentlemen to the

[13]Calvin M. Woodward, *The Manual Training School* (Boston: Heath, 1887), p. 173.
[14]*Ibid.*, p. 171.
[15]*Ibid.*, p. 172.

acre."[16] Charles Ham was less restrained in his endorsement of the new approach. "I made an exhaustive study of the methods of the St. Louis school, and reached the conclusion that the philosopher's stone in education had been discovered."[17]

Woodward joined the critics of classical education. He championed science and technical studies as necessary alternatives to Greek and Latin. He based his arguments on an analysis of the "obvious needs of our people." The development of polytechnical education was related, he said, to a succession of events in our history. "The first great want was for civil engineers, who should locate and construct the vast network of railroads, which continually grows thicker and closer all over our land, with their thousands of bridges and tunnels." Next chemists were wanted, "men skilled in the analysis of soils, ores, manures, poisons, noxious gases, and the various products of industry."[18] When placer mining was exhausted, the seekers of precious metals found their treasure locked in veins of rocky mountains. They were irretrievable without the aid of geologists, mechanics, and manufacturers of tools and machinery. The machinery itself depended on the exploitation and development of the mining and manufacturing of iron, lead, copper, zinc. From these developments grew massive needs in the field of building and architecture. Even in the ancient occupation of tilling the soil, men began to hope that revolutionary progress might ensue if the experimental methods of science were applied to agriculture and horticulture.[19] In the face of such social realities, Woodward could not resist the temptation to ridicule an educational tradition which set boys to conjugating Greek and Latin verbs for six or seven years.

Woodward studied efforts of various European countries where more practical educational programs were being developed as alternatives to traditional literary-oriented schooling. Prussia, Belgium, and France, he observed, were establishing industrial schools for children of laborers and factory operatives which centered on specialized training in skills such as engraving, coloring, dyeing, lace-making, weaving, and glasswork. This arrangement, said Woodward, was suited to the European social system, wherein the lives of workingmen were destined "to run smoothly in grooves cut for them before they were born." The situation was quite different in American society, Woodward held, because "with us every boy is a natural candidate for the office of president, and no one shall dare to place any bounds to his aspirations and his social possibilities."[20] European-style training, beyond its use in

[16] *Ibid.*, p. 222.
[17] *Ibid.*, p. 172.
[18] *Ibid.*, p. 247.
[19] *Ibid.*
[20] *Ibid.*, pp. 248–249.

charitable and reformatory schools, had no place in America—"at least
for the present," Woodward concluded.

Woodward's claims about the value of manual training in aiding
upward social mobility pointed to the type of opposition he anticipated
as he entered the lists against traditional educators in NEA meetings.
Anyone who suggested the use of tools and handwork in school could
expect to encounter the suspicion that he was an advocate of low-status
education. Manual experiences were associated with education for the
dull, the academic and social failures as represented in charity or reformatory schools.

Over a period of years in the eighties and nineties Woodward mar-
shaled a variety of arguments against his critics. He was particularly
stung by the charge of his most noteworthy opponent, William T. Harris, that manual training was nothing more than an education for the
"lower faculties," and indirectly for "lower students." In order to counter the formidable arguments of Harris and other NEA orators, Woodward felt impelled to defend manual training in terms of the dominant
psychological rationale of the period, the theory of training mental
faculties. He agreed with Harris, he said, that the

> first and greatest faculty to be trained is sense-perception. . . . Knowl-
> edge and experience and memory and generalization are necessary to
> the operations of logic, and manual training is particularly strong in
> furnishing the knowledge and experience, in establishing the major
> premises essential to logical reasoning. Tool instruction and tool prac-
> tice are full of meaning, and should always be strictly logical.[21]

Thus the foundation for sound learning in manual experience could be
established. But the most striking and peculiar function of manual training, Woodward asserted, was its potential for

> cultivating a capacity for executive work, a certain power of creator-
> ship. Every manual "exercise" involves the execution of a clearly
> defined plan. . . . However, at proper times . . . pupils are set to forming
> and executing their own plans. . . . Memory, comparison, imagination,
> and a train of reasoning—all are necessary in creating something new
> out of old. This power of intervention, of creation, is the highest active
> power of intellect of which we are capable.[22]

Harris should have been reassured that his own concern for the
higher faculties and leadership training was as precious to Woodward
as it was to the foremost philosopher of education himself. But somehow
or other Harris, remained unconvinced, and the two men remained in

[21]C. M. Woodward, *Manual Training in Education* (New York: Scribner, 1890), p.
204.
[22]*Ibid.*, p. 206.

different camps. Both were elbowed aside in the trade-training movement that was to follow.

Woodward would never concede that he was less interested than Harris in quality education. In fact he was convinced that manual training had a general message for all education. One of his most famous phrases was the statement, "we claim to train the whole boy: the hand and the heart" as well as the head. He pointed out that for many boys the regular school was unpalatable. They left school in droves, to the hurt both of themselves and of the society. Manual training, Woodward maintained, could rekindle interest in learning:

> There comes a time in the life of every boy when he craves with an irresistible appetite what may be called food for his physical nature; when the senses are most acute; when he is exquisitely conscious of his growing strength, his increasing power over the external world; when his budding manhood opens the door into the great workshop of nature, and he is satisfied with nothing less than actual contact with concrete forms and tangible forces.[23]

Woodward's language and psychology have a quaint and dated quality. Yet while the immediacy of the manual training issue faded, some of Woodward's basic pedagogical hunches proved to be far from obsolete. He had argued that educational programs limited to verbal exercise would fail to satisfy the young, especially when compulsory attendance laws would require all to sit in schoolroom seats until young manhood or womanhood. Woodward sensed that children and youth need kinds of learning experiences in which they can employ their sensory, physical, esthetic, and executive "powers" in order to attain intellectual and personal growth.

C. VOCATIONAL TRAINING BEGINNINGS

In the eighties and nineties, the American high school began to emerge as the secondary-level extension of the common school. There was a rapid increase both in the student population and in new additions to the curriculum. It was a turbulent time, a time of rapid business and industrial growth characterized by ruthless competition and the possibility of fantastic success. Prosperity was intermittently shaken by devastating depressions and social violence. The drive for success had seized American society. It was becoming clear that the need for more education was essential not only to advance but simply to survive in the new economy.

[23] *Ibid.*, p. 209.

The public high school came to the fore as it learned something of value from its predecessor and chief competitor, the academy. Academies had become popular by offering what the people wanted. One of the repeated demands was for more practical subjects. Courses in drawing and domestic science began to make their appearance. There was steady pressure for greater provision of commercial training. Edmund J. James of the Wharton School of Finance and Economy at the University of Pennsylvania delivered a major address at the American Bankers Association meeting in 1892, "A Plea for the Establishment of Commercial High Schools." Businessmen in Chicago, New York, Philadelphia, and other major cities stepped up demands for such services from the high schools. Commercial courses within regular high schools or separate commercial schools began to flourish at once. By 1896 the NEA was pleased to welcome the new Department of Business Education to its ranks.

An important development that accompanied the expansion of the high school was the introduction of elective subjects, an idea which received publicity and support from the prestigious President of Harvard, Charles W. Eliot. Elective offerings provided an arrangement which eased the way for competitors to the dominant classical tradition. Natural sciences and modern languages became lusty contenders together with the newer practical offerings. The proliferation of subjects led to confusion which verged on chaos; and the NEA, beginning in the 1890's, launched its important Commissions, designed to restore order to the curriculum and straighten out relations between the lower schools and the colleges.

While the NEA debates over manual training and other new subjects waxed eloquent, the pressure of the new economic and social realities heightened during the nineties. There was an urgent need for a vast number of workers prepared to perform the myriad functions required by ever-growing industrial and business organizations. Businessmen were turning to the high school to produce the army of trained clerks, typists, stenographers, and bookkeepers they required. At the same time came the call for some kind of trade training to meet the needs of expanding industries. Just as had been the case in commercial education, some of the earliest attempts to meet these urgencies came from private schools outside the public system.

Although some business leaders were giving enthusiastic support to manual training in the eighties, others were impatient with the lofty rhetoric that accompanied the movement. As Lawrence Cremin said, "what they wanted was practical trade training to free them from growing union regulation of apprenticeships."[24]

[24]Lawrence A. Cremin, *The Transformation of the School* (New York: Vintage Books, 1961), p. 33.

The first full-fledged school to offer specific trade training was started in New York City in 1881 by Colonel Richard T. Auchmuty. Auchmuty was a prominent architect from a wealthy New York family. His New York Trades School was organized to provide specific instruction in carpentry, bricklaying, plumbing, plastering, stonecutting, printing, and tailoring. Auchmuty avoided any fancy talk about providing "cultural education" or the training of mental faculties. His school offered carefully designed short courses aimed at teaching specific trade skills.

Auchmuty gave a straightforward explanation of his goals and the need for schools like his.[25] He argued that modern factories had made the apprenticeship system dysfunctional. Boys were rebelling against the long years of apprenticeship training, and masters no longer cared to teach them. Furthermore, Auchmuty said, labor unions were coming under the control of "foreigners" who conspired to put narrow limits on the number of available apprenticeships. The result was that native American boys were in danger of being shut out of the trades. New factory methods had outdated the tradition of learning through apprenticeship in a workshop. The alternative was clear, Auchmuty said. *Schools* to teach the trades would have to be created to replace the apprentice system. A side-benefit for employers would be that the graduates of training schools would be free from union control and could probably be hired at lower wages. That his argument was convincing to the business community was evidenced by a $500,000 endowment provided by J. P. Morgan in 1892.

Auchmuty made no effort to conceal the fact that his school was based on an antiunion bias, and labor unions were quick to see the threat. A plan aimed at destroying union control over apprenticeship threatened a vital interest of trade unionism. The violence of union reaction is suggested in their favorite appelation for the trade schools, "breeding schools for scabs or rats."

Other schools were established upon the new conception of trade training education as contrasted with the ancient tradition of apprenticeship. In 1883 the Hebrew Technical Institute was founded in New York by the Jewish community to facilitate the integration into American society of a growing number of Jewish immigrants.

In Philadelphia, the Williamson Free School of Mechanical Trades was established in 1891 by the philanthropist Isaiah V. Williamson. Williamson shared the contemporary anxiety over the decline of apprenticeship. His school, free to indigent boys approved by the

[25]See Richard T. Auchmuty, "An American Apprentice System," *The Century*, New Series, Vol. 15 (November 1888–April 1889), pp. 401–405.

board of trustees, was friendly to the manual training idea but it super-imposed courses of a more vocational nature on the manual training base.

In addition, a few corporations began to establish training schools for their own employees. Perhaps the first of these was the school opened by the R. H. Hoe Company of New York in 1872. The Hoe Company was being pressured by its customers for an improved quality of printing press. More sophisticated workers were required to produce such machines. Free courses were open to Hoe employees in English, mechanical drawing, arithmetic, algebra, and geometry; and all of this work was related directly to the needs of the firm. Graduates of these courses were given preference for promotions, on the assumption that they would be more reliable in handling the work needs of the company. Thus the trend was established that in the new work-world rewards would go to those with proper *school certificates*.[26]

In the eighties and nineties the public schools were reluctant to make the move toward thoroughgoing trade training. NEA meetings began to reflect the new pressures, however, and occasionally a plea was made to get schoolmen to take the plunge. Thus delegates in 1889 were told

> Instead of saying, we will not teach trades, we should aim to provide a large and increasing series of trade schools, until all boys and girls, too, in all trades, shall have the benefit of well-devised and thorough instruction therein.[27]

There is no indication that anyone paid attention to this speech by Mr. Selim H. Peabody in 1889. It seemed to be nothing more than another plea to add one more set of courses—trade training—to the already crowded school curriculum.

Time would show, however, that lurking behind the apparently mundane subject of vocationalism were some disturbing philosophical

---

[26]For a fuller account of these early trade schools, see Melvin Barlow, *History of Industrial Education in the United States* (Peoria, Ill.: Bennett, 1967), pp. 43–45. An indication of the growing pressure for trade training education by the turn of the century is indicated by the shift in Calvin Woodward's arguments for manual training. In a chapter prepared for the U.S. Commissioner of Education's Report in 1903, Woodward pointed out that well-equipped manual training shops were useful for evening trade training courses. Woodward admitted there was truth in the charge that relatively few of the manual training school graduates became mechanics. He replied that those who did not enter higher technical training were so valuable that they tended to be groomed for supervisory positions. If the number of graduates were increased significantly, he said, they would demonstrate that they had work skills needed for industry. (Calvin M. Woodward, "Manual, Industrial and Technical Education in the United States," *Report of the U.S. Commissioner of Education*, Chapter XIX (1903), pp. 1034–1039 *et passim.)*

[27]Selim H. Peabody, "The Value of Tool Instruction as Related to the Active Pursuit in which Pupils Subsequently May Engage," NEA *Proceedings* (July 1889), p. 103.

questions of profound import for both public education and for the meaning of democracy in a technological society. The major interest groups of the progressive era would find themselves drawn into debates on these matters.

part II

Interest Group Pressures for a New Education in an Industrial Society

INTRODUCTION

A study of the debate over vocationalism in education makes it possible to identify some characteristic pressures and responses that emerged as we entered the corporate-technological stage of our history.

Clearly apparent was American industry's drive to compete successfully for profits in world markets, and its desire that American schools become the instrument for achieving national wealth and power.

Equally evident was the pursuit of prosperity by the individual laborer. The workingman's struggle led to a growing awareness of the strategic importance of formal education as a means of personal advance. This resulted in growing demands that schools provide practical services to that end.

The progressive period was marked, too, by the emergence of nationwide interest groups seeking federal solutions to educational problems. Industrialized America was a society in which powerful organizations emerged with nationwide constituents. In the rough-and-tumble of the post-Civil War period, the threat of social chaos often loomed large. In the absence of the ability of any one group to dominate policy, the tendency grew for rivals to join in appeals to the federal government for actions which might advance mutual interests. In education, this meant a willingness to depart from the sacred doctrine of local control. As education became critically important for sustaining a prosperity based on science and technology, business, labor, and farm leaders had no trouble in championing plans designed to get help from Washington.

Progressive-era leaders were preoccupied, too, with desires to reform institutions to shore up traditional values. A rash of critiques appeared in both popular and scholarly writings which pointed with alarm to some of the concomitants of the technological society. There was concern over the decay of democratic participation and the weakening of institutions—concern about growing depersonalization and vulgarization of life. But hope was strong that science could open new avenues to human good; and proposals flowered for reforming the system.

Progressive rhetoric was marked by pious platitudes and clever rationalizations, as well as by genuine efforts to criticize and innovate. Such was the case in the river of words surrounding the move toward vocationalism in education. As we turn to those who spoke on the vocational-liberal studies controversy, we ought not be surprised to find conflicting values and motivations. Such confusion represented a true reflection of the dissonant state of the American psyche. The outer mood was confident, but underneath there were anxieties about where the turbulent forces of change might lead.

2/ The National Association of Manufacturers Takes a Stand on Vocationalism in Education

One of the earliest and most powerful voices demanding that schools teach the skills needed by the new industry was that of the National Association of Manufacturers. The NAM was organized in 1895, at a time when American industry faced an urgent need to take stock of its condition. Many manufacturers had been ruined or badly shaken in the depression of 1893–1894. Thomas B. Egan, who acted as Chairman of the first organizational meeting, lost no time in announcing an article of faith from which the association took its mandate: the prosperity of any locality, he said, was dependent upon the prosperity of the businesses in it; and therefore the proper test for any proposed public policy was whether it would be good or bad for business.[1] Half a century later, Eisenhower's Secretary of Defense, Charles E. Wilson, restated the proposition when he said, "For years I thought what was good for our country was good for General Motors, and vice versa."

The men who came together to form the new Manufacturer's Association were motivated by the clear desire to survive in the face of economic depression. Their interest in education emerged as they made a broad-based analysis of the causes of their predicament and formulated a coordinated program of policies to overcome obstacles to progress. Speakers at their conventions pointed out that the pell-mell construction of railroads in the seventies and eighties had led to rapid expansion of many industries like steel, toolmaking, roller bearings, and the like. When the national railroad network was completed by the 1890's, many of the new factories which had fed its construction were dangerously overextended. Perceiving the hazards of overproduction, the manufacturers moved quickly to enlarge domestic and foreign markets.

The Association developed a number of recommendations for im-

[1]NAM, *Proceedings*, 1895, pp. 7–8.

proving the domestic situation. First they asked the President to elevate the Secretary of Commerce to Cabinet rank. Secondly they sought action to secure a uniform classification of freight rates to facilitate trade in the national market. Finally they created a committee to secure reform of the patent office, which had proven itself incapable of keeping up with the innovations of rapid technological change.

Perceptive businessmen and bankers saw that the promise of large profits lay in high volume, low unit-cost production. This led to a rapid increase in use of the corporate device. Combinations of business units occurred on a wide scale. The trend was in the direction of larger plants with more modern, efficient machinery, and with larger labor forces.

The response of manufacturers to a decline in prices was to cut costs. Wage costs were reduced by layoffs, longer hours, or changes in hourly pay rates. Scientific time-and-motion studies were introduced to increase labor output, and capital was invested in the purchase of up-to-date equipment which lowered production costs.

Each new move solved some problems and introduced others. Thus investment in new machinery increased fixed costs, which could lead to peril in times of depression. Complicated equipment required more highly trained operatives, and they were hard to find. Moves to lower labor costs were resisted by the unions. Many manufacturers were unable to adapt to the swift flow of changes that followed one upon another.

There is no doubt, however, that the Association felt confident in its decision to promote aggressive expansion into international commerce. The decision to compete more vigorously with nations who for decades or centuries had dominated commerce was a reflection of the self-assurance of American industrialists. They shrewdly set to work to analyze what handicaps they confronted and what policies were to be pressed. Gradually they identified a series of federal actions required to improve their positions in foreign trade.

Charles Heber Clarke, Secretary of the Manufacturer's Club of Philadelphia, described at the first meeting of the Association both the opportunities and the difficulties he foresaw in entering markets south of the Rio Grande. He pointed, for example, to Britain's advantage in shipping. American machinery sold to Brazil had to be shipped by way of Liverpool. The NAM, he said, should demand federal subsidies to help create an American Merchant Marine fleet. Clarke then turned to the need for a new Central American Canal to open markets on the west coast of South America to American manufacturers. It was clear, he said, that the federal government should finance such a project. Other pleas made at this meeting or shortly thereafter called for proper tariff protection and the expansion and improvement of consular service to help open the markets of the Far and Middle East, as well as those of Latin America.

In 1898 President Search of the NAM picked up Clarke's tactic of analyzing the kinds of advantages held by European competitors. He warned that Germany had become the most dynamic force in foreign trade, and that its industrial power was based squarely upon its elaborate system of vocational and technical schools. England was learning from Germany's example, Search said, and the United States had better do the same. If American manufacturers were to lock horns with veteran industrial giants, they would have to learn to improve the technical quality of their products. This was possible only through formal technical training for workers. Search argued that ultimately the system depended on the "individual man." If American workmanship was to be improved, America's schools, colleges, and universities would have to devote more attention to teaching technical and scientific knowledge. The classical and literary studies had their place, Search conceded, "but it is unfair to the great material interests of the land to leave out of account the obvious demands of industry and commerce." Where public education was concerned, the time had come to realize that "considerable sums should be diverted from the main educational channels to be put into commercial and technical schools."[2]

A review of the activities of the NAM in its early years shows, then, that the decision to promote vocational training was one key component in a concerted drive to win a new role for American industry in the growing competition for world markets. As the twentieth century opened, manufacturers were convinced that they had identified their needs and problems. They felt they had found in German education the model to be followed to secure more efficient workmanship. Plans were made to send emissaries to visit German schools, and "missionary" educators from Germany were invited here.

Winning consent to the idea that American schools should be adapted to the needs of American industry according to the German model turned out to be harder than was expected. The truth is that even in this era of business hegemony, the businessman's faith that what was good for him was good for America was not universally accepted. When businessmen had turned to corporate combinations to overcome the chaos of rampant individualism, other Americans joined the trend toward forming interest-group organizations. One consequence of the return of prosperity in the late nineties, for example, was a rapid growth in the strength of the American Federation of Labor. The AFL felt seriously threatened by the NAM's recommendations for the modifica-

[2]Presidential address, NAM, *Proceedings*, 1898.

tion of the school system and prepared to offer stubborn resistance.

Some educators, too, had grave doubts. One of their concerns was philosophical. If the purpose of the American revolution had been to break free from the class-oriented traditions of societies across the Atlantic, they were suspicious of the manufacturers' call to return to the European educational pattern. Self-interest, too, was involved. If the German model were followed, vocational schools would be administered separately from the main system. Who would be running the new vocational school system? Would money and power be diverted from the public schools to these suddenly favored newcomers?

The debate that followed was characterized by rugged interest-group battling and by philosophical conflict, as the values involved were gradually uncovered and examined.

A. THE NAM IN ACTION

By the early 1900's manufacturers were ready to make a formal drive for vocational education. Their readiness was shared by other interest groups: Settlement-house leaders, labor and farm spokesmen, feminists, and a growing number of educators. One way or another they were all impelled by new problems generated by the emerging technological society.

At the famous first meeting of the Douglas Commission on Industrial and Technical Education (1906), it was reported that hearings throughout Massachusetts had revealed massive support for vocational education from a great variety of interests and callings.

In the following year President Theodore Roosevelt sent a paper to the first symposium of the newly formed National Society for the Promotion of Industrial Education which sounded major themes about to be amplified for national attention. "We contend for the markets of the world," he said, and warned that "our most formidable competitors are the nations in which there is the most highly developed business ability, the most highly developed skill." The prize would be won, said Roosevelt, by "the countries of greatest industrial efficiency."[3] Roosevelt paid conventional compliments to the American public schools, but he pointed to a basic flaw. The system, he said, fails "to give the industrial training which fits a man for the shop and the farm." It is curious, he went on, that we have developed high quality schools for the men at the top—our engineering schools rank with the best in Europe, but "we

[3]Letter from Theodore Roosevelt to Dr. Henry Pritchett, in "A Symposium on Industrial Education," National Society for the Promotion of Industrial Education *Bulletin*, No. 3 (September 1907), pp. 6–9.

have done almost nothing to equip the private soldiers of the industrial army—the mechanic, the metal worker, the carpenter."

Roosevelt went on to add that an education which provided "industrial intelligence" would add dignity to labor, provide protection against immigrant job competitors, and provide for workers and farmers formal educational programs equivalent to those already available to professional and managerial groups. He welcomed, too, the formation of a superordinate interest group like the National Society for the Promotion of Industrial Education, which could bring together a variety of otherwise antagonistic parties. The President wanted help in furthering a new educational vision. The schools were to become efficient instruments for securing national industrial supremacy, in a way that would serve both the material ambitions and democratic aspirations of American farmers and workers. That indeed would be a political brew with a wallop.

1. The First Report of the NAM Commission on Industrial Education (1905)

The NAM had been in action several years by the time Theodore Roosevelt gave his blessing to vocational education. We have noted the conviction of the Association's leaders that American industry would fail in international competition unless the quality of its products matched that of its rivals. Industrialists were keenly aware of a serious and growing shortage of skilled workers who could adapt to constant changes in factory processes. With the German model as a guide, they saw themselves confronted with two major handicaps. First, they were getting little or no help from the schools. Second, they faced a rapidly growing union movement committed to controlling conditions of employment and preventing the use of cheap labor which employers felt was essential to their survival.

The surge in the strength of organized labor is illustrated by the growth of its membership from 500,000 in 1897 to nearly two million in 1903.[4] The American Federation of Labor doubled its membership between 1898 and 1900 and trebled it between 1900 and 1904.[5] With the growth in numbers and power came rising unrest. Industrial disputes, strikes, and lockouts increased at an alarming rate.

Employers saw in the union movement a threat to their right to control their enterprises. Most employers had no experience in dealing

---

[4]John R. Commons et al., *History of Labour in the United States* 4 vol. (New York: Macmillan, 1921–35), Vol. IV, pp. 13, 15.

[5]Lewis L. Lorwin, *The American Federation of Labor* (Washington, D.C.: Brookings Institution, 1933), p. 59.

with unions and resented bitterly the need to cope with union representatives in addition to handling the challenges of their competitors.
David M. Parry, in his presidential address to the NAM in 1903, expressed management's resentments in a bitter denunciation of union
power. "Either a man has the right to run his own business or he has
not. If he has not . . . it means that individual liberty is destroyed and
we must bargain with such liberties as we may be allowed to possess."[6]
Organized labor, he said, "knows but one law, and that is the law of
physical force—the law of the Hun and Vandals, the law of the savage.
All its purposes are accomplished either by actual force or by the threat
of force."[7]

The unions, said Parry, were not only making freer use of the harsh
weapon of the strike but were also trying to get Congress to serve their
purposes. They were pushing hard for an eight-hour workday law. They
were seeking restrictive legislation against immigrants. Through the
apprenticeship system, they set limits on admission to training programs for the vitally needed skilled mechanic. When employers sponsored private trade schools to circumvent apprenticeship, the unions
hurled charges of "scab hatcheries" at them and fought to deny jobs to
the graduates of such schools.

Parry argued that England was being destroyed industrially by
similar thrusts of organized labor. He called on American manufacturers to unite to fight the union menace. A few voices condemned his
militant spirit, but the majority supported him. A declaration of principles was approved which affirmed the right of employers to hire and fire
as they saw fit and proclaimed that "in the interest of the employees and
employers of the country, no limitation should be placed upon the
opportunities of any person to learn any trade to which he or she may
be adapted."[8]

The rationale thus was established for the formation of a Committee
on Industrial Education to formulate recommendations for managerial
action.

2. The 1905 Report

The first detailed report of the Committee on Industrial Education
was presented in 1905 by its chairman Anthony Ittner, a firm supporter
of Mr. Parry. Ittner asked that the report be read by a secretary with
good delivery because, he said, "I want this report to strike this conven-

---

[6] Albert K. Steigerwalt, *The National Association of Manufacturers, 1895–1914: A
Study in Business Leadership* (Grand Rapids, Mich.: Dean-Hicks Company, 1964), p. 109.
[7] NAM, *Proceedings*, 1903, p. 17.
[8] *Ibid.*, pp. 166–167.

tion right between the eyes." Figures were cited on the school dropout rates: 80 percent were lost before reaching high school, 97 percent before graduating from high school—kinds of figures which would be repeated endlessly in the years of debate to follow.

Ittner said that the schools, with their impractical and boring programs, failed to meet the needs of ordinary boys. Furthermore the apprenticeship system, which had once prepared youth for work, had nearly broken down as a result of changing industrial conditions and the obstructionist attitudes of the unions. Manual training and technical schools were fine for the handful who attended them, but they failed to reach the vast majority. Ittner's report asserted bluntly: "To authorize and found and organize trade schools in which the youth of our land may be taught the practical and technical knowledge of a trade is the most important issue before the American people today."[9] Only through education could the cruel effort of the unions "to monopolize the opportunity to live" be thwarted.

Ittner and his committee underscored their conviction that the only recourse was to follow the pattern of the technical and trade-school system of Germany—"at once the admiration and fear of all countries. In the world's race for commercial supremacy we must copy and improve on the German method of education."[10] The virtues of the German plan were described in detail. The German system was free from the handicap of union meddling. Generally speaking, German trade schools had been first established by private industrialists, with commercial and trade organizations following their lead. State and municipal aid then followed.

Ittner's report quoted with approval a statement by Professor H. H. Belfield of Chicago who argued against beginning with *public* trade schools: "The initiative should be taken by corporations or private individuals." With a proper foundation, these schools might eventually be added to the public school system. Belfield stated that his investigation of European schools had showed that if large manufacturing establishments maintained their own schools, they would rid themselves of strikes. "When they shall educate their own workmen, these workmen will be loyal to the company rather than to an outside organization."[11]

Ittner's report concluded with an affirmation of the wonderful future which could be designed for American workingmen if the German model were copied.

[9]NAM, *Proceedings*, 1905, p. 143.
[10]*Ibid.*, p. 145.
[11]*Ibid.*, p. 149.

3. A Period of Clarification: 1905–1910

The 1905 Report put the question of industrial education squarely on the NAM agenda. The years which followed provided opportunities for debate within the organization and for interaction with other interested groups. Major goals remained constant, but amplifications, modifications, and changes did occur. We shall look at several themes which were stressed during these years: (a) the NAM's analysis of the kinds of labor needed in modern manufacturing; (b) their criticisms of American schools; (c) the virtues manufacturers saw in German education, and the lessons they drew for American schools; (d) the attitude of NAM toward federal financial support; and (e) summary trends which eventually made possible an accommodation with other groups.

B. LABOR NEEDS OF MANUFACTURERS

All parties agreed that the apprenticeship tradition of worker-training was failing or was irrelevant to the needs of large-scale manufacturing. The Director of Cooper Union, Charles R. Richards, prepared a lengthy report for the New York State Department of Labor in 1909 on the problems of obtaining skilled labor. Richards gave a detailed summary of the apprenticeship problem which was referred to repeatedly in years to come.

> The apprenticeship system is a survival from a period when only one class of industrialists existed, viz., the master-workman who was both merchant and craftsman and who in his own person bought and sold and practiced all the operations of the trade. The apprentice, who was in turn to become the master, was at once both assistant and learner, and he received a training which it was to the advantage of the master to make as thorough and complete as possible. . . . When, however, the capitalist appeared and with him the fixed body of wage earners, the apprenticeship system lost its natural place in the industrial order. The master-merchant became the financial director and the master-craftsman became the shop director or the wage earner. The first of these is in no position to perform the function of teacher, and the others have no interest in so doing.
>
> The modern organization of industry on the capitalist basis means the employment of numbers of workmen as wage earners whose sole responsibility is the forwarding of the productive tasks assigned to them. Such organization generally also means extended division of labor. . . . With the entire working force engaged upon production, it is to no one's interest to turn aside and instruct the learner, and such instruction, if in any sense comprehensive, can be given in the direct course of production only at a certain immediate loss.

Under these conditions, the employer of today, drawing his workmen from the general labor market, that in some cases is largely fed by immigration, no longer feels the same individual necessity and responsibility for the training of beginners, and hesitates to assume the cost and inconvenience of such a provision. The maintenance of a thorough apprenticeship system, having become exceptional, imposes in a sense a penalty upon the manufacturer who undertakes it inasmuch as he has no guarantee that apprentices will remain in his employ. Furthermore, the great subdivision of labor that characterizes all modern industries on a large scale imposes peculiar difficulties in the way of a thorough and comprehensive training, inasmuch as such a training involves a shifting of the apprentice from one branch to another that lessens his productive value. All these conditions make the employer slow to assume the trouble and expense of a thorough apprenticeship system. . . .

Another difficulty, and a very large one, that faces the apprenticeship question is the unwillingness of the American boy to submit to a long period of training at low wages for the sake of future opportunities. The tendency of the American boy is toward a short cut; he resents the rules and restrictions of the apprenticeship period and turns to openings that yield larger immediate returns. . . .

Another cause that holds back a bright boy from the apprenticeship is the low wages paid. . . . Organized labor, with its mind almost solely upon the advancement of the standard of living, and the employer, with his mind almost solely upon the increase of profits, have neither been concerned to advance the wages of the apprentice, and, with no influence to press them upward, these wages have remained extremely low.

Owing to these many conditions, apprenticeship in the sense of a broad and thorough training of the first-class workman has given place in many establishments and in many of the industries where it formerly prevailed to a so-called apprenticeship that trains in only a narrow range of work and fits only in some special line of skill.[12]

In the 1907 NAM session on industrial education, manufacturers spelled out the nature of the labor problem from their point of view. There were needs for two kinds of labor, they said: skilled mechanics to build machines and maintain them, and unskilled workers to run them. "A dull machine hand may manipulate the screw machine, but it takes a mechanic of intelligence and skill to read the drawings and to make the jigs and fixtures required in building the machine."[13] The

[12]Charles A. Bennett, *History of Manual and Industrial Education, 1870 to 1917* (Peoria: Manual Arts Press, 1937), pp. 523–525, citing *Industrial Training*, Part I of Twenty-sixth Annual Report of the Bureau of Labor Statistics, prepared by Charles R. Richards (State Department of Labor, Albany, 1909), pp. 14–24 and 27.
[13]NAM, *Proceedings*, 1907, pp. 129–130.

latter type of worker would understand the overall process of production and could adapt to change.

What manufacturers wanted was a generous supply of each type of labor: let the laws of the marketplace determine wage levels. Artificial shortages or union restrictions were evils that ran counter to nature's laws. Ittner, in particular, was committed to the idea that short trade training courses could provide workers with specialized skills and felt that the union's insistence on lengthy four-to-seven-year apprenticeship programs was a curse both to employers and to workers.

> Let us, each and all, work toward the end that every young man living on that portion of the earth's surface covered by the protecting folds of "Old Glory" may have the widest, fullest and freest opportunity to learn the trade of his choice, without detriment or hindrance of any kind whatsoever, regardless as to whether the country or any portion of it has twofold or tenfold more skilled workmen than there is any real need or place for; and likewise regardless as to whether the wage of a skilled artisan falls below the wages of a common laborer or not.

Fortunately, said Ittner, this country had no laws preventing a skilled workman from returning to common labor:

> The way will always be open for skilled workingmen to turn their hands to common labor should they find it financially to their interest to do so. The right to learn a trade should be as free as air and sunlight, and all artificial and arbitrary hindrances or barriers from whatever sources must sooner or later be removed. This is the law and gospel as embodied and enunciated in the immutable and everlasting principle of "the Fatherhood of God and the universal brotherhood of man."[14]

Immigrant workers played an important part in the labor supply problem. The NAM had a permanent Committee on Immigration which took the position that free access to the labor market might be restored by the importation of willing workers from Europe. Here again, the unions sought to interfere. In the 1911 NAM convention, Secretary of the National Liberal Immigration League John F. Carr pointed out that unions and the Federal Immigration Commission sought to restrict immigration on what they termed economic, moral, and social grounds.

Carr urged the Association to oppose these new efforts to change immigration policies. He told the manufacturers that his studies showed immigrants were less prone to crime than native-born Americans; that they sought charity less frequently during financial panics; and they

[14]*Ibid.*, p. 114.

were less diseased than native Americans because "defectives" were barred from entry. Furthermore, he said, immigrants had demonstrated their facility in adjusting to the realities of the labor supply problem. When there was a labor shortage, they came in droves; when times were bad, they returned to their European birthplaces.

Manufacturers needed a mobile work force, said Carr. "The new immigrant labor with its orderly swarming back and forth across the ocean answering our need, is vital to our industrial life, and there is menace to that life in the present attitude of Congress."[15] Even efforts to introduce literacy requirements into immigration procedures should be rejected, he asserted; for "the economic needs of the nation are for the rough manual laborer, and not for the clerk or professional man. . . ." Furthermore, "the illiterates who remain among us are not a menace. They are never anarchists." It was bad enough that America's own working population was subject to compulsory school attendance. Such laws only contributed to the problem of an inadequate supply of unskilled labor. Boys with many years of schooling, said Mr. Carr, don't want to dig ditches for sewers and subways. Clearly, industry must depend for unskilled labor "more and more upon countries with a poorer school system than our own."

Secretary Carr had been willing to concentrate his cold eye on the problem of obtaining unskilled labor from "uncivilized" regions. Other manufacturers, however, were concerned with securing skilled workers.

C. NAM CRITICISM OF AMERICAN SCHOOLS

In 1911, N.A.M. President Kirby asserted that

> the great importance of a thorough system of industrial training as a means of building up in this country an industrial supremacy over other nations is getting to be more generally understood and the subject is more in the public mind than ever before.[16]

The Association recognized that the educational task was more formidable than they had first believed. It now seemed so huge, in fact, that they were ready to renounce their earlier hopes that industrial training could be handled by private trade schools with philanthropic support. They had to take a harder look at public education. When they measured the schools against the needs of manufacturers, they found them utterly deficient.

[15] NAM, *Proceedings*, 1911, pp. 45–50 *et passim*.
[16] *Ibid.*, p. 72.

It was the rage of the era to measure institutions by efficiency criteria. Thus the industrialists, whose own operations were being revolutionized by Taylorism, spoke in terms of efficiency in passing judgment on the schools. They rolled out the statistics of cost against performance and were dismayed at the results. What were the American people getting, they asked, for an annual outlay of $450 million and a school plant investment of $1 billion?

H. E. Miles, then chairman of the Committee on Industrial Education, said he would describe how the school system would look if it were submitted for judgment to an international panel of impartial experts.[17] The public school system would be shown to rest "on theories instead of reality." Educators insisted their objective was that all students finish elementary school through grade eight, with most continuing to complete high school. The facts, on the other hand, were that only half of the children in school finished sixth grade; one in three completed the grammar school course; and only one out of thirty graduated from high school. The great majority of children from working families were ready for industrial training at age twelve or fourteen, and almost nothing suitable was provided for them.

A realistic appraisal of the situation in industrial nations, said Miles, reveals that children are divided educationally into three classes:[18] (1) "The abstract-minded and imaginative children who learn readily from the printed page." Most of these come from families whose ancestors were in the higher occupations, although many come from humbler origins. (2) The "hand-minded" children who have great difficulty with the printed page. More than half of all children are in this group: they leave school at the sixth grade or earlier. (3) An intermediate class which falls in between the other two.

In the face of these facts, Miles went on, the schools provided a literary education which satisfied the needs only of the first group of children—of one in thirty—while they were guilty of the most inexcusable neglect of the other twenty-nine.

Miles' analysis was influenced by what manufacturers had learned about the German system. The 1905 report pointed to German schools as a model, and delegations had been sent to study the German system intensively. Dr. George Kerschensteiner, educational philosopher and architect of the famous Munich vocational schools, was brought to this country as advisor—an early instance of the educational expert being sent to a "developing country."

The manufacturers learned that if American schooling neglected

[17] *Ibid.*, pp. 187–188.
[18] NAM, *Proceedings*, 1912, pp. 156–158.

the practical needs of the majority, German education was its polar opposite. An intricate variety of trade and technical education programs had been developed to meet the needs of each class of workers. At the top were the research-oriented "technical colleges" (*Technische Hochschulen*),[19] which provided university-level training in areas such as architecture, engineering, pharmacy, veterinary science, mining, forestry, agriculture, business-oriented economics, and military and naval studies. Much of the success of German industry was due to the research produced at these schools. The Germans were among the first people to demonstrate the tangible rewards of research and developmental activities. Just below the technical colleges were the intermediate technical schools (*Gewerbliche Mittleschulen*) for engineers who were less research oriented. Industry avidly sought the graduates of these schools. The *Werkmeisterschule* for foremen came next. Below these was a bewildering variety of trade schools. Special schools existed for almost every trade known to the industrial world, with training periods ranging from seven-week "refresher" courses to complete seven-year programs. In 1900 Prussia had twenty-one different schools for the building trades alone.

American manufacturers were intrigued, too, with the German continuation school: an innovation designed to reach the mass of semiskilled and unskilled industrial workers. These schools were created primarily to provide part-time education for employed youth in the fourteen to eighteen age group. As early as 1900 the United States Commissioner of Labor saw these schools as "the keystone to the whole scheme of industrial education as offered to the laboring class proper."[20]

By 1910, NAM leadership was strongly drawn to the continuation-school idea. The issue provided the occasion for a rift between the first chairman of the Commission on Industrial Education, Anthony Ittner, and his successor, H. E. Miles. In the era of the NAM's worst feud with the unions (1903–1910), Ittner had argued vociferously that privately owned, all-day trade schools could produce finished workers for industry. Such schools would replace union-controlled apprenticeship programs. What had caught the attention of efficiency expert Miles was the expense of fully equipped trade schools. He was struck by the contrast in cost between American-type trade schools and German continuation schools. In the latter, the shops of industry provided the setting for trade-skill learning and thus saved the schools the expense of elaborate

---

[19]See U.S. Commission of Labor, *Seventeenth Annual Report* (Washington, D.C.: Government Printing Office, 1902), pp. 870–890 *et passim*.
   [20]*Ibid.*, p. 890.

modernized equipment. Miles said his studies showed that the cost of continuation schools was $15.00 per pupil per year—less than half of the cost of American elementary schools. In the few existing American trade schools, costs ran from $180 to $250 per pupil per year. Mr. Miles had no difficulty in drawing the conclusion that the continuation school was a promising model. A somewhat similar program endorsed by Miles was the cooperative work-study plan pioneered by Herman Schneider in Cincinnati, in which two shifts of boys alternated between a week of school and a week of work.

In response to the cost analysis of Miles, Ittner indicated that he was hurt by the rejection of his trade-school recommendations. Lauding Germany became monotonous, Ittner said. "When Brother Miles is a year older he will think differently" about the speed with which we can overtake Germany. [21]

Miles' efficiency orientation was in line with current trends, however, and the interest of the manufacturers in George Kerschensteiner could not be diverted. Part of Kerschensteiner's plan provided that the work-experience dimension of the continuation schools should be used to give American working-class children insights into the nature of the arts and sciences. He hoped that work-related studies would induce young people to seek further knowledge of the relationship of their work to the broader context of twentieth century life. He hoped also to develop a kind of citizenship-training which would enable the individual to see himself as organically related to family, work, and society, but in a way that would free him from the German tradition of educating students "to perform blind service to a strictly defined State organism."[22]

The manufacturers ignored Kerschensteiner's thoughts on citizenship and seized upon those ideas of his that promised practical payoff. According to efficiency criteria, continuation schools could produce impressive results at a fraction of the cost of trade schools. This was the fact upon which they concentrated, although they were also taken with selected portions of Kerschensteiner's general philosophy. They listened attentively, for example, to his assertion that

> the first aim of education for those leaving the elementary school is training for trade efficiency, and joy and love of work. With these is connected the training of those elementary virtues which efficiency and love of work have in their train—conscientiousness, industry, perseverance, responsibility, self-restraint, and devotion to an active life.[23]

[21]NAM, *Proceedings,* 1911, pp. 201–202.
[22]See Diane Simons, *George Kerschensteiner* (London: Methuen, 1966), p. 30.
[23]*Ibid.,* p. 35.

What a difference such attitudes could make in American factories, where, as Miles had said,

> our factory children look upon a shop too much as upon a jail. There has developed among a considerable part of the adult factory workers a dislike, almost a hate of work.[24]

D. THE NAM'S 1912 POSITION ON INDUSTRIAL EDUCATION

By 1912, when various forces were culminating in a final drive for the enactment of federal legislation, the NAM was ready to state its considered position. Its recommendations bore clear signs of the influence of studies of German schools.[25]

For the majority of children (14–16) in industrial areas, the proper type of education should be German-style continuation schools. The NAM urged that such schools be established in every industrial community in the land. They should be day schools and provide at least five hours of school instruction per week for which the employer should pay wages.

> It is the experience of some manufacturers that after a little schooling, a boy can take hold of a new machine and in a week or so do three-fourths as much as a grown man, while a boy without schooling will take a month or two to do half as much as a man.[26]

The instruction in these continuation-style schools should be "exceedingly practical;" a shop atmosphere should permeate all work in the school. Courses should concentrate on material related to the theory and practice of a given industry. Mechanical drawing, shop mathematics, and hand work such as pattern-making, molding, or machine-shop work should be taught in connection with the making of practical objects like tools, gasoline engines, or benches. For girls, academic instruction should be related to the making of dresses, hats, baked goods, and similar products.

Courses in citizenship should be included "to make an industrial worker who is a good citizen, wise as to his rights and obligations." Statements on this subject were left at a very general level.

The vocational schools should be administered jointly by practical men from the vocations and educators. NAM members were sceptical of "impractical educators." They felt that manual training had been

[24]NAM, *Proceedings*, 1912, p. 154.
[25]*Ibid.*, pp. 156–157 *et passim.*
[26]*Ibid.*, p. 159.

diverted from its industrial purposes by the "culturists," and they were determined not to let that happen again.

The Wisconsin plan for the administration of the new schools was recommended. In Wisconsin, industrial education was put into the hands of separate state and local boards of control. At the 1911 NAM meeting, an even more desirable administrative arrangement modeled on the German pattern was advocated.

> Up to fifteen years ago the continuation schools of Germany were under the Department of Education, but they found that they never got practical educators until they took it away from that department and put it into the Department of Commerce and Labor.[27]

As a result, it was said, "Germany has moved twenty-five years ahead of us." The ideal was thus projected that a new system of schools for the majority of American children should be administered not by educators but by men of business in collaboration with representatives of labor. Political realities put this goal beyond reach, but the NAM had by now accepted the idea that administrative boards should have a tripartite composition with representatives from industry, labor, and schools. Interaction with other groups in the National Society for the Promotion of Industrial Education may have led the NAM to pull back from its earlier advocacy of outright business domination of vocational schools. But emphasis on the European dual system of administration—with industrial education outside the main school system—was maintained; and it aroused bitter opposition from American labor and school men.

Various plans were cited with approval in the NAM statement such as the cooperative work-study plans of Fitchburg, Massachusetts, and corporation schools established by huge companies like General Electric or Westinghouse, which gave complete three- or four-year apprenticeship programs, evening schools for the upgrading of personnel already in industry, and industrial education programs for girls. The Association also made clear that it supported with equal conviction commercial and agricultural courses comparable to industrial training programs.

The full-time trade schools, which had been advocated so strongly by Mr. Ittner, were ruled out as a favored solution. Mr. Miles' figures on their cost as compared with that of the continuation schools had been convincing. But, again using Germany as their model, the Association placed some trade schools at "the apex of the pyramid." Such higher trade schools, it was said, would be open to the abler youth who completed work in the continuation schools. These schools, as in Ger-

[27]NAM, *Proceedings*, 1911, p. 198.

many, were to provide advanced training for those who would become "the engineers and captains of production."

The rationale for this structure, it was held, would not be complete without consideration of its foundation at the elementary level of education. Prevocational or manual training should be provided for all children in the lower grades. Operating on the assumption that 90 percent of children would not continue in school beyond the eighth grade, the Association recommended several plans. One would be to extend continuation school opportunities to children fourteen years old and over who were required by compulsory education laws to continue part-time schooling until age sixteen. A second would be to develop for the fourteen-year-olds three elective courses of two or three years' length: a cultural course for the 10 percent who would go on to higher studies, and commercial and industrial courses for the rest. "The commercial and industrial courses should be intensely practical and make the best sort of intelligent, efficient working people, with as much culture included as may be."[28] The Association also looked with favor on plans which reduced elementary schooling to six years and then divided children into three tracks, cultural, commercial, and industrial.

Finally, this system of education needed to be complemented everywhere by centers of vocational guidance, "so that the great majority of the children who now enter industry with no direction ... may enter under advice, intelligently and properly into the progressive and improving occupations."[29]

E. ATTITUDE OF NAM TOWARD THE FEDERAL GOVERNMENT

NAM leaders over the years had been concerned about the financing of their ambitious programs of industrial, commercial, and agricultural education. By as early as 1907 they were willing to assume that federal aid would be required to supplement state and local support. They were impressed by the dividends that agriculture had received under programs financed by the Morrill Act of 1862 and the Hatch Act of 1887.

> It is largely due to this governmental assistance that our agriculture has been marvelously improved, made more scientific, and that the industrial army of agriculturists are to-day the happiest and in many respects the best informed and most reliable of American workers.[30]

[28]NAM, *Proceedings*, 1912, p. 169.
[29]*Ibid.*, p. 176.
[30]NAM, *Proceedings*, 1911, p. 193.

Manufacturers now asked that comparable resources be made available for industrial and commercial education. In annual conventions, the NAM endorsed various bills—the Davis bill, the Page-Wilson bill, and others down to Smith-Hughes—which were designed to promote this end.

It may seem strange that an organization so committed to free enterprise, and so fiercely suspicious of efforts to expand the "socialistic" tendencies of the government in Washington, would readily endorse federal support and regulation for public education. A closer look at the record of the NAM in the first decades of its existence shows, however, a consistent pattern. When proposals were made to use federal taxes for groups or interests outside the sphere of business, the NAM objected. But when the issue was the advancement of business welfare—with which the public welfare was equated—the manufacturers felt no hesitancy in appealing for federal action and financial support. One need only recall NAM support of measures like federal standardization of freight rates, the expansion of the consular service, subsidies for an American merchant marine, and moves to construct a Central American Canal, to see that their endorsement of federal support for industrial education was quite predictable.

F. SUMMARY TRENDS

The National Association of Manufacturers was created in the last decade of the nineteenth century to meet the needs of the new technologically oriented American industry. The corporate combinations that emerged were hierarchically organized and dependent on the cultivation of a wide variety of specialized skills. At the upper levels of industry there was a need for research-oriented scientists and engineers, with managerial skills. American higher education, with its Colleges of Engineering, Schools of Business Administration, and general Liberal Arts training, began to organize itself to meet these needs. Industry's need for a pool of unskilled labor was being satisfied by the influx of immigrants and rural Americans to the cities. The great lack was the wide variety of workers in between. The apprenticeship system, which had originated in a handicraft stage of production, was adequate for an ever-shrinking percentage of workmen. It was irrelevant for most purposes of the new manufacturing. The skill needs of modern industry could be met only through formal education. Manufacturers realized this and turned their attention to the public schools.

The model they chose was the educational system of their most feared economic competitor. In the German example they found a complete system of schools tailored in mirror-image fashion to the skill gradations required by industrial modes of production. Furthermore, it was a system of industrial education which made use of the equipment of industry, so that school costs could be held down. As American observers saw them, the German schools produced not only skilled workmen, but workers who were content in their jobs and loyal to the economic and political system. The message seemed clear. Schools in the United States had to be patterned immediately after this model if American industries were to meet the challenge of German competition.

Yet as one reads the sometimes ecstatic endorsements of the German system, one encounters occasional notes of anxiety even in the *Proceedings* of the NAM. The fact is that these industrialists, while riveted to the requirements of their enterprises, could not escape their acculturation to American values. As early as 1903 a Mr. Samuel Jones of Ohio expressed alarm at the rhetoric of efficiency which was beginning to predominate.

> I heard from this platform yesterday, the monstrous doctrine announced from a well-meaning man that labor was a commodity like brick and sand and coal, to be bought and sold. Under the stars and stripes, under the Declaration of Independence, we heard that doctrine preached here yesterday. I am sure that this was nothing but a mistaken notion on the part of a well-meaning man.[31]

When German education was praised, the afterthought was often, "Of course we can't literally copy the German system. We must adapt it to American traditions and conditions."

There were those, even among the hard-driving businessmen, who hesitated to give all-out endorsement to an educational system which seemed to deliberately perpetuate class lines. The Horatio Alger success ethic required a fairer chance. Even Anthony Ittner felt the importance of that: "Train the free-born American boy to the end that he may have a fair field and an open path to work onward as a free American citizen."[32] The idea of differentiated school systems and the belief in access to success for all were brought together somewhat awkwardly in the assumption that the masses would fulfill the roles decreed for them by destiny while the occasionally able and ambitious lad would move into upper strata. The class-oriented European education had always provided for these sports—"the clever boys"—too.

It was a mark of the time that themes of social uplift fit neatly with ideas for business betterment. Concern was expressed frequently for

[31]NAM, *Proceedings*, 1903, p. 167.
[32]NAM, *Proceedings*, 1905, p. 150.

the human waste resulting from the high level of school dropouts. The new skill-oriented schooling could save young men from becoming wastrels and enable them to share in the golden standard of living. The newly trained American workingman

> will advance greatly in general intelligence as well as in technical skill; he will be a better citizen and a better man, of more value to the state as well as to his home and family. He will cease to spend his spare time in saloons and loafing places and in useless or wasteful ways. A trained mechanic and artisan will then be the peer of any man in the community in which he lives, and the standard of American manhood will be as high as that of any other nation on earth.[33]

Frequent statements announced the need for workmen with "industrial intelligence"—for potential shop leaders whose perspective would not be limited to knowledge of one specialized skill. Insight and adaptability would enable factory personnel to adjust to the flow of changes which could be expected.

Occasionally a speaker claimed that there were kinds of educative possibilities in shops and offices which never could be provided in classrooms. Such activities could save pedagogical practice from dullness, which kills the desire to learn. There were brief assurances, too, that "cultural subjects" and citizenship education would be provided in addition to trade training.

One may acknowledge the existence of these subthemes in the talk of the manufacturers; yet their main concern clearly focused on the technocratic goal of using the schools to produce the skills and attitudes which industry required. The industrialists did not achieve literally the program which they recommended. They met opposition. We shall try to understand what did happen by examining the stands taken by other parties to the issue.

[33] *Ibid.*

3/Organized Labor and the Industrial Education Movement

American workers and their unions were as deeply involved in issues surrounding the industrial education movement as were manufacturers and businessmen. However, the American Federation of Labor was more hesitant about formulating a position than was the NAM. It had more ideological conflicts to resolve.

The Federation's first considered statement appeared in 1910, in a report from its Committee on Industrial Education, headed by John Mitchell, of the Mine Workers Union. In order to understand the AFL's struggles with the question of vocational education, we must first note several nineteenth century developments which affected the kind of thinking that AFL leaders brought to the subject. These were the emergence of a trade-union philosophy committed to working within the going economic system; and transformations in the nature of work which undermined the traditional apprenticeship mode of training workers.

A. THE EMERGENCE OF A TRADE-UNION PHILOSOPHY

The American labor movement came into being as a significant force in American life in the 1820's and 1830's with the formation of the Political Workingmen's Parties, and of local and national trade unions. Differences in emphases and styles between the Workingmen's Parties and the trade unions, however, reflected a major alternative for American labor. The issue was whether the labor movement should become a force for social and economic change through political action, or whether it should concentrate on advancing the economic welfare of workers through narrower trade union action.

By the 1820's and 1830's American workers were becoming aware that the factory mode of production was forcing them into the status of a permanent wage-earning class. Independent craftsmen and mechnics were being reduced to the vulnerable status of hired hands whose

43

financial survival was in the control of the owners of the new factories. This change in economic status threatened them just at the time that they had gained new political rights to vote, free from property or religious restrictions. They responded by forming Workingmen's Political Parties in Philadelphia, New York, and New England.

In Philadelphia the labor movement began in 1827. It took the form first of the Mechanics Union of Trade Associations, which included all the organized workers of the city, and was then transformed into the Workingmen's Party. It was a short-lived movement, but its direction was clear. Workers desired equal citizenship. To get it they decided they needed two essentials—more leisure and access to free public education.

The case for a ten-hour workday was stated in political terms. The workingmen linked economic inequality with political inequality and hated both.

> We are fast approaching those extremes of wealth and extravagance on the one hand, and ignorance, poverty, and wretchedness on the other, which will eventually terminate in those unnatural and oppressive distinctions which exist in the corrupt governments of the old world.[1]

The result, they said, was that the working class, "entirely excluded from the advantages derivable from our free institutions, for want of knowledge and correct political information had been subject to gross impositions." Labor's political impotence resulted, they felt, from the fact that workers labored from sunup to sundown and so were unable to exercise their rights as citizens; while the leisured rich had time to dominate political life and pass laws that were beneficial to their class.

In New England, the Association of Farmers, Mechanics, and Other Workingman similarly fought the drift toward class polarization. They saw a growing tendency for men associated with banks, chartered monopolies, and manufacturing to emerge as a new economic aristocracy; while free farmers and mechanics receded into the role of factory operatives. The self-employed "honest workmen" were alarmed by what happened to those forced to take work as factory hands. The Association declared that the factory system

> which presents so fair an outside show [represents] perhaps the most alarming evil that afflicts our country. The cheapness and facility of procuring the manufactured articles are no recompense for their in-

[1]John R. Commons et al., *History of Labour in the United States*, I, (New York: Macmillan, 1961), p. 192, citing *Mechanics' Free Press*, May 1, 1930.

jury to the health and morals of the rising generation. To look at the poor and spiritless beings as they pour out of the factory to their hurried meals at the sound of a bell; to see the lazy motion of their jaded limbs, and the motionless expression of their woebegone countenances, must give a pang to the feeling heart which can never be forgotten. This factory system is essentially opposed to the spirit of our institutions, since from its nature, it must throw large bodies of people together, and by degrees render them wholly dependent upon a few employers, and forever crush that spirit of independence which is the only safeguard of freedom.[2]

It soon became clear that the opportunity for political participation required not only the margin of time and energy which could come from a shorter work day, but also the knowledge and skill which resulted from formal education. The *Mechanics Magazine* in 1833 estimated that in the United States there were 1,000,000 children between the ages of five and fifteen who were not attending school at all. The next year the number of illiterate children was estimated at 1,250,000. In a suburb of Philadelphia hundreds of boys, seven years old and upward, were said to be employed daily "from *dawn till eight* in the evening."[3]

In 1829 the Workingmen's Party of Philadelphia put public education at the head of its list of priorities. A preamble section of the political platform declared that "real liberty and equality have no foundation but in universal and equal instruction which has been disregarded by the constituted guardians of the public prosperity."[4]

The Party explained their support for a leading candidate as follows:

. . . he is the friend and indefatigable defender of a system of general education, which will place the citizens of this extensive republic on an equality; a system that will fit the children of the poor, as well as the rich, to become our future legislators; a system that will bring the children of the poor and rich to mix together as a band of republican brethren; united in youth in the acquisition of knowledge, they will grow up together, jealous of naught but the republican character of their country, and present to the world the sublime spectacle of a truly republican government, in practice as well as in theory.[5]

We may note that early nineteenth-century workers, while repelled by the harsh divisions of class distinctions, assumed that American society could be egalitarian—"a band of republican brethren."

[2] *Ibid.*, p. 320, citing "Address to the Workingmen of Massachusetts." *National Trades' Union*, November 1, 1834.
[3] *Ibid.*, p. 182, citing *Mechanics' Free Press*, Nov. 21, 1829.
[4] *Ibid.*, p. 224, citing *Mechanics' Free Press*, Jan. 24, 1829.
[5] *Ibid.*, p. 228, citing *Mechanics' Free Press*, Oct. 2, 1830.

There might be distinctions of wealth and rank, but there would be no such radical gaps that some lived in dire poverty and human indignity while others enjoyed the privileges of wealth, leisure, learning, and power. Ths distinctive feature of American society, they felt, was its promise that all its members could win the opportunity to live with self-respect and power to participate. Access to leadership would be open to all. Those distinctions which might emerge would be based on what Jefferson had called the aristocracy of talent rather than the aristocracy of privilege. Access to a free education of equal quality was the cornerstone on which to build the American democratic republic.

The workingmen's groups were clear about their educational priorities. They wanted free tax-supported schools so that they and their children could be released from the pauper school shame. They wanted an open ladder system of education with free infant schools at the lowest rung. They opposed the lottery system as an undignified way of raising revenue, designed to exploit the weaknesses of some heads of families. They supported the efforts of public normal schools to obtain competent teachers. They championed publicly elected school boards with broad representation, including members of the working classes. They opposed the granting of public funds to private schools—especially to the academies. They attacked child-labor practices, which prevented access to schooling.[6]

Where the curriculum was concerned, the working men were less clear. They did oppose deadly dull instruction which killed the desire to learn. Yet they were somewhat unsure about the inclusion of practical studies. In the main, they put stress on the quality of general education, but there was support among the followers of Robert Owen for the manual-training approach of Fellenberg's school in Hofwyl. In New York City, in particular, Frances Wright and other Owenites demanded a system of public education which would

> combine a knowledge of the practical arts with that of the useful sciences. . . . Instead of the mind being exclusively cultivated at the expense of the body . . . or the body slavishly overwrought to the injury of the mind, they hope to see a nation of equal fellow-citizens, all trained to produce and all permitted to enjoy. . . . As the *first* and *chief* of their objects, therefore, the Mechanics and Working Men put forward a system of Equal, Republican, Scientific, Practical Education.[7]

[6]For a general treatment of the educational policies of the early labor movement, see Philip R. V. Curoe, *Educational Attitudes and Policies of Organized Labor in the United States,* Chaps. 1–2 (New York: Teachers College Press, 1926).

[7]Commons, *op. cit.*, p. 284, citing New York *Working Man's Advocate,* September 18, 1830.

1. The Emergence of Trade Unions

We have noted the attitude toward education of the early workingmen's organizations in order to understand the original value orientation which motivated them. They subscribed to the democratic-republican ideal and they wanted to secure the conditions which would enable them to experience it as reality. They were radical reformers, not in the sense of aiming to overthrow the system, but in the sense of wanting to *get in* on the promises verbalized by it. The early efforts to win power through labor party political action ended, however, in defeat. The Workingmen's Parties, with their goal of establishing a republic of independent farmers and mechanics, foundered partly under the shock of economic depressions and partly over splits on ideological questions. After the decline of these parties in the early thirties labor's next move was to seek a different kind of power through trade union organization.

Labor shifted its tactics to trade union defense not only because of political defeats but because there was an accelerated change in the status of the worker from that of independent artisan to factory operative. The nature of work changed under the advent of merchant and industrial capitalism. Improved highways and canals broke the isolation of communities and formed larger markets. Broader markets required changes in modes of production. The small shop in which a master mechanic worked with several journeymen, with a retail store attached, was replaced by a more efficient and profitable system in which merchant-capitalists contracted with master mechanics who jobbed out the work. Under the stress of increasing competition, masters were reduced to contractors whose task it was to get work produced at the cheapest price. Soon the master resorted to cutting wages and using unskilled labor—children, women, convicts, or immigrants. Trade skill operations were broken down into simple components so that untrained hands could learn them quickly. The term "apprentice" often became an archaic term applied inaccurately to any child hired as a wage-earner.

As a response to the new situation workingmen decided to concentrate on strengthening trade unions into economic defense groups. Economic survival took priority over political utopianism.

Thus a pattern evolved that was repeated throughout the nineteenth century. Laboring men periodically were attracted to political action to win a reformed social order that would embody egalitarian republican ideals. When such efforts resulted in rebuff or frustration they turned to economic trade union action to secure survival or hopefully a share in prosperity within the industrial system.

In the forties some workers were attracted to the social utopian theories of Robert Owens and Fourier. Attempts to create egalitarian communes as alternatives to the main system were, however, short-lived. After the Civil War workers once again were drawn to idealistic political-social reform efforts. Under the stress of economic depression and political repression some rallied to new socialist or anarchist movements. The main move, however, was toward the Knights of Labor who flourished briefly in the seventies and eighties. The Knights concentrated on organizing unskilled as well as skilled workers into industrial unions. They had broad and grand objectives: the reconciliation of workers and employers (their constitution pledged the Order to persuade employers to agree to arbitrate all differences in order to avoid strikes); the establishment of cooperative institutions to supersede the wage system; the securing of equal rights for both sexes; and the attainment of an eight-hour work day by the use of labor-saving machinery.

When the Knights of Labor attempted in the mid-eighties to take over leadership of the skilled trades they precipitated a bitter fight, however, which led to the breakaway of the American Federation of Labor in 1886.

In the nineties many laboring men joined farmers in the Populist Movement's attack on "the vested interests." When Populism went down to defeat, however, the stage was set for the triumph of Samuel Gompers' philosophy of trade unionism: avoid attachment to political parties; avoid utopian ideologies; concentrate on bargaining techniques which put money into the worker's pocket; stick to the union—reward its friends and punish its enemies. Labor had chosen to fight for improved material conditions by becoming another interest group within the existing economic system.

The tensions within labor between the motivation to seek democratic social reform versus the tendency to concentrate on trade-union defense would show when labor had to decide on which policies for American education it would support as we turned into the twentieth century. Labor's attitudes toward the industrial education reform movement, for instance, were influenced by another development which was at least as important as ideological concerns—changes in the nature of the work processes.

B. CHANGE IN THE NATURE OF WORK AND ITS SIGNIFICANCE FOR AMERICAN LABOR

The trend toward specialization of work was accelerated during the Civil War when there was a revolutionary shift from production via the hand tools of the craftsman to production by the power-driven machinery of the factories. This led to radical changes in the methods of hiring and training labor, which in turn precipitated bitter conflict between the new industrialists and the union organizations.

The craft system and apprenticeship training had prevailed into the nineteenth century. In this ancient tradition, a boy was apprenticed to a master with whom he lived for from five to seven years. Apprenticeship laws required that the master not only teach him the skills of the craft but provide general education and moral training. Thus a New Haven Act of 1656 provided that if masters did not teach apprentices "to read the Scriptures and other good and profitable printed works in the English tongue and to understand the main principles of Christian religion necessary to salvation," the apprentice could be withdrawn and placed with another master who would do so.[8]

The significant education for an apprentice derived from the family-shop setting through which he related to the local community. He learned by living in the total situation. The factory system disrupted these traditional arrangements. Paul Douglas in his classical study *American Apprenticeship and Industrial Education* provides a graphic description of the nature of the change.

> If the ordinary craftsman was deeply affected by the substitution of power-driven machinery for his hand tools, much more deeply and more subtly was the apprentice. For him it meant a revolutionizing not only of his methods of work but of his entire social status as well, both at home and in the shop.
>
> His home had formerly been at his master's. He had lived and worked familiarly with him, receiving his board and clothing in return for his services. Now, with the growth of industry, the master could no longer house all of his apprentices. He had to let them find their own shelter, and commute their former benefits into a cash allowance. . . .
>
> Within the shop the change was equally great. The master was no longer literally a "master-workman," in close personal touch with each boy. The very nature of machine production had fixed a gulf between the two. The tasks of the employer were becoming more and more exclusively those of the business man, his immediate concern was buying and marketing rather than craftsmanship. His contact with his apprentices grew rapidly infrequent and impersonal. In brief, master and apprentice had stood in the relation of father and son; they now stood in the relation of employer and employee.
>
> The training the apprentice received changed no less than his

---

[8]R. F. Seybolt, *Apprenticeship and Apprenticeship Education in Colonial New England and New York* (New York: Teachers College Press, 1917), pp. 52–60.

station. Machine production does not require the all-round skilled
workman because it increases the division of labor and splits a trade
into many different jobs. . . . The mastery of the whole gamut of
machines within a trade becomes well-nigh impossible. . . . Apprenticeship accordingly became specialized.

The purely cultural training of the apprentice fared of course even
worse. The master who did not see him from one week's end to the
other could hardly be expected to teach him his letters or his cate-
chism.[9]

The threats to the security of journeymen workers grew in intensity
after the Civil War. Ruthless competition in the business world put new
pressures on employers to cut labor costs. Employment of children
increased; European immigrants (skilled and unskilled) were recruited;
and some employers moved to fill their works with cheap black labor
from the South. The National Labor Union claimed in 1866, for example, that Boston employers were importing blacks from Portsmouth,
Virginia, to serve as strike breakers.[10]

Labor organizations responded by seeking to control entry to apprenticeship. They still clung to the idea that no child should be in
industry unless he was actually learning a trade. When the unions saw
large numbers of untaught children in factories, they protested that
these children were being denied their apprentice rights to training.
The National Unions in the sixties and seventies sought to secure union
control over apprenticeship by turning to the state legislatures. Apprenticeship laws were passed in Massachusetts, Pennsylvania, New
York, Illinois, and Ohio requiring that written indentures be signed
before an apprentice could begin work. The truth, though, was that
"apprenticeship" was irrelevant to factory conditions. This was demonstrated by the ease with which most employers evaded the laws. They
simply stated that they hired minors as "general workers" rather than
as apprentices. Employers sought other means to oppose union efforts
to control entry to work. In New York, for example, employers welcomed the opening of Colonel Auchmuty's Trade Training School in
1881. The Colonel was an enemy of union control of apprenticeship
training. He maintained that the unions were led by new "foreign
elements" who tried to establish restrictions which would deny access
to skill training for native-born American boys. When Auchmuty's
school furnished strikebreakers for a local strike, it confirmed the worst

[9]Paul H. Douglas, "American Apprenticeship and Industrial Education," *Studies in
History, Economics and Public Law*, Vol. 95, No. 2 (New York: Columbia University and
Longmans, Green, 1921), pp. 55–56.
[10]Curoe, *op. cit.*, p. 71.

of labor's suspicions. For decades, thereafter, union leaders poured scorn on private trade schools as "scab hatcheries."

Since state laws had proved ineffective, and local unions were too weak to regulate apprenticeship, labor's tendency at the end of the century was to seek national regulation through strong national unions. The American Federation, with its powerful craft unions, emerged as the dominant labor organization. As late as 1890, only seventeen of forty-eight trade unions had attempted to regulate apprenticeship through their national bodies. By 1904, however, 70 out of 120 national unions had enacted apprenticeship regulations. This represented an increase in the percentage of workers in unions with such controls from 16.5 percent in 1890 to 54 percent in 1904.[11]

By the early 1900's, when the issue of industrial education came into prominence, both labor and management had strong national organizations. Both groups realized that the traditional method of apprenticeship was irrelevant to the facts of the factory system.

Moreover, the new industrialism was developing needs for a new kind of work force. New machine processes were continually introduced to the workingman. At the same time there was an increasing tendency among workers to move from factory to factory and city to city. The person who possessed only one routine skill could be lost. What was required of the new worker was a general knowledge of the factory system and higher skills to move within it: the ability to read blueprints and complicated instructions, to do shop mathematics, to practice safety and hygiene rules. Convention orators seemed to have this kind of situation in mind when they made oft-repeated pleas for "industrial intelligence." They were talking about some measure of insight into the total set of processes involved in an industry, as compared with the narrow mastery of only one skill. The belief began to grow that only "industrial education" could produce "industrial intelligence."

C. EVOLUTION OF THE AMERICAN FEDERATION OF LABOR'S ATTITUDES TOWARD THE INDUSTRIAL EDUCATION MOVEMENT

In broad terms the history of the labor movement between 1865 and 1900 is one of accommodation: accommodation to the proliferation of corporate enterprise, to the development of an unmistakable class structure, to the disappearance of traditional democratic hopes for a society of independent small craftsmen and entrepreneurs. Al-

[11]Douglas, *op. cit.*, pp. 69–70.

though the outcome of industrial agitation was far from settled by 1900, it is accurate to say that the labor movement survived the century mainly by accepting for its members the very working class status it had been the purpose of the early reformers to abolish.[12]

Rush Welter's statement in *Popular Education and Democratic Thought in America* summarizes important aspects of labor's stance as the move to introduce industrial education into the schools began in earnest. "Accommodations" had not been made without a struggle. In the sixties and seventies, men like William Sylvis of the National Labor Union and leaders of the Knights of Labor had tried in vain to introduce producers' cooperatives, to counter pressures which were pushing workers downward from the status of independent artisan-entrepreneurs to the position of factory employees.

When the social reform efforts of the National Labor Union and the Knights failed, several varieties of socialists, communists, and anarchists sought to lure American workers to European revolutionary movements with other aims—the overthrow of the corporate capitalist system.

As the American Federation of Labor ascended in power Samuel Gompers pulled the workers away from these radical alternatives. In his book *Seventy Years of Life and Labor* Gompers made clear how his conviction grew, from bitter labor struggles in New York, that workingmen would delude themselves if they followed such utopian reformers. Their energies, he said, would be dissipated by ideological factionalism; *their* heads would be fractured when intellectual agitators urged them to take to the streets.[13]

Gompers' own rejection of socialist alternatives was predicated upon his belief that the profit system would permit a kind of accommodation to allow workers to improve their position within it. Trade unions as interest groups would develop the powers and the techniques to increase workingmen's share in the growing national wealth; unions would act with sufficient responsibility to win eventual acceptance by the employers and the public; they would provide a quality of community to satisfy the members' needs for solidarity; and they would resist all efforts to be diverted from pursuing single-mindedly the goal of "more and more." The American Federation fought bitter battles for union control in the early nineties against Daniel De Leon and other socialists. Gompers and his followers won decisively. As the twentieth

[12]Rush Welter, *Popular Education and Democratic Thought in America* (New York: Columbia University Press, 1962), p. 177.

[13]For Gompers' campaigns against the socialists, see also Gerald N. Grob, *Workers and Utopia* (Evanston, Ill.: Northwestern U. Press, 1961), Chaps. 8 and 9.

century opened, American workers had chosen to take their chances within capitalism and, in the main, had accepted middle-class values and aspirations. The AFL experienced a spectacular increase in membership as the new century opened.

In spite of the Federation's renunciation of revolutionary doctrine the very success of the union movement frightened the manufacturers. As we recall, NAM President Parry in 1903, armed with the conservative version of social Darwinism, had opened an era of hostility to all of labor's efforts to challenge the prerogatives of management. Trade unions, Parry argued, interfered with the industialist's freedom to act in accord with his own self-interest, which had been granted him by "the natural order of the universe."[14] One of the weapons the NAM chose to employ against the unions was an expanded system of trade-school education. It was the NAM's endorsement of industrial education as an anti-union tactic which stirred the initial interest of the Federation in the subject.

The Federation appointed its first Committee on Education in 1903 and passed a resolution which concluded rather lamely that "the subject of manual training and technical education to be given by trade unions is of such general character that this convention would not very well recommend any plan or policy that would apply equally to all unions. . . ." Committees on education appointed in 1904 and 1905 did not even report. In 1906 a resolution was passed, without discussion, that the Committee on Education conduct investigations into the subjects of apprenticeship, the career lives of graduates of the trade schools, manual training programs, and schools of technology. Conflicts within union ranks slowed the AFL's efforts to define a stand. Some craft unions, like the carpenters, saw no need to concede any departure from their tradition of apprenticeship; other leaders were convinced that technological change required workers to take new approaches. Gompers himself started with the position that if the new technology required upgrading of skill through schooling then unions should establish their own schools such as the one being tried by the Typographers Union. In practice it wasn't quite that simple. Workers did not respond well to the idea of attending such schools; and the unions as well as employers found they did not have the energy, funds, or talents to run large-scale school programs.

The alternative was to ask the public schools to assume skill training functions. But the unions had ambivalent feelings toward public school leadership. The Federation at the turn of the century was nervous

[14]For examples of management's commitment to the doctrine of social Darwinism, see NAM, *Proceedings*, 1903, pp. 13–62, 114–130, and 199–237.

about sporadic antiunion sentiments emanating from meetings of the National Education Association. For several years in a row, the AFL set up committees to investigate the attitudes of teachers toward labor unions and children of working people. They were concerned that teachers were unduly influenced by the dominant business ethic and that children might be taught a distorted view of labor's role in society. They were not of a mood to turn over industrial training to public schools without careful consideration.[15]

With the establishment of the Massachusetts Commission on Industrial Education in 1906 and the founding of the National Society for the Promotion of Industrial Education (NSPIE) in 1907 events took a new turn. In both of these forums labor heard a strong plea from progressive allies that public schools should assume major responsibility for industrial education. When Gompers accepted membership into NSPIE labor was brought into a working relationship with corporate managers even while warfare between the two was raging elsewhere.

The President of NSPIE, Professor Charles Richards, spoke to somewhat sceptical AFL delegates at their 1907 Convention. He urged them to keep an open mind and to cooperate in forthcoming deliberations. The union leaders decided that the subject was of sufficient importance to merit their serious attention. In 1908 Gompers appointed a commission of fifteen, chaired by his trusted lieutenant, mineworkers' leader John Mitchell. The committee was charged with the task of making an exhaustive investigation of approaches to industrial education in this country and abroad. The Federation's attitude on the subject was reflected in a resolution passed at the 1908 convention.

> There are two groups with opposite methods, and seeking antagonistic ends, now advocating industrial education in the United States. ... One of these groups is largely composed of the non-union employers of the country who advance industrial education as a special privilege under conditions that educate the student or apprentice to non-union sympathies and prepare him as a skilled worker for scab labor, thus using the children of the workers against the interests of their organized fathers and brothers in the various crafts. ... This group also favors the training of the student or apprentice for skill in only one industrial process, thus making the graduate a skilled worker in only a very limited sense and rendering him nearly helpless if lack of employment comes in his single subdivision of a craft. ...
>
> The other group is composed of great educators, enlightened representatives of organized labor and persons engaged in genuine social service, who advocate industrial education as a common right to be open to all children on equal terms to be provided by general taxation and kept under the control of the whole people with a method or

[15]See, for example, AFL, *Proceedings,* 1902, p. 165; 1903, p. 29.

system of education that will make the apprentice or graduate a skilled craftsman, in all the branches of the trade.[16]

D. THE MITCHELL REPORT AND SUBSEQUENT DELIBERATIONS ON INDUSTRIAL EDUCATION

John Mitchell provided aggressive leadership for his committee. Various types of schools were visited in many parts of the country. Conferences were called to hear the views of a wide variety of spokesmen from outside labor as well as from within the ranks. The committee consulted with Charles F. Richards of NSPIE; Dr. Herman Schneider, founder of the University of Cincinnati's cooperative work-study program; Paul Hanus of Harvard; Frederick Fish, Chairman of the Massachusetts State Board of Education and President of AT & T; Arthur Dean, Chief of the Division of Trade Schools of the New York Department of Education; Dr. Elmer E. Brown, Chief of the U.S. Bureau of Education; Dr. Henry Pritchett, President of the Carnegie Foundation; A. Lincoln Filene, the Boston business leader; and Frank A. Vanderlip, President of the National City Bank of New York.

While the investigating committee had exposed itself to many points of view, its 1910 report concentrated on recommending policies which would protect trade union interests against the assaults of industrialists.[17] It reflected Samuel Gompers' kind of trade unionism.

As the Federation leaders sharpened their perception of the alternatives, they decided to join those who were insisting that industrial education be included in the public school program. They clarified what they were *for* by making it the converse of what they were against. If NAM President Ittner supported private trade schools with short courses to produce workers with skills of immediate use to industry then Mitchell's committee expressed adamant opposition to flooding the market with narrowly trained workers produced by industry-controlled schools. Mitchell took the position that if the technical and industrial education of workers had become a public necessity such training should properly be offered through the public schools. Labor above all, though, should be on guard against efforts of industrialists to influence and control public school programs.

[16]AFL, *Proceedings*, 1908, p. 234.
[17]The complete final report was printed in *Senate Documents*, U.S. Congress, No. 936, Vol. XL, 62nd Cong., 2nd Sess., 1911–12 ("Industrial Education: Report of the Committee on Industrial Education of the American Federation of Labor"), pp. 5–114. At the request of the AFL, the U.S. Bureau of Labor prepared an exhaustive survey of nearly every industrial and trade school in the U.S. Mitchell's committee referred to it at length. See U.S. Commission of Labor, *Twenty-Fifth Annual Report, Industrial Education* (Washington, D.C.: Government Printing Office, 1911).

The Mitchell Committee's suspicions of the industrialists was confirmed, for example, by its findings on the cooperative work-study program in Fitchburg, Massachusetts. A group of manufacturers had worked out an agreement with the high school in which the school provided academic instruction to boys indentured to the manufacturers. The employers could decide how many boys they would take and which would be retained or dismissed. Unions in the area charged that antiunion propaganda was taught, and that boys from prounion families were not accepted as apprentices, or were subject to dismissal. The public school thus failed to protect the educational rights of all its students and let itself be turned into a tool for private interests. Moreover, the Committee complained of new school guidance bureaus which used fancy rhetoric about "guidance" and "careers" but did little more than recruit boys to fill dead-end jobs for local industries.[18]

On the other hand, there were points on which labor and the industrialists were beginning to agree. The two factions shared an enthusiasm for the benefits of higher education which had come from the federally aided land grant universities. They could agree that the time was ripe for additional federal grants to extend practical subjects down into the secondary schools. Labor and management also shared the suspicion that impractical schoolmen were incapable of administering effective vocational training programs. They were ready to agree that workers and managers should be represented on public boards to advise and supervise such programs.

Where pedagogical details were concerned, there was still uncertainty and confusion. Part of this derived from the predominance of skilled trade unionists in the AFL who had to keep one eye on the interests of skilled artisans—the "aristocrats of labor"—and another on the welfare of the larger numbers of workers who were to hold semiskilled jobs in the new factories.

There was ambivalence, too, about the kind of future that workers should aspire to in the new industrial society. Many had come to share the view of labor leader, Samuel B. Donnelly, who said at the first meeting of NSPIE that the time had come to admit that "the American workingman will always remain a workingman." Industrial education was needed to fit him for his place in society. The worker's fate would not be deplorable, said Donnelly, so long as he could advance to the highest grade of employee in mechanical and artistic ability. If he hewed to the union, "the higher remuneration is a sufficient inducement."[19]

[18]Senate Documents, No. 936, 1912, pp. 98–100.
[19]NSPIE *Bulletin*, No. 1, 1907, pp. 34–35.

On the other hand, the 1910 AFL Report began with a different emphasis. It spoke of the growing need for men who could act as foremen, supervisors, or managers. The Committee wanted to assure access to education which would make it possible for children of workers to rise to the ranks of management.[20] As Mitchell put it in a strange phrase "assuming that the social stratification is vertical," the goal was to see that every boy had his chance to rise. The question of just where to rise was not answered clearly. Some of the skilled craft leaders thought in terms of their own role as "the aristocracy of labor." If unions could control entry to the labor market, those with necessary and exacting skills such as machinist and typographer could look forward to high compensation. Others, however, wanted to keep open for their children the chance to break out of the wage-earning status altogether to reach the salaried positions of foreman, manager, or executive or even the professional status of doctor, lawyer or engineer. The idea that any boy could go as far as his ability and character would take him led labor to resist any educational scheme which put children of workers into separate school systems. Trade schools, separate from the general school system, might deny students access to the chance of "moving up." Both labor and business leaders were steeped in the "rags to riches" stories of *Joe the Bootblack* and *Sam the Newsboy*.[21]

In reading the Mitchell Report and subsequent Federation statements on industrial education one can feel the continuing pull of these several orientations. On the one hand there was what might be called the "honest workman" orientation. Spokesmen for this position were ready to settle for skill-training courses which would improve the standard of living of union members as workers. They were ready to assume that "the American workingman will always remain a workingman." With that, they were impatient with lofty philosophizing and wanted no-nonsense, practical courses that would lead to good jobs and fatter pay checks. Others, as we have seen, were worried about measures that would lock their children into a permanent working class status. They wanted to incorporate industrial education into public schooling in a way that would make it consistent with the American success ideal. Industrial education *and* social mobility was their goal.[22]

There were still others who began to conceive of industrial educa-

[20]U.S. Congress, *Senate Documents*, No. 936, Vol. XL, 62nd Cong., 2nd Sess., 1911–12, pp. 5–7.

[21]See Irving J. Wyllie, *The Self Made Man in America: The Myth of Rags to Riches* (New York: Free Press, 1954).

[22]For an insightful account of the "honest workman" and "upward mobility" orientations see Berenice Fisher, *Industrial Education: Americans Ideals and Institutions* (Madison: U. of Wisconsin Press, 1967).

tion as a means for a new educational enlightenment. They spoke in the tradition of democratic social reforms. They were few in numbers but could be quite eloquent. They began to see the possibilities of a broad school reform movement in which the industrial component could help vitalize the entire school program. Such a new education might make urban schooling relevant to the realities of an industrial society; it might utilize techniques to give students chances to be active, doing, inquirers instead of mere lesson-sayers; and it might cultivate attitudes and skills necessary to humanize life in the age of technology.

All of them were sure about two things. They were unhappy about the experience their children were getting in urban schools, and they were determined to beat back any ambitions the industrialists might have to influence or control industrial education for their own benefit.

Labor was willing to add its voice to the general call for industrial education as a school-reform movement.

One can sense a note of personal experience in the workers' indictment of the deadly quality of urban classrooms. A bill of complaints was presented:

> first, a lack of interest on the part of the pupils; and secondly, on the part of the parents, and a dissatisfaction that the schools do not offer instruction of a more practical character. The pupils become tired of the work they have in hand, and see nothing more inviting in the grades ahead. They are conscious of powers, passions and tastes which the school does not recognize. They long to grasp things with their own hands and test the strength of materials and the magnitude of forces.[23]

In the face of the general complaint and ideological differences over what to do, the Mitchell Committee chose to avoid making specific recommendations. It contented itself, in the main, with presenting lengthly descriptions of industrial eduation programs which had already gotten underway. It described (1) trade union schools with technical education programs, (2) examples of public trade schools that had appeared since 1906, including cooperative work-study schools and continuation schools, (3) apprenticeship schools established by large corporations such as General Electric, Western Electric, International Harvester, and the railroad companies, (4) private philanthropic trade schools, (5) the Hampton and Tuskegee Institutes for Negroes, and (6) brief references to industrial education programs for girls.

Most labor leaders were too busy with other matters to be educational philosophers. As the movement for industrial education gathered momentum the general tendency was to concentrate on policies which

[23]AFL, *Proceedings*, 1909, p. 137.

safeguarded trade-union interests. Mr. J. M. Lynch, a delegate at the 1912 convention, probably expressed the feelings of the majority. "We cannot stop the trend in the direction of this kind of education in the school; but we can if we cooperate with the educators, have it come our way."[24]

The Mitchell Report did alert the Federation to the fact that significant matters were at issue in the vocational education drive. AFL leaders watched carefully efforts to enact state and federal legislation. The Federation's affiliation with NSPIE enabled it gradually to clarify, with other interest groups, the aspects of consensus which could be written into a federal bill.

In 1913 an effort began in Illinois to enact the "Cooley Bill," which would have created a State Board for Industrial Education separate from the general school board. The AFL joined a number of educators in vigorous opposition to this proposal to establish a dual school system. The bill violated labor's emerging principle that vocational and technical training should be supplementary to general education. In 1915, as support for the Smith-Hughes bill was gaining momentum, the Federation said its support would be dependent upon an amendment which would require states to accept a unit system of administration as opposed to Cooley-type dual control.[25]

When Smith-Hughes actually became law, the Federation was in a predicament.[26] The Act did not *require* a unit system of control by the states. States were given the choice, either to designate the State Board of Education to administer vocational education, or to create a separate board for that purpose. Concomitantly, however, the Act specified that labor had to be represented on any boards concerned with vocational education whether at the federal, state, or local level. The Federation compromised its position on "dual administration" and settled for representation on the advisory boards.

It is ironic to find that shortly before making this concession, the

---

[24]*American Federationist*, December 1909.

[25]American Federation of Labor, *Proceedings*, 1915, pp. 323–324. See also Edwin G. Cooley, "The Argument for Industrial Education from the Success of Germany," NSPIE. *Bulletin*, No. 15, 1911, p. 178. Cooley's reports on German schools were influential in promoting the rage about German industrial education. When he sponsored the "Cooley bill" for a dual system in Illinois, he became the bete noire of labor and liberal groups as an advocate of Prussianizing American education. Cooley's own writings show though that he was not an uncritical admirer of all that was German. He was opposed to letting "the man be merged in the artisan" and warned that the general education of the elementary school should never be replaced by any purely vocational training. Nevertheless, he argued vigorously for a separate system of schools for the 90 percent, aged fourteen and older, who would not go to college. See his "Principles That Should Underlie Legislation for Vocational Education," NSPIE. *Bulletin*, No. 16, 1912, p. 146.

[26]See Curoe, *op. cit.*, p. 135.

AFL was presented at its 1915 Convention with a report that contained the most perceptive and sensitive analysis of the value issues concerning industrial education that it had ever considered. It broke away from the narrow concern for union welfare and raised the philosophical questions about the role of vocational training in a democratic society.[27]

The report began by saying that in considering what educational policies to support labor ought to consider such questions as what a true education consists of, who should be educated, how far and by what methods, and who should do the educating. The purpose of education, the report said, is to bring us "nearer to the perfection of our nature." In its broadest sense, "education" ought to be seen as a process including all the effects on character of the pattern of community life, of forms of government and law, of industrial arts, and of social, economic, and civic life. Questions about a good education for children could not be entertained adequately without reflecting on the quality of life in the total society.

The report noted that past statements by the AFL indicated it supported the new move for industrial education but with some misgivings. Without safeguards, vocationalism could be made so subordinate to commercial interests that "the opportunities of the workers' children for a general education will be limited, which will tend to make the workers more submissive and less independent." To prevent this it proposed that labor reject narrow skill-training and endorse only policies supportive of "a full development of American freedom and of American manhood and womanhood."

> We hold the child must be educated not only to adapt to his or her particular calling . . . but that they should be educated for leadership as well; that they should have the power of self-direction and of directing others; the powers of administration as well as ability to assume positions of responsibility.
> It is not only essential that we should fit our boys and girls for the industries, but it is equally essential to fit the industries for the future employment of our young men and women.[28]

What good would it do, the report asked, to have industrial education programs if children were "to be fastened to a machine, requiring but the repetition of a few muscular motions"?—"Vocational education is not enough; extreme specialization must be abolished."

The report argued that commercial interests in the past had put pressure on the public schools to train a huge supply of cheap labor

[27]AFL, *Proceedings*, 1915, pp. 321–325.
[28]*Ibid.*, p. 322.

merely so that profits could be increased. Teachers and administrators faced these pressures and sometimes bowed to them.

> It is for labor to say whether their children shall receive a real education in our public schools, or whether they are to be turned out as machine-made products fitted only to work and to become part and parcel of a machine instead of human beings with a life of their own, and a right to live that life under rightful living conditions.[29]

Feeling this way, writers of the 1915 report opposed the dual administration of public education which the Smith-Hughes Bill was to permit. As we have seen, the Federation shortly afterward backed away from a firm stand on the issue in return for guarantee of union representation on boards for vocational education.

The Federation continued to be torn by its several value orientations. These conflicts were apparent as it periodically considered various alternatives for industrial education programs. Mr. Frank Glynn, Director of Vocational Education in Wisconsin, was invited in 1917 to describe the system of vocational schools pioneered in Wisconsin under *dual* administration.[30] Wisconsin was commended for organizing the most exceptional opportunity for democratic education yet known in America. The vocational schools were designed to work hand in hand with labor, farmer, and employer. Mr. Glynn said that Wisconsin's vocational schools met agriculture's needs, providing for every worker from the mechanic who makes the tractor to the farmer who raises and harvests the crop. He assured the Convention that the new system of vocational education was administered by practical men made up of representatives of labor, agriculture, and business. The new system said Glynn, is for 90 percent of the people and is arranged so that every working boy and girl between fourteen and seventeen must spend at least eight hours per week out of his working time in school. He was not bothered that this seemed to be a paltry amount of time for general education. On the contrary, he asserted that "It is not, however, the usual academic education which the young person left school to evade, but rather it is a new type of instruction which fits the boy for gaining [sic] occupations and the girl for efficient homemaking." A state educational system was, at last, providing something for "those who are forced by economic conditions to enter employment at an early age" instead of offering only a "culture curriculum" tailored to those who are college-bound.

[29] *Ibid.*, p. 323.
[30] AFL, *Proceedings*, 1917, pp. 267–270.

One can sense the pull of conflicting values in the 1915 and 1917 statements, pulls which reflected dilemmas for education in a society which aspired to be both industrial and humane. Both statements acknowledged the great need in all facets of society for more technical training. Labor could join industry in asking schools for practical courses offered by practical men. The 1915 report sensed, however, that such training programs could move too far in the direction of turning public schools into instruments for serving the needs of business and industry.

E. BLACK WORKERS, AFL, AND INDUSTRIAL EDUCATION

It is clear by now that the discussions on vocational education reflected the pressures, confusions, and conflicts in values of the larger society as Americans entered the twentieth century. The question was whether the new technological-urban realities could be combined with the values of the democratic ideal. The issue remains in doubt. Nowhere has this been more apparent than in the case of American black citizens.

The Mitchell Committee Report followed very closely the descriptions of vocational programs drawn up in the Commissioner of Labor's 1910 report, *Industrial Education.*[31] Often the wording was repeated verbatim or with very close paraphrasing. This is true of the accounts of the two schools for blacks: the Hampton Normal and Agricultural Institute of Virginia, and the Tuskegee Institute of Alabama.

There were some interesting omissions or shifts in emphasis in Mitchell's summation of the Department of Labor's survey. The Commissioner of Labor's Report pointed out that there were very few vocational programs for Negroes in the North. In the South, such schools were supported by private philanthropy. It pointed out that the intention in the South was to discourage Negroes from seeking city or industrial employment and to encourage them to return to the farms. "This field is free from competition and from face feeling." The skills taught were those that would be helpful on the farm: "blacksmithing to shoe his own horses . . . enough carpentry to shingle his own roof or build his own barns, etc."[32] Girls were taught what was useful for homemaking, or the skills for the kind of employment open to them—laundry work, cooking, sewing, being nursemaids. Teacher training in the normal school branches was stressed for both boys and girls. There was a

[31]Commission of Labor, *op. cit.*, pp. 311–799.
[32]*Ibid*, p. 312.

strong emphasis on "uplift and enlightenment." The prospectus of one school announced that its purposes were

> To train them to be intelligent, faithful, trustworthy; to instill in them right moral principles, to teach them dignity of labor; to encourage them to buy homes and farms and to become good and desirable neighbors and citizens.

Production of such useful and dependable citizens who would be happy down on the farm, away from the competition of city labor markets, seemed sensible. The trouble with such a solution to "the problem" was that technology was already invading Southern agriculture and eliminating the rural reservations.

The Commissioner's Report warned that schools for Negroes were not to be compared with those for whites, because they were handicapped by lack of funds and unable to obtain qualified teachers for most of the work.

> While thus hampered they still must aim to give a good training in industrial work, for in practically all trades the regular apprenticeship is not open to the Negro youth, so if a school starts a boy (or girl) in a trade it must give sufficient training to enable him to compete with the man who has served an apprenticeship.[33]

The Mitchell Report omitted these references to the condition of black workers and stuck to reprinting descriptions of the programs offered at Hampton and Tuskegee.

This reluctance to talk about the real problems of black people in the work world is understandable in terms of the depressing trade union record of racial discrimination. Discriminatory treatment was present from the moment that black persons were freed from slavery. Just after the Civil War, blacks chose to organize separately from whites despite some efforts of the National Labor Union to win them over. The chief reason for separate organization was "the exclusion of colored men and apprentices from the right to labour in any department of industry or workshops . . . by what is known as 'trade unions.' "[34] When blacks tried to enter the trades, they were rebuffed by their white fellow workers. In 1869 a black printer who was refused admission to a local union took his case to the convention of the National Typographical Union. He was rejected there, too.

When black workers were brought North in considerable numbers at the time of World War I, they received harsher treatment from

---

[33] *Ibid.*, p. 311.
[34] John R. Commons *et al.*, *History of Labour in the United States*, II (New York: Macmillan, 1961), p. 135, citing *Chicago Workingman's Advocate*, Jan. 1, 1870.

northern workers than did the immigrants from foreign lands. After the war, in the depression years of the early twenties, blacks had to give way to whites in competition for jobs or run the risks of race riots or lynchings. Gompers himself deplored discrimination against black workers and made efforts in AFL conventions to secure fairer treatment for them. In the South, he felt he had to accede to white prejudice; and he accepted separate black unions in the few places where they were organized. When racism flared up in the twenties, Gompers chose to defer to the prejudices of the International Unions rather than precipitate a conflict within the Federation.[35]

The difficulties of black people must be seen against the bitter conditions of poverty which all urban workers suffered in the last decades of the nineteenth century. Robert Hunter in *Poverty* pointed out that one-third of the people of New York were dependent upon charity at some time in the eight years prior to 1890.[36] In the years around 1900, approximately 20 percent of the population of New York and Boston were unemployed or in distress.

The industrial workers of the North were confronted constantly by new sources of cheap labor: children, women, immigrants, and blacks. In the harsh struggles for survival, the black person had the special handicap of being visible. Ovington, in *Half a Man: The Status of the Negro in New York,* points out that in the competitive urban situation, the status of the black people worsened in the period from 1850 to 1914. The free blacks in New York prior to the Civil War represented a small percentage of the population. Black people were always active in domestic service: but they worked also as shipbuilders, riggers, coopers, caulkers, tailors, printers, carpenters. They occupied a considerable position in the catering and restaurant business. Some of the better-known barber shops and drug stores were black-owned.

Hard times came after the Civil War when black workers had to compete with immigrants, particularly the Irish. The 1900 census showed only a few black men working at the trades. They found that the unions, which were a boon for white workers, had become an agency to force them out of work. As Ovington succinctly put it:

> If they are the only available source of labor, colored men can work by the side of white men; but where the white man strongly dominates the labor situation, he tries to push his black brother into the jobs for which he does not care to compete.[37]

[35]Gompers, *op. cit.* pp. 37–39.
[36]Robert Hunter, *Poverty* (New York: Macmillan, 1909).
[37]Mary White Ovington, *Half a Man: The Status of the Negro in New York* (New York: Longmans, 1911), p. 93. Ovington's picture of the black man's condition in relation to labor unions and the world of work is supported by the evidence compiled in W. E. B. DuBois' classic study, *The Philadelphia Negro* (Philadelphia: U. of Pennsylvania, 1899).

In trying to give a balanced picture, Ovington did find certain areas in which able blacks were making gains in the 1900's. There was an increase of black physicians and dentists, although New York doctors would not admit black interns to hospitals for training. The black graduate had to go to Philadelphia, Chicago, or Washington for hospital training.[38] There were increases in the number of black lawyers, actors, musicians, and ministers. In a poignant observation, Ovington pointed out that blacks had been notably successful in one business venture. "The Negroes of the city die in great numbers, and the funeral is all too common a function." The wealthiest black in New York City was an undertaker.[39]

After viewing all of the setbacks and gains for the black worker in the work world of New York, Ovington was forced to conclude: "No group of men in America have opposed his progress more persistently than skilled mechanics, and, should he graduate from some school of technology, he would be refused in office or workshop."[40] Racism was widespread in American society. Union workers probably were no more or no less racist than others.

It is no wonder then that the Mitchell Committee had little to say about vocational education for black people. Indeed, very little was said on the subject by any of the groups who spoke so profusely about the virtues of industrial education.

[38] *Ibid.*, p. 114.
[39] *Ibid.*, p. 109.
[40] *Ibid.*, p. 113.

4 / Industrial Education and Progressive Reform

We have noted how leaders of industry and labor called on American schools to modify their programs. They were joined by an array of other interest groups in the progressive era.

The progressive movement, which began in the late nineteenth century and continued until World War I, was headed by middle-class and professional groups, whose roots were in the new cities. The progressives shared some concerns with their populist predecessors. Both were concerned with the corrosive effects of economic and political power concentrations. Traditional values of individual initiative and community solidarity seemed threatened by the rise to power of new financial giants and big-city political bosses. Both progressives and populists tried to check the chaos and disorder which accompanied the onrush of change. The populist movement, however, was primarily a rural, small-town phenomenon, antagonistic to the new urbanism. The progressives, on the other hand, were prepared to accept urban life as inescapable reality. They were ready to do battle against ugly aspects of the cities and to transform them so that they could embody once again beloved values of older American communities. To take on this formidable task progressives were prepared to use the organizational and scientific skills of trained experts.

It is not surprising, then, to find progressive groups in the forefront of the concern about industrial education. The schools in the cities were undergoing an unprecedented expansion. They were confronted with new waves of impoverished, non-English-speaking immigrant children, and with multiple pressures to retain more children in school longer. The schools were handicapped in facing these challenges by inadequate finances and by demoralizing political intrusions. The problem of simply keeping up with accelerating expansion took most of the schools' energies. The question of thinking seriously about what kinds of education might be effective for urban poor children had hardly been considered as the century opened. The truth is that schools at the end of the nineteenth century were ill equipped in resources, personnel, and theory to meet the unprecedented problems of the mushrooming cities.[1] The recitation method of learning, a survival technique of the one-room schoolmaster, was transported into the new brick, factorylike schools of the city. Latin still held a preeminent position in the high schools. Gradually these traditional school practices were brought under criticism by various groups in the cities—by leaders of industry, business, and labor, and by progressive groups like the settlement house workers, who lived daily with the cruelties of the slums.

Progressive reform was not a simple phenomenon. Robert H. Wiebe has identified two major groupings within progressivism. One was motivated by the desire to bring urban disorder under control by scientific expertise and social control; while the major goal of the other was to reduce human misery by humanitarian social reform.

> By 1905 urban progressives were already separating along two paths. While one group used the language of the budget, boosterism, and social control, the other talked of economic justice, human opportunities, and rehabilitated democracy. Efficiency as economy diverged further and further from efficiency as social service.[2]

The two sectors occasionally came together in the desire to face common enemies. Both, for example, wanted to replace the chaos, conflict, and poor social service of the city with conditions that would be more orderly, rational, and efficient. Both were enraged by municipal corruption, which they felt was a product of the unholy alliance of greedy "interests" with power-hungry political bosses. They could agree on the need to replace a corrupt spoils system with efficient bureaucracies guided by qualified experts. They shared, at least for a while, a confidence in the voice of the people. The antidote to the poison of political bosses, in cahoots with corrupt financiers, was direct democracy in the form of the initiative, referendum, and recall. "Efficiency" guided by scientific expertise would replace "waste."

But there were conflicting intentions concealed in the loose rhetoric of reform. While business-oriented progressives were alarmed by waste, it was financial waste that bothered them most. When they discussed educational waste, they pointed to the "low yield of school products" measured on the yardsticks of cost accounting. Or, they deplored the impractical curriculum which failed to serve the requirements of business and industry. The humanitarian reformers, on the

---

[1]See Joseph Mayer Rice, *The Public School System of the United States* (New York: Century Company, 1893) for one of the earliest studies to show how bad things were.

[2]Robert H. Wiebe, *The Search for Order* (New York: Hill and Wang, 1967), p. 176.

other hand, were appalled chiefly by the "human waste" as represented in the lives of slum dwellers eroded by poverty, vice, crime, despair.

The differences in emphases were clear and tended to grow sharper as the progressive era unfolded. Their biases were reflected in the kinds of city each group desired to create.

> The reform-minded business man . . . usually pictured the ideal city as an extension of his commercial values. Desiring continuous services that were also inexpensive, he resented taxes that would take away with one hand the benefits he was extracting with the other. His modern city was a business community; a clean, attractive appearance, an atmosphere of growth and progress, raised the general level of the economy.[3]

This viewpoint excluded much that the humanitarian progressives cherished: the cultivation of trained, self-reliant citizens capable of vigorous democratic participation; the creation of communities with rich social services—playgrounds, kindergartens, health and hygienic facilities, adult education programs, social centers where immigrant generations would be brought together to share the music, the art, the dance of old traditions. In short, humanitarian reformers wanted, through public financing, to create neighborhood communities which would be centers of order, sanity, and mutual support against the impersonality and dissonance of the new cities. Eventually they turned to the federal government for programs and funds. They always assumed, however, that American society contained the will and the capacity to introduce the needed reforms.

The dual value orientations of progressivism—efficiency and social control on the one hand and rejuvenated democracy and social service on the other—were both represented in the efforts to introduce vocationalism into the schools.

A. SOCIAL SERVICE GROUPS AND INDUSTRIAL EDUCATION

The year 1906 was a critical one in the drive for vocational, or industrial, education. It was the year of the publication of the *Report of the Massachusetts Commission on Industrial and Technical Education,*[4]

---

[3] *Ibid.*, p. 175. For a detailed elaboration of the effects of the Taylorist brand of efficiency on American education, see Raymond E. Callahan, *Education and the Cult of Efficiency* (Chicago: U. of Chicago Press, 1962).

[4] Commonwealth of Massachusetts, *Report of the Commission on Industrial and Technical Education* (Boston: The Commission, 1906), hereafter referred to as the "Douglas Commission Report."

and the year in which the National Society for the Promotion of Industrial Education (NSPIE) was organized. These two events may be seen both as the culmination of several decades of pressures to institute a more practical curriculum, and as the beginning of concerted moves which led to enactment of the Smith-Hughes Act in 1917.

As noted earlier, dissatisfaction with public schools had been growing among the new businessmen and industrialists since the Civil War. In Massachusetts, long before the Douglas Report, Yankee manufacturers had been nervous about their ability to meet international competition. At the World's Fair in Paris in 1867, English and American manufacturers discovered that their wares were inferior to those produced on the continent. Leading Massachusetts manufacturers expressed their concern by sending a petition to the Legislature in 1869. In it they pointed to the lack of skill in drawing and other "arts of design" on the part of American workingmen. The next year the legislature responded by making drawing a required study in all public schools of the state. A State Director of Art Education was appointed, and all towns of more than ten thousand inhabitants were required to maintain evening school courses in drawing.[5] This speedy response may be contrasted with the resistance to other demands for curriculum change in the nineteenth century. The kind of art intended was made inescapably clear: "The end sought is not to enable the scholar to draw a pretty picture, but to so train the hand and the eye that he may be better fitted to become a breadwinner."[6]

We have noted, too, the interest of businessmen in commercial education and manual training. They were relatively satisfied with the former; but they became increasingly sceptical about the capacity of manual training programs to produce the kind and amount of skilled workers they now needed. By the late nineties New England industrialists were prominent in the drive for "real trade schools."

At the same time, additional support for industrial education was coming from a variety of groups concerned with ameliorating the plight of the urban poor.

When muckrakers like Jacob Riis[7] called attention to the appalling conditions of immigrant slums, they touched the consciences of some of the affluent. In New York, for example, Grace Dodge, daughter of

[5]Reported in an introductory section on the history of industrial education in the Douglas Commission Report, pp. 10–12 *et passim*.

[6]United States Bureau of Education, *Circulars of Information*, "Drawing in the Public Schools: The Present Relation of Art to Education in the United States," No. 2–1874 (Washington D.C.: Government Printing Office, 1874), p. 10.

[7]See, for example, Jacob Riis, *How the Other Half Lives*, (New York: Sagamore Press, 1957) and *The Children of the Poor* (New York: Scribner's, 1892).

one of New York's wealthiest merchants, was active in founding organizations like the Children's Aid Society, the Association of Working Girls Societies, and the Kitchen Garden Association. The latter was changed in 1887 to the Industrial Education Association, committed to promoting manual training classes in schools, especially at the elementary level.

In New York City, too, the wives of prominent business and professional men organized the Public Education Association in 1895. One of the PEA's objectives was to professionalize school administration, but it stated that its major concern was with

> the schools below 14th Street where the system had been longest at work and where it has had to deal with a peculiar environment, an almost foreign population in some localities—and where, if the system had not adapted itself to, or conquered, that environment, it was clearly no system for the city at all.[8]

The disorder and discontents of the seventies, eighties, and nineties forced attention to the plight of the inhabitants of urban slums. The New York census showed it to be the home of 1,500,000 people, of whom 80 percent were foreign born or of foreign parentage. The new immigrants were largely non-English-speaking people: Russian and Polish Jews, Italians, and newcomers from the Balkans or Eastern Europe. Sol Cohen has shown that the New York reformers, in their eagerness "to do something about these slum dwellers," seized upon education and the public schools as the Great Panacea.

> The public school was cast as the great immigrant assimilating agency. The school also was cast as the . . . prophylactic for crime, vice, pauperism, juvenile delinquency, and the other social ills of of the city. Finally as those who led the reform movement in New York may have been antiforeign and anti-immigrant, they were also sincerely concerned with the plight of the slum dweller. The public schools were cast as a major agency in their program for the amelioration of slum life and a major agency in their program of constructive social reform.[9]

After the turn of the century the Public Education Association spawned a rash of reform committees whose titles indicate the social service functions the Association sought for the public schools: Truancy, Compulsory Education, Special Children, Hygiene of School Children, School Lunch, Parents Meeting, Visiting Teacher, and Committees on Vocational Education and Vocational Guidance Surveys. Between 1914

---

[8]Sol Cohen, *Progressives and Urban School Reform* (New York: Bureau of Publications, Teachers College, Columbia University, 1964), p. 4, citing Public Education Association, *Annual Report*, 1896, pp. 8–9.

[9]*Ibid.*, p. 8.

and 1917, the PEA's major project was an unsuccessful attempt to get the New York City public school system to adopt Henry Wirt's Gary Plan, with its platoon school and industrial education orientation. Urban reform groups thus furthered the cause of industrial education in their efforts to encourage the public schools to renounce narrow academic programs, and perform instead a series of social service for the urban poor. Convinced of their own virtues these middle class reformers had no idea that their well-intentioned efforts had a patronizing quality that vitiated deep-rooted social change. As the twentieth century unfolded we would discover slowly and painfully that there are profound differences between "doing good for people" and giving them power to work on their own problems.[10]

1. The Role of the Settlement House Leaders

Another response to industrialism came from the Settlement House Movement. New York's problems with its immigrants were replicated in the experiences of the other great cities of the East and Midwest. Jane Addams, in collaboration with Ellen Gates Starr, founded Hull House in Chicago after returning from Toynbee Hall in London in 1889. Other settlement houses patterned after Toynbee Hall and Hull House sprang up in industrial cities of the East—in New York, the University Settlement and the Henry Street Settlement, for example, and in Boston, the South End House and the Civic Service House, founded in 1901 for immigrants of the North End. Frank Parsons, "father of the vocational guidance movement," taught in the Breadwinners Institute of the Civic Service House, and from his experience founded the Boston Vocation Bureau. Robert Woods was the head worker in the South End House and became the historian of the settlement house movement.[11]

The settlement house leaders had interests broader than sponsorship of vocational education; Woods' account in *The Settlement Horizon* makes it clear, however, that many of their activities did center on the industrial education question.

Woods states in *The Settlement Horizon* that a central aspiration of these reformers was ". . . to rear a generation *better equipped both technically and morally* for a highly integrated industrial system."[12]

[10]See Michael B. Katz, *The Irony of Early School Reform* (Cambridge: Harvard U. P., 1968).

[11]See Robert A. Woods and Albert J. Kennedy, *The Settlement Horizon* (New York: Russell Sage Foundation, 1922) and *Handbook of Settlements* (New York: Russell Sage Foundation, 1911).

[12]Woods and Kennedy, *The Settlement Horizon*, p. 220. (Italics added.)

The settlement house leaders brought more than moral fervor to their task. They were new-style, university-trained professionals in close contact with pioneer scholars in the social sciences. They saw their task as multifaceted: (1) to develop insights into the dynamics of the industrial system and the needs of the people in it, (2) to develop pilot programs that would demonstrate how the needs of city people should be met, (3) to act as an agent for disseminating findings so as to influence other institutions like the public schools, and (4) to secure legislation and public tax money to meet problems spawned by the new industrialism.

The settlement house movement became involved with industrial education from its inception. Settlement houses were just being established when the depression of 1893–95 sharpened the misery of slum dwellers. Settlement people became particularly sensitive to the problems of youth aged twelve to sixteen as they left school and looked in vain for work. As industrial processes became more complicated, employers grew increasingly reluctant to hire these untrained children. They were the last hired and the first fired. They drifted from job to job and could look forward only to a lifetime of marginal employment. They would be lucky if they did not drift into alcoholism or crime.

The discontents and the rebelliousness of boys in this category became apparent to the settlement people. Many youth felt the need for additional training but could find no help in the public schools. The settlement houses were not so slow to respond. They began to introduce classes in sloyd,* carpentry, printing, garment cutting, shoe repair, plumbing, and bricklaying for boys; and in cooking and sewing for girls. They quickly found, however, that the settlements were not equipped to offer adequate trade training. Costs were prohibitive; it was almost impossible to obtain qualified teachers; and the unions were very suspicious. "Most important of all, the community unit of trade training was seen to be district and city rather than the neighborhood."[13] In the face of their limitations, settlements threw their support behind efforts to get industrial education programs introduced into the public schools. They made headway in securing evening trade classes and sought expansion of manual training programs.

Settlement workers also became active proponents of free kindergartens. The rationale for justifying these programs has a familiar sound.

> One cause for the poor showing made by many boys and girls both in class and in shop is paucity of provision for really educative play. As

---

*A Swedish system of manual training.
[13] *Ibid.*, p. 139.

running, jumping, and climbing lead to increasingly accurate accommodations between mind and the larger motor muscles, and club relations coordinate thought and deportment, craftwork makes adjustment between the constructive facilities and hands. No amount of formal instruction can take the place of the free movement of a child's mind as he endeavors to find himself.[14]

Over a half century later these ideas would be enunciated again as if for the first time. Under the label of perceptual-motor training, they would appear in Head Start programs for urban poor.

It is important to note, however, that the settlements were interested in more than converting school officials to the idea of introducing more practical offerings. Their pilot demonstrations were intended to illustrate the value preferences which humanitarian reformers felt were necessary to make life decent in the new era. They wanted nothing less than to create models in which people could learn to exert democratic control over institutions and events. They confidently expected that this could happen in the enormous complexity of the new cities.

Examples of the kind of aspirations settlement people held are found in movements they sponsored in relation to the campaign for industrial education. They turned, for example, to the establishment of arts and handicrafts programs. In the spirit of Ruskin and William Morris, their goal was to unite the designer and workman—to produce people capable of combining utility and beauty.

In 1897 the American Society of Arts and Crafts was founded in Boston, a forerunner to the National League of Handicraft Societies of America. Gustave Stickley of the United Crafts of New Jersey envisioned a new democratic art that would come from the people rather than from a leisured elite.

> A simple democratic art should provide (the people) with material surroundings conducive to plain living and high thinking, to the development of the sense of order, symmetry, and proportion.[15]

Stickley resisted an attitude of rebellion toward the machine. The purpose of craftsmanship, said Stickley, is to relate production to man's total needs. If machinery, in the hands of thoughtful and conscientious workmen, could aid in achieving this goal, there was no need to reject it. The only threat lay in the machine's domination over man's work, leisure, and tastes. The way to avoid industrial slavery was to insure the

---

[14] *Ibid.*, p. 141.
[15] *The Craftsman*, Vol. I, No. 1, Eastwood, New York (October 1901), i–ii. For a fuller account see Berenice M. Fisher, *Industrial Education* (Madison: U. of Wisconsin Press, 1967).

worker's control over all phases of production.

Apart from his beliefs in industrial democracy, Stickley's ideal assumed that the artist and the worker would be combined in one person. Others like Jane Addams and Mary Simkhovitch were leery of promising such a possibility to the immigrant. They recognized that the immigrant would have to make his way in an industrial situation where specialization was a hard fact and much work would be mechanical and routine. They favored crafts programs but felt workers might have to limit craftsmanship to an avocation or to an income supplement. They did feel that workers should be taught to appreciate design in products and initiated art appreciation programs to contribute to that end.

The settlement house workers and their allies clearly hoped to sponsor programs which would nourish the aesthetic impulse. But specialization and commercialization made it difficult if not impossible to realize holistic visions of art integrated with use.

The struggle between art for use and art for personal development was reflected in the discussions of the Department of Art of the NEA founded in 1884. Some educators stressed the importance of art for skilled workmen in order to better prepare them for the competition of foreign labor. Others spoke of the moral effects of art or handicraft on uncouth workers. These men might not only learn skills but be "kept out of rum shops."[16] This quality of moral uplift was a recurrent theme in the complex thinking of the progressives. It is illustrated in a statement by Robert Woods:

> Even simple handicraft demands accuracy, neatness, order, perseverance, initiative . . . while appreciation of property created by one's own labor brings about a new attitude toward thoughtless destruction.[17]

Another concern of the reformers was the cultivation of worker insight into the cultural origins of his industry. This process was emphasized in Jane Addams' work at Hull House and reflected the ideas she had developed in her association with John Dewey. Miss Addams was horrified by the fact that men had lost all sense of the relation of their work to the larger society and to human history. She was equally dismayed that the young had no knowledge or appreciation of the traditions of crafts which their parents had practiced in Europe. In response to this ignorance, Jane Addams opened the Hull House Labor Museum. In it she hoped that both young and old workers would gain an understanding that contemporary modes of production were an outgrowth of long, historic processes. Settlement house programs, she held, should

[16]NEA, *Addresses and Proceedings*, 1885, pp. 607–614 and 275–283.
[17]Woods and Kennedy, *The Settlement Horizon*, p. 140.

help people of the cities retain a sense of organic relationship both to the human past and to the larger contemporary social order. The public schools should learn from this example.

A third reform value is illustrated by the School for Printers Apprentices, managed by the Hudson Guild in New York. The Guild was proud that it was able to create a school by obtaining the cooperation of unions, employers, and educators. This accomplishment illustrated the ideal of collective action and provided "an important object lesson in seasoned and responsible industrial democracy."[18]

It was hoped this school would become a prototype to be emulated by the public schools. The Apprentice School for Printers combined technical training with courses teaching communication skills and social insights—English, history of printing, economic problems of the trade, principles of unionism, and "the science of cooperation." This last item was emphasized in other aspects of settlement house programs. As Woods put it, ". . . industrial recruits, settlement workers believe, should include discipline in the art of democratic association."[19] Skills of the democratic process should be included in all trade-training programs. At their own centers, settlement leaders used club work for this purpose.

> Detailed, specific drill and discipline in working together with constant and varied emphasis on motives which govern cooperative effort, are the core of a coming phase of education. The type of personal initiative and leadership developed in this atmosphere, when qualified with the sense for results that trade schools give, produces persons who soundly fill out their part in trade organization and in a more developed system of the organization of industry as a whole.[20]

Settlement house workers sponsored neighborhood consumer cooperatives and spoke of industries in which democratic forms of administration would produce "a new sense of reciprocity throughout, create a larger product, and share it on a better understanding and more equitable basis."[21]

Employers, even in the business reform group, had little patience with such talk. A few like A. Lincoln Filene, manager of Filene Sons and Company, Boston, were ready to try profit sharing plans and felt that such a move might head off agitators trying to win the ear of immigrants. Most business leaders, like those in the NAM, however, regarded such ideas as downright subversive.

[18]*Ibid.*, p. 217.
[19]*Ibid.*, p. 219.
[20]*Ibid.*
[21]*Ibid.*, p. 220.

B. SETTLEMENT HOUSE LEADERS AND THE EVENTS OF 1906: THE DOUGLAS COMMISSION REPORT AND THE FOUNDING OF NSPIE

1. The Douglas Commission Report

Settlement house leaders and their allies played a leading role in events surrounding the Douglas Commission Report and the founding of the National Society for the Promotion of Industrial Education. We have seen that settlement people in the nineties had come to the conclusion that the public schools needed to be reformed to meet the practical needs of urban children. They had found allies among businessmen (both conservative and progressive) among labor leaders, and among some educators (including both those who were to identify themselves as vocational educators and those inclined toward "progressive education").

Social workers became involved in a number of developments which preceded formal moves to support industrial education. In Massachusetts, the Legislature, in 1905, created a Commission on Industrial Education "to inquire into the advisability of establishing industrial schools." In the following year, when a permanent commission was empowered to establish such schools, Robert Woods, of the South End House in Boston, served as temporary chairman during the period of organization and development. For three months Woods traveled throughout Massachusetts talking with manufacturers, union leaders, and educators to get ideas for drawing up a plan for industrial education in the state.[22]

In Chicago, meanwhile, Jane Addams was promoting the cause of industrial education. She found a sympathetic audience in the Superintendent of Schools, Ella Flagg Young, who in the nineties had been Dewey's chief advisor on elementary education at his University of Chicago Laboratory School. Miss Addams was invited to make one of the main speeches at the founding convention of NSPIE.

When the Douglas Commission Report was published in 1906, its chairman acknowledged that the interests of people like Jane Addams were different from those of the practical men of industry. The opening paragraph of the Report acknowledged the existence of two distinct forms of interest in industrial education as "manifested by two classes of people." The first was the "theoretical interest felt by students of social phenomena and by expert students of education"; the second, "a

---

[22]Woods and Kennedy, *The Settlement Horizon.*

more practical and specific interest felt by manufacturers and wage-earners."[23]

The first group, said the Report, was represented by men and women "who have been brought into intimate contact with the harder side of life as it appears among the poorer people in the cities, who are grappling with the variety of problems of children to which city life give use." The second group consisted of manufacturers and workers who were aware that new factory processes required new industrial skills. The plea from this group was for *industrial intelligence:*

> the mental power to see beyond the task which occupies the hands for the moment to the operations which have preceded and to those which will follow it—power to take in the whole process, knowledge of materials, ideas of cost, ideas of organization, business sense, and a conscience which recognizes obligations.[24]

Thus the division between humanitarian reformers and the advocates of trade-training was apparent from the early stages of the vocational education movement.

The year of 1906, however, was a time for consolidating agreements. All parties affirmed their conviction that the public schools were "too exclusively literary in their spirit, scope, and methods." They reaffirmed their faith in the common school but said it needed to be changed to meet "modern industrial and social conditions." They agreed, too, that manual training, while well-intentioned, had been captured by the "culturists" and was therefore ineffective for the task at hand. It had become "a sort of mustard relish—an appetizer . . . severed from real life."[25] The purpose in 1906 was to *promote* industrial education; the need had to be dramatized to win public support. The Douglas Commission employed typical progressive-style tactics. It conducted hearings to sound out public opinion, and it hired a social science expert.

Hearings were conducted throughout Massachusetts which led the Committee to conclude that there was "widespread interest in the general subject of industrial education."[26] Many kinds of people were interviewed—manufacturers, workers, farmers, housewives, school officials—and everyone seemed to favor it. Some hoped industrial education would prevent juvenile delinquency. Some saw it as the answer to the economic problems of industry. Others felt the state should "do

[23]Commonwealth of Massachusetts, *Report of the Commission on Industrial and Technical Education* (Boston: The Commission, 1906), p. 4.
[24]*Ibid.,* p. 5.
[25]*Ibid.,* p. 14.
[26]*Ibid.,* p. 4.

something," almost anything, to help urban youth relate to the complex city environment. Some women wanted industrial education to offer training to actual and potential housekeepers and mothers.

It is interesting to note that the Commission found almost everyone in favor of something vaguely called "industrial education," but that the Commission was not able to learn just what that term meant to the people who favored it. The Commission reported that with two or three exceptions out of 143 witnesses, "when the question was asked, 'Have you any plan to propose for meeting the need of which you speak?' the answer was, 'I have not thought so far,' or 'I leave that for the Commission to decide.' "[27] We may recognize this as an early manifestation of the yearning to find some magical solution to the school problems of the industrial age. The 1906 version was: "industrial education will provide the way—but don't ask us what it is."

The Commission also hired Susan Kingsbury, a Ph.D. investigator from Simmons College, "a trained student of sociological problems," to write a report on the condition of Massachusetts children between the ages of fourteen and sixteen. Her report of one hundred and two pages, filled with charts and statistics, provided vivid testimony to the "wasted years" of children between these ages. Miss Kingsbury was a social science reformer, and the humanitarian leanings of her writings dominated this first report. Her findings were cited by speakers of all persuasions for years to come. With allowances for the details of time and place, her description of the educational problems of urban children is distressingly familiar.

Miss Kingsbury found 25,000 children aged fourteen and fifteen who had dropped out of school and worked intermittently. But school officials reported that this figure hid the seriousness of the educational problem. There were many other children who remained in school because there was "nothing else to do." In addition to those who had departed physically, thousands of other students had left school mentally.

Miss Kingsbury found that the desire to drop out of school often had nothing to do with the class from which the child came. She concluded it is the age "which brings the child the desire to begin to *do* something." He wants to learn to produce in the industrial world, she said. "At fourteen he is physically ready and mentally and morally anxious to cease imitating and to become creative."[28] In probing the factors that

[27] *Ibid.*, p. 6.
[28] *Ibid.*, pp. 85–86. Later studies suggest family need may have been greater, and was hidden by a reluctance to admit financial need. See Paul Douglas, "American Apprenticeship and Industrial Education," *Studies in History, Economics and Public Law*, XCV, No. 2 (New York: Columbia University, and Longmans, Green, 1921), pp. 88–95.

made children want to leave school, Miss Kingsbury discredited the widely held opinion that it was primarily because a child's parents wanted a supplemental income. Over and over parents asked, "What shall we do with him?"

When it came to a solution, everyone connected with the Commission wanted to hear that the answer lay in industrial education. Miss Kingsbury obliged; but with the caution of an academician, she cast her answer in the form of a question. It is pointless to blame the teacher, she said. "Is it not rather the subject taught and the way of teaching it, in addition to the numbers taught, which are responsible?" And in the progressive mode she asked, "Do not all of these faults prevent the consideration of the individuality of the child?"

The Commission's report produced recommendations consistent with a consensus which had been growing for some time. The grade schools were urged to add instruction and practice in "the elements of productive industry," including agriculture and the domestic arts, to be taught so as to secure cultural values for children as well as benefits for industry. High schools were asked to relate the content of mathematics, science, and drawing to their application in local industries. Finally, the Commission recommended the appointment of a state commission on industrial education, whose task it would be to create a separate industrial school system. The commission on industrial education was to function independently from, and parallel to, the State Board of Education. Thus a system of dual administration, which visitors from Germany had been praising, was endorsed.[29]

When the new Commission got down to practicalities, much of the reform tone of Miss Kingsbury's report began to fade. In its first report of the following year, the Commission concentrated almost solely on the wishes and needs of the manufacturers. It launched a direct appeal for trade training courses, concentrating on the specifics of time and place for each of the offerings.[30]

2. The National Society for the Promotion of Industrial Education (NSPIE)

Soon there was a growing feeling that what was good for Massachusetts might be good for the nation. Shortly after the publication of the Douglas Commission Report in April of 1906, action started in New

---

[29]The schoolmen of the state never really accepted the idea of a second school system operating as a rival to the public schools. The Massachusetts General Court in 1909 ordered consolidation under a single State Commissioner who was to have two deputies: one for the common schools and one for industrial education.

[30]Commonwealth of Massachusetts, 1907.

York City which led to the founding of NSPIE. In June, Charles R. Richards, Professor of Manual Training at Teachers College and future President of Cooper Union, and James P. Haney, Director of Art and Manual Training in New York City, met with thirteen men at the Engineers Club. They shared a conviction that there was a strong sentiment across the nation to advance the cause of industrial education.

Their plans resulted in the call for an organizational meeting at Cooper Union in November. About 250 people, including industrialists, labor leaders, educators, and social workers responded to the invitation. A constitution was adopted, and Dr. Henry S. Pritchett of M.I.T., who had been prominent in promoting engineering education, was elected President. M. W. Alexander of General Electric was Vice-President; V. Everit Macy of New York, Treasurer; and Charles R. Richards, Secretary. Members of the Board of Managers included Milton Higgins, Worcester manufacturer; Anthony Ittner of the NAM; Frederick Fish, President of AT&T; Frederick W. Taylor, the consulting engineer; Jane Addams and Robert Woods from the Settlement Houses; Samuel Donnelly of the New York Building Trades and F. J. McNulty of the Electrical Workers from the unions. The Board also included heads of several technical high schools and the principal of an industrial arts school; the Secretary of a New York municipal improvement association; a banker; and the president of a southern education association. With the exception of revolutionary radicals, the Society managed to bring together about as diverse a collection of Progressive-era spokesmen as one could imagine.[31] The Society reflected the emerging progressive conviction that the problems of the industrial age required national solutions; and it represented the capacity of progressives to bring together groups with divergent values for the purpose of furthering specific reforms.

The diversity of interests was frankly acknowledged. The founders stated that the purpose of the Society was "to unite the many forces making toward industrial education the country over." They recognized, too, that there existed "no substantial agreement as to the practical form" which the new education should take.[32] The Society's functions were to study the range of possibilities, to seek areas of agreement on concrete proposals, to act as a clearing house of information, and to "educate the public."

Because President Pritchett was ill, the Society's opening conference was chaired by the ubiquitous Nicholas Murray Butler of Columbia University.[33] Butler did not let his role as chairman interfere

[31] *Bulletin* No. 1 (1907), pp. 5–15.
[32] *Ibid.*, pp. 7–8.
[33] *Ibid.*, pp. 17–19.

with his giving a long speech to open the convention. He assured members that the Society had "taken hold of one of the most important and far-reaching of our social and industrial problems." He set the tone of reconciliation. On the one hand, he shared tha anxiety of industrialists who were worried about the head start enjoyed by European rivals; but he assured union members that "if we can make labor worth more, labor is perfectly sure to get more." (He was perfectly aware of that favored word in Gompers' vocabulary.) Butler also expressed some of the uneasiness which general educators continually felt in the presence of vocational education enthusiasts. The first task of the public school is to make American citizens, he said; and therefore care must be taken not to introduce trade education too early. He made it clear that he was not defending old-fashioned, narrow elementary schooling but was encouraging the new education which made "a constant appeal to the general powers of the child, while laying a sound foundation for the special trade or industrial education which is to follow."

Mr. Frank Vanderlip, Vice-President of the National City Bank of New York, expressed an admiration for the German system which was shared by many at the meeting. He was optimistic that the introduction of industrial education would enable America to improve its economic position *vis à vis* Germany.[34]

Frederick Fish of AT&T announced his conviction that what helps our industries helps our national life: anything that stands in the way of industrial improvement should be frowned upon and eliminated.[35] He felt that the nation had gained enormously from industry's ability to do things upon a large scale; but he expressed some perturbation about the tendency of the system to reduce large numbers of men to the status of machine tenders. The real case for industrial education was that it would contribute also to our artistic, ethical, and spiritual development.

Jane Addams, Director of Hull House, spoke the language of the progressive-liberal in urging government support for industrial education as a first step in improving the condition of the lower classes. She too praised Germany, but with a different emphasis from that of the manufacturers.

> Much has been said this evening concerning German education, but I suspect they have developed those fine, technological schools in very much the same spirit as they have developed legislative protection for the working man. Modern legislation in Germany secures for the working man old age pensions, it cares for him when he is out of

[34] *Ibid.*, pp. 20–23.
[35] *Ibid.*, pp. 24–30.

work . . .; it proposes to limit the amount of interest upon the money he borrows, and all this is done not primarily that industry may be advanced, but because Germany has waked up to the fact that human welfare is a legitimate object for Governmental action.[36]

To compete with Germany, she said, Americans must adopt a similar point of view. Jane Addams saw a New Deal kind of lesson in the activities of Imperial Germany.

The NSPIE founders were right in their estimate of the mood of the country. Soon after the Society's first meeting, individuals and organizations of almost every type began declaring their support for "industrial education." It became as right as "motherhood." Significantly, many organizations committed themselves to the general principle before concrete proposals were clarified. Thus the NEA in 1907 called for the establishment of "trade schools" (undefined), at public expense "whenever conditions justify their establishment."[37]

When NSPIE sent out questionnaires to inflence people, one person who responded was President Theodore Roosevelt. He expressed his profound personal interest in NSPIE's cause.[38] Later in 1907, in his annual message to Congress, the President said:

> Our school system is gravely defective in so far as it puts a premium upon mere literacy training and tends therefore to train the boy away from the farm and the workshop. Nothing is more needed than the best type of industrial school, the school for mechanical industries in the city, the school for practically teaching agriculture in the country.[39]

Commenting on the rash of interest in industrial education, the New Hampshire State Superintendent of Schools declared, "We are besieged with public documents, monographs, magazine articles, reports of investigations too numerous to mention, etc., etc."[40]

NSPIE leaders were more realistic than some of the Johnny-come-lately enthusiasts. They realized that differences within the Society's membership had to be confronted and resolved. They had to try to find out what they were talking about. The period between 1907 and 1910 was a time of interaction and consensus-seeking.

NSPIE's Secretary Richards addressed the American Federation of Labor convention in 1907. The Society's leaders knew that there was

---

[36] *Ibid.*, p. 39.

[37] NEA, *Declaration of Principles*, 1907, p. 29.

[38] NSPIE *Bulletin* No. 3, 1907, pp. 6–9.

[39] Theodore Roosevelt, "Annual Message, December 3, 1907," *The Abridgments, 1907*, Vol. I, pp. 30–31.

[40] Henry C. Morrison, "Vocational Training and Industrial Education," *Educational Review* (October 1907), p. 1242.

apprehension among labor leaders about the Douglas Commission Report. They knew that labor had to be won over if the industrial education movement was to succeed. Richards' speech stirred the AFL to action. A resolution was passed which expressed labor's opposition to private trade schools "used as a weapon against the trade union movement," but which also expressed approval of efforts to raise the standard of industrial education and to teach "the higher techniques of our various industries."[41] The resolution was followed by the creation of the Mitchell Committee, which developed the detailed outlines of labor's position in 1910.

NSPIE began to publish a series of bulletins which carried its ideas throughout the country, including an important symposium on industrial education. The symposium[42] elicited responses to eleven questions from a list of business and labor leaders. The results helped to clarify the issues between the two groups. What began to emerge was an agreement that some kind of industrial education was a legitimate item of public expense. Each side, however, wanted to have a decisive say in the control of training programs with respect to who should enter them and what kind of instruction should prevail. It was also clear that for both labor and the manufacturers, industrial education meant trade training. There was precious little reference to the rhetoric of settlement house reformers or progressive educators, with their common concerns about democracy, science, and culture for the masses.

On a day at the end of the convention in 1908, Jane Addams saw how things were going. She pointed out that "the place we have arrived at . . . is the relation of industrial education to public schools as represented by the trade school." Her misgivings reflected the gap between the ideals of the Settlement House reformers and the narrower trend that was developing. "If we are not on guard," she said, "the manufacturers may capture the public school as, forty or fifty years ago, the business men captured the public schools."[43]

To avoid misuses of public education, said Jane Addams, the Society ought to explore ways in which industrial education could be incorporated into the public schools so that it would serve the welfare of the whole community. She also challenged the assumption "that industrial education is one thing and cultural education is of necessity another."[44] She sought to verbalize for her tired and uncomprehending audience

---

[41] American Federation of Labor, Report of the Committee on Industrial Education, Senate Document No. 936, 62nd Cong., 2nd Sess., Vol. 4 (Washington, D.C.: Government Printing Office, 1912), pp. 21–22.

[42] NSPIE *Bulletin* No. 3, "A Symposium of Industrial Education," 1907.

[43] NSPIE *Bulletin* No. 5, 1908, pp. 92–93.

[44] *Ibid.*, p. 94.

the point of view that her friend John Dewey had been arguing: that a study of the intellectual, technological, and social changes related to the changes in work processes in the industrial era could serve to enliven the quality of general education. Jane Addams tried putting it in these words:

> Modern industry embodies tremendous human activities, inventions, constructive imaginations and records of devotion. Every factory filled with complicated machines has in it the possibilities of enormous cultural value if educators have the ability to bring out the long history, the human as well as the mechanical development, which it represents. It is this cultural aspect of industrial training which is applicable to these boys of fourteen who are not yet fit to earn their living. . . .

It is the task of education, Miss Addams continued, to help the child understand the environment in which his days will be spent. The schools should capitalize on the fourteen-year-old child's interest in the world of work: "The records of many high schools show that if he is not thus educated, he bluntly refuses to be educated at all." Boys should be given the opportunity to perform with their own hands at least one basic technique on which the life of the community depends. The proper approach, she was arguing, was not to train fourteen-year-olds with specific trade techniques useful to industry, but to use the processes of production and commerce in the community to give children richer educational experiences. She was weak on details, but her general idea was that youth should be given a chance to participate directly in the real work of the community in a way that would deepen their insights into the urban era. "To live intelligently in an industrial community and to interpret it in terms of culture, we must have educated people who know it from the standpoint of technique."[45] Her words were recorded in the *Proceedings;* but the Society's membership was bent on pursuing other goals.

By 1910 and 1911 the drive for industrial education had reached a new stage. The NAM, influenced by its own cost accounting studies, had dropped its earlier allegiance to private trade schools. It had accepted the idea of trade training at public expense, but had shifted its support to the continuation school idea because of its lower cost. The Association was willing to accept joint membership with union representatives on Boards for Industrial Education, but it favored the dual system of administration. The Mitchell Committee Report (1910) showed that labor

[45] *Ibid.*, pp. 94–95.

had shed some of its earlier misgivings. It was ready to agree to some form of trade training, although labor still insisted that public sponsorship be free of antiunion bias. Whether industrial education programs should be administered by "dual or unitary" arrangements remained a divided issue.

Even while the struggle over dual control was going on, NSPIE found enough agreement within its ranks to advance the general cause. A 1910 Survey of the Society[46] showed that a wide variety of industrial education programs had emerged in the preceding five years. A number of school experiments were developed from 1910 to 1917. Among these were the prevocational or intermediate industrial schools; the continuation schools; the work-study cooperative schools; the all-day vocational or trade schools; and the apprenticeship or corporation schools. The idea was accepted that no single approach could meet the various needs to be served.

The Survey also showed that twenty-nine states had begun some form of industrial education; ten provided for technical education, eighteen for manual training, eleven for domestic science, nineteen for agricultural training, and eleven for industrial and trade courses.

In spite of the increased activity, the aggressive leaders of NSPIE were dissatisfied. They could claim with justification that relatively few children were actually affected and that there was still more talk about action than solid change in the public schools. No one expressed this criticism more effectively than did Jesse D. Burks of the Bureau of Municipal Research of Philadelphia. He noted that only one half of thirteen hundred city school systems had introduced some form of handwork or manual training. He shared the conviction of municipal researchers that the cities could be reformed by the application of scientific research. Burks urged that the "striking discrepancy between ideas and achievement" be reduced first, by scientific surveys of school systems to gather facts and then, by plans of action to implement "a safe, progressive, and rational program of education."[47]

Burks anticipated by several years the emphases that were to emerge in NSPIE's next stage. In order to encourage the public schools to accept industrial education reform, the society was ready to join the school-survey rage, and to increase its effectiveness in lobbying for both

[46]NSPIE *Bulletin* No. 11, 1910: "A Descriptive List of Trade and Industrial Schools in the United States." I am indebted to the scholarship of W. Richard Stephens for pointing out how school surveys were used by NSPIE leaders to promote the cause of vocational education. See his *Social Reform and the Dawn of Guidance* (Terre Haute. Indiana State University, 1968).

[47]NSPIE *Bulletin* No. 11, 1910, p. 145.

state and federal legislation. A key factor in spurring both efforts was the appointment of the energetic Charles Prosser as Executive Secretary in 1912.

The urge to get results intensified between 1910 and 1912. Several factors were responsible. The appearance of Frederick Taylor's *Principles of Management*[48] in 1911 triggered a wave of increased criticism of the economic inefficiency of the schools. Taylor argued that his principles could produce efficiency and economy in every area of life and urged that they be applied with equal force to all social activities: "to the management of our homes; the management of our farms; the management of the business of our tradesmen, large and small; of our churches, our philanthropic institutions, our universities, and our governmental departments."[49]

The muckraking journals—*McClures, Saturday Evening Post, Outlook*, and the *Ladies Home Hournal*—began attacks on the social and economic inefficiency of the schools and urged the application of Taylor's principles to school administration. Soon the professional education journals as well were featuring articles by leaders in educational administration like Frank Spaulding, Franklin Bobbitt, and Ellwood Cubberly, who urged the application of scientific management to education.[50] Spaulding, for example, recommended the dollar as the criterion for judging the efficiency of both school administration and school programs. He described how he had been using this criterion since 1904 in his schools at Newton, Massachusetts. He told an NEA audience in 1913, "Academic discussion of educational issues is as futile as it is fascinating. Which is more valuable, a course in Latin or a course in machine shop?" Spaulding announced that when he found he could secure more pupil recitations in English for a dollar than he could in Greek, he decided "to purchase no more Greek instruction."[51]

By the end of 1911 the stage was set for the ambitious NSPIE leaders to take advantage of the new efficiency mood. James Munroe, a leading Boston industrialist and then President of NSPIE, took up the challenge at the November meetings. He opened by arguing that the addition of industrial education throughout the elementary school

---

[48]Frederick Taylor, *The Principles of Management* (New York: Harper, 1911.) For a detailed account of events connected with Taylorism, see Raymond E. Callahan, *Education and the Cult of Efficiency* (Chicago: U. of Chicago Press, 1962), Chaps. 2–3.

[49]*Ibid.*, p. 8.

[50]Raymond E. Callahan in *Education and the Cult of Efficiency* (Chicago: U. of Chicago Press, 1962) has given a detailed account of the influence of the business efficiency movement on public education.

[51]Frank Spaulding, "The Application of the Principles of Scientific Management," NEA *Proceedings*, 1913, p. 265.

could certainly reduce "the inconceivable waste of our human resources." Beyond that, he maintained that

> the effect of industrial education upon the general welfare, the direct effect in increasing industrial efficiency and prosperity, and the indirect influence in diminishing the number of incompetents, unfortunates, and other social wrecks and burdens, would be so great as literally to reform our industrial and social structure. . . . What the community wants . . . of the school is efficiency.

Munroe urged every good citizen to join NSPIE "to keep down the present awful waste of our vast human resources."[52]

The next question was how to stir the sluggish public and stand-pat school administrators. Munroe set forth his strategy in a book, *New Demands on Education,* published in 1912. Echoing Burks, he called for using the mechanism of the educational and industrial survey under the direction of an "educational engineer." To his own question about ending the waste in education, Munroe answered:

> What every other business does when it finds itself confronted with possible bankruptcy through preventable waste, losses and inferiority of output. It calls in engineering commercial experts to locate causes and to suggest reforms. We need "educational engineers" to study this huge business of preparing youth for life, to find out where it is good, where it is wasteful, where it is out of touch with modern requirements, where and why its output fails; and to make report in such form and with such weight of evidence that the most conventional teacher and the most indifferent citizen must pay head.
>
> Such engineers would make a thorough study of (1) the pupils who constitute the raw material of the business in education; (2) the building and other facilities for teaching, which makes up the plant; (3) the school boards and the teaching staff, who correspond to the directorate and the working force (4) the means and methods of instruction and development; (5) the demands of society in general and of industry in particular upon boys and girls—this corresponding to the problems of markets; and (6) the question of the cost, which is purely a business problem.[53]

NSPIE was ready to move into various school systems, survey their programs, find them inefficient and out of touch with the needs of industrial society, and then urge them to reorganize with vocational education at their center. The Society began at once to conduct school

[52]James P. Munroe, "President's Address," NSPIE *Proceedings,* 1911, pp. 49–56.
[53]James P. Munroe, *New Demands in Education* (New York: Doubleday, 1912), p. 20–21.

surveys across the country in places such as Richmond, Virginia; Minneapolis; and Richmond, Indiana.

3. The Move to Secure Federal Aid

NSPIE's second major effort after 1910 was the securing of federal funding for vocational education. This had been a goal from the first NSPIE Convention in 1908, when delegates had voted to transmit to the President of the United States and to Congress a report prepared by Henry Pritchett of M.I.T. to call special attention to the importance of "this whole matter from the standpoint of our national and economic welfare."

By 1912, NSPIE leaders had witnessed legislative gains in a number of states—Massachusetts, New York, Connecticut, Indiana, Ohio and Wisconsin. Yet the diversity of vocational programs and the unevenness of support prevented the kind of effective national effort that NSPIE leaders desired. They decided to focus their efforts on obtaining federal legislation, which might bring order and resources across the board. Support from a number of sources was growing; the time seemed ripe to add impressive NSPIE resources of skill, energy, and money to the cause. The hiring of Charles Prosser in 1912 as Executive Secretary of the Society was a move which ensured the full-time leadership required to coordinate efforts. Prosser had been head of the pioneering vocational education program in Massachusetts, under the general superintendency of David Snedden. He proved to be an effective and powerful lobbyist while he held his Society office between 1912 and 1915. Prosser virtually authored the Smith-Hughes bill. We shall follow the work of Snedden and Prosser in more detail later in this study.

a. Coalition with the Agriculturists

Lawrence Cremin has rightly pointed out that agrarian protest played a powerful role in advancing the more practical kind of schooling that was represented in the vocational education rationale.[54] It is true that when labor committed itself to support federal aid for voca-

---

[54]Lawrence A. Cremin, *The Transformation of the School*, pp. 41–50, provides a brief lucid account of the role of the agriculturists in the vocational movement. For a more extensive account of the role of farm organizations in the political maneuvering which led to passage of the Smith-Lever and Smith-Hughes Acts, see Lloyd E. Blauch, "Federal Cooperation in Agricultural Extension Work, Vocational Education and Vocational Rehabilitation," U.S. Office of Education Bulletin, 1933, No. 15 (Washington, D.C.: Government Printing Office, 1935). For an account of the changes farmers were seeking in agricultural education see Ann Keppel, *"Country Schools for Country Children"* (unpublished Doctoral Thesis, University of Wisconsin, 1960).

tional education in 1910, a key element had fallen into place. Without the powerful help of the farm interests, however, it probably would have been impossible to marshal the coalition of votes that was required to pass the Smith-Lever and Smith-Hughes legislation.

The farm interests, after all, had led the way in getting federal support for education. The Morrill Act of 1862 had launched the Land Grant Universities, and the Hatch Act of 1882 had provided federally assisted agricultural experiment stations. By the early 1900's the combination of scientific study and research with skillful dissemination and feedback from farmer practitioners was recognized as one of the bona fide revolutions produced by American society. (Fifty years later Soviet Premier Khrushchev would come to the Garst farm in Iowa to try to learn why the labor of less than 10 percent of our population could feed the country, with an embarrassing surplus to spare, while one out of every two Russians was required for farm work.) The efficiency-minded American progressives were already duly impressed. They expressed their admiration for the results of the federally supported A & M Colleges, and they invited farm leaders to speak at NSPIE conventions.

In spite of new gains, there was serious concern about agriculture in the 1900's and new discontents among the farmers which made them ready to join the campaign for vocational education. With the rapid growth of the cities, farming had become more of a commercial proposition. The significant buyers became the great canneries and packinghouses which shipped across the nation. Farmers who could not master sophisticated production techniques were being squeezed out of competition in the new national arena. Even while the United States was becoming a national society and gaining in numbers and power, this very fact produced new anxiety about the adequacy of its food supply. There was an unprecedented growth in population; and city people were learning to enjoy better standards of eating during a time of growing prosperity. Meanwhile the flight of farm youth from the country to the enticements of the cities accelerated. In short, agricultural production was increasing but not as rapidly as was consumption.

The problem was complicated by agricultural change. There was a reduction in the amount of public land available for farming and a rapid depletion of soil and soil fertility.[55] The time to pay the price for the abuse of our natural resources was approaching. The educational import of this situation was obvious. Reformed agricultural practices required the application of greater agricultural intelligence. New

[55]Charles R. Van Hise, *The Conservation of Natural Resources in the United States*, (New York: Macmillan, 1936).

methods had to be developed for dry farming and for the use of irrigation. Farmers were needed who could do their work more skillfully and intelligently, and who were equipped to handle complex machinery and business records. Progress in agriculture was dependent, in large part, on the extension of education and research.

Under the impact of these changes, farmers gradually dropped their traditional scepticism about schooling. When the Populist political effort of the nineties failed, they were ready to seek answers to their problems through education. At the college level, farmer-dominated legislatures stepped up efforts to insure that the land grant colleges improved their effectiveness in promoting technical advances in agriculture and disseminating practical programs for farmers. As farmers confronted the complexities of their work and witnessed the loss of their children to the cities, they turned to the schools with new expectations.

Farm journals began to abound with charges that the content of rural education was sterile and irrelevant. It was judged to be too "literary"—failing to provide live and practical instruction for boys so that they could profit from work in the farmer's institutes and experiment stations and thus find new challenges in modern farming. It failed to provide the kind of domestic science that would teach girls to make farm homes attractive and contemporary.

Cremin has pointed out that farm journals like *Wallace's Farmer* and William Dempter Hoard's *Hoard's Dairyman* led the criticisms:

> Wallace agreed with the contributor who insisted on abandoning "the cut and dried formula of a period when a man was 'educated' when he knew Greek and Latin," and suggested that there be less adherence to textbooks, more concern with the all-around development of children and increasing attention to the rudiments of agriculture. [56(a)] "It is hard," he wrote, "for many a middle-aged farmer to get a clear idea of what is meant by protein, carbohydrates, nitrogen-free extract, etc. Now, these terms are no harder than many which the pupils learn and which are of no earthly use to them in their everyday lives."[56(b)] The teachers' guides should come not from high schools, normal schools, or colleges, but from farmers themselves, who know best what their children need. Instead of depending on textbooks, teachers should experiment in the classroom with seeds, with the Babcock milk tester, with honeycombs, or with any other practical material, being careful to "get the fodder down low enough for the lambs."[56(c)]

[56]Cremin, *op. cit.*, p. 44, citing *Wallace's Farmer*, (a) Jan. 19, 1913, p. 68; (b) Mar. 6, 1908, p. 338; (c) Feb. 18, 1910, p. 332 and Aug. 28, 1914, p. 1165.

Hoard in his *Dairyman* deplored the deadly quality of rural school practice which, he claimed, had not changed in sixty years. To redress the situation, teachers would need a whole new outlook. They would have to master elementary botany, agricultural chemistry, and sanitation.[57] Hoard wanted to abandon the tradition of equating "culture" with a knowledge of Latin. He wanted to give "culture" a new democratic meaning which would include teaching girls how to care for family health and how to beautify the home, while boys would learn how agricultural science and technology could revolutionize farm production.[58]

In Wisconsin the farm organizations were active in criticism of the State University, calling it "a cold storage institution of dead languages and useless learning which costs several billions of bushels of wheat each year."[59]

Theodore Roosevelt's experience as a Dakota rancher in the 1880's helped sensitize him to the problems of farmers. He took action consistent with the new mood. He appointed a Commission on Country Life, which reported in 1909 that farmers were unanimous about the need for better educational facilities in the rural districts. The question was being pushed vigorously by national organizations like the Patrons of Husbandry and the Farmers Educational and Cooperative Union.[60] President Roosevelt also backed the Davis Bill in 1907, which called for supporting instruction in agriculture and home economics in secondary agricultural schools, and mechanic arts and home economics in city secondary schools.

The coalition had not yet been formed, however, which could get a measure like the Davis Bill through Congress. In the years immediately ahead it became increasingly evident that "industrial education" had both rural and urban supporters. They shared a disgust for "literary" schooling and agreed that only reforms which added practical and applied sciences could satisfy them.

By 1910 labor had joined farm groups supporting the Davis-Dolliver bill. When these two came to NSPIE seeking its support, the Society's leaders were eager to support the general cause but found flaws in the specifics of the legislation. After a short period of delay, Charles Prosser became the head of NSPIE's lobbying activities in the state legislatures and in Washington. A period of fascinating politicking

---

[57]Hoard's *Dairyman*, July 19, 1895, p. 419.

[58]Cremin, *op. cit.*, p. 45.

[59]Theodore Saloutos and John D. Hicks, *Agricultural Discontent in the Middle West, 1900–1939* (Madison: U. of Wisconsin Press, 1951), p. 128.

[60]Country Life Commission, *Report*, Senate Document 705, 60th Cong., 2nd Sess., pp. 5–53 *et passim*.

went on until the enactment of Smith-Hughes, including a *quid pro quo* agreement whereby the Smith-Lever Act for the farmers was passed (1914) in return for support of the agriculturists for Smith-Hughes, which became law in 1917.

part III

Public School
Responses to Pressures
for Vocationalizing Education

INTRODUCTION

"Industrial organization quietly forces its peculiar impress upon each and all." Frank Tracy Carlton, NEA Report on *The Place of Industries in Public Education*, 1910, p. 9.

The torrent of discussion about industrial education was one sign of a national awareness that American society had entered a radically new stage of social development. There was a sense that all institutions were being transformed by the urban-industrial syndrome. The vocational education movement was a manifestation of onrushing social change. At times its leaders appeared strong enough to initiate a new set of schools aimed at serving the training needs of industry. Even if this threat to the common school tradition could be warded off, critical questions remained. What responses *would* the public schools make to the industrialization of the United States?

During the last three decades of the nineteenth century, schools had been under increasing pressure to be more responsive to the needs of the work world. The NEA reflected these trends by instituting new departments for areas such as manual training and commercial education. Public-school men were not prepared, however, for the vigor and force of the new thrust toward trade training of the early 1900's, nor for the measure of support that gathered behind NSPIE. NEA leaders could hardly fail to be aroused when they heard powerful voices within NSPIE advocating the establishment of a system of vocational schools separate from and parallel to general public education. The urgency of the matter was underscored when Massachusetts followed the recommendations of the Douglas Commission and actually established a dual system of schools.

1910 was a year for stocktaking, and the NEA joined the AFL and the NAM in issuing a position paper: "A Report of the Committee on the Place of Industries in Public Education." The report was the product of a committee appointed by the Department of Superintendence in February 1908, with Jesse D. Burks, of the Bureau of Municipal Research of Philadelphia, as chairman. At that time, it had been decided to broaden the work of an ongoing committee concerned with reviewing the status of manual training; the new assignment was to study "the entire question of the place of industries in public education."[1]

The committee recognized that the most significant fact in the past fifty years had been the industrializing of the United States. Nevertheless, Charles Richards, in a review of the history of industrial education, was forced to conclude that "the school and the industrial establishment have preserved their separateness during this period."[2] He acknowledged that some responses had been made: for example, the opening of private evening schools, the creation of engineering schools and institutes of technology, the introduction of courses in manual training and industrial arts. Chairman Jesse Burks[3] reported, however, that manual training, where the main effort had been made, was "an isolated, abstract, and unprofitable fad" and that there was no agreement among leaders in education as to the place of manual training in the schools. Burks acknowledged "the remarkable interest in industrial education, which is now probably the dominant factor in the educational thought of the country." The message was clear, he said, that the situation demanded "immediate, cooperative action." At the same time, he gave expression to the great uncertainty about what to do. Many programs were in an experimental stage, he said; and "several years of further study and experience are needed to demonstrate just what types of industrial education are destined to find a permanent place in the American public school system."

The most perceptive observations were those set forth in an introductory paper entitled: "Notes on the History of Industrial Education in the United States." The author was Frank Tracy Carlton, Professor of Economics and History at Albion College in Michigan, and one of the new breed of progressive, mid-Western social scientists. He shared the new inclination to trace the source of social change to economic factors.

[1]NEA Report on *The Place of Industries in Public Education*, 1910.
[2]Charles F. Richards, "Some Notes on the History of Industrial Education in the United States," NEA *Report*, 1910.
[3]Jesse Burks, "Introductory Address," NEA *Report*, 1910.

Thus he held that "social progress is vitally and intimately connected with modifications in the methods of doing the world's work."[4] He acknowledged industrialization as the source of change but argued that men have tended to be unaware of two different kinds of consequences flowing from it. On the one hand, he said, the world of the twentieth century was being transformed into one vast neighborhood. New means of communication could help men free themselves from ancient parochialisms and open the possibilities for enriched human relationships. On the other hand, the specialization of work in industry tended to confine workers' lives within very narrow limits: "occupations have been specialized and sub-divided until the life of the individual is cramped."

In a time of such pervasive change, Carlton argued, the very meaning and scope of basic terms such as morality, law, justice, liberty, patriotism, and education were shifting. He commented on education as an example. Using the perspective of the new anthropology, he pointed out that in primitive cultures, all education was informal; it consisted of the learnings picked up from daily life in the group. In preindustrial America, formal education at higher levels was for a privileged few who spent years, for instance, learning an ancient language. For the majority, it had consisted of learning the rudiments of literary and arithmetical skills. Under contemporary industrialism, however, "the home was shorn of its industry and playground and the shop if its apprenticeship system." The result was one that the reformers never ceased repeating: that the school was now forced to offer services which previously had been taken care of by other institutions. Pedagogically, schools were now obligated to include not only verbal training but the "doing" kinds of learnings. Thus shops, laboratories, gardens, and kitchens were finding their way into schools.

Specialization in work according to Carlton had resulted also in new class divisions. American society, split by interest groups and class differences, found it more and more difficult to agree on "any customary or new standard of education." Fundamental differences of opinion divided people over what the public school should be about.

These differences were manifest in the debate over how the schools should respond to industrialization.

> Today one class of men who are insistently urging that the public school emphasize industrial and trade education, do so because they wish an increased supply of workers who are mere workers or human automatons. Many influential employers in the United States are de-

[4] Frank T. Carlton, "The Industrial Factor in Social Progress," NEA *Report*, 1910, p. 8.

manding in no uncertain tones that the public schools be utilized to
turn out narrowly trained industrial workers who may become passive
links in the great industrial mechanism of the present age. Systemati-
zation and specialization are the favorite watchwords of this class. The
application of factory methods to the school is demanded in the name
of efficiency and economy. Standardization, not individual treatment,
is the ideal of the businsss man.[5]

Formerly, Carlton said, manufacturers had opposed manual training
when it was a form of general education because of its costs. Now, when
the industrialists needed skilled workers, they wanted to turn public
education into schools for apprentices.

There are other people though, continued Carlton, who stand for
the proposition that "the public school system should train efficient
workers who are also thinking men and women capable of enjoying art,
literature, and leisure, and who will be able to intelligently consider the
political and social problems which will inevitably arise in the twentieth
century." They demand that "a well-rounded development be given
each child, and that each student be prepared for useful and efficient
work in the community."[6] The two views are almost diametrically opposed, said Carlton; but the difference is that the first group is agreed
on its goals, while the second group remains divided on the proper
scope of educational programs.

Carlton called for educators who were progressive to take their
stand with the second group. They should work for the proposition that
industrial or vocational education should be included in formal schooling because industry is "the determining factor in fixing the conditions
of living, working, playing, association and resting." The great problem
of the United States, he said,

> the one which towers above all others, is to *universalize opportunity*
> for decent health and comfortable living; not for a few, but for all; it
> is to give to each and every child in this great and rich land of ours,
> the heritage of a child—decent home, surroundings, sufficient and
> proper food, opportunity to play, and a chance to use hand and brain
> in some form of constructive work. *This* is the social, political, and
> educational problem of the age; and the peculiar form in which it is
> presented to the present generation is due to industrial advance.[7]

Carlton urged that care be taken about how industrial education
would be introduced into the schools. It should serve to counter the
evils of specialization which could diminish men.

[5] *Ibid.*
[6] *Ibid.*, pp. 12–13.
[7] *Ibid.*

Vocational training must be indissolubly linked with other forms of training which will broaden the outlook of the student, which will make him a citizen as well as an efficient worker with hand or brain. The aim of modern education should be, if the aim be anything more than the production of a nicely articulated industrial system, to produce men, not machines.[8]

Under the lash of industrial change, educators were forced to review all aspects of school programs. Whether they realized it or not, the value issue which Carlton described revealed itself in every matter they examined.

[8] *Ibid.*, p. 13.

5/Vocational Guidance

> [My father] therefore sometimes took me to walk with him and see
> joiners, bricklayers, turners, braziers, etc., at their work, that he might
> observe my inclination, and endeavor to fix it on some trade or other
> on land.
>
> Benjamin Franklin

The introduction of vocational guidance into public education was
a product of the industrial education movement. A study of events
surrounding its origins shows that the tension between the "efficiency"
and "humanitarian" reform values, which Carlton described, was present from the beginning.

It is not surprising to find a call for school guidance accompanying
the drive for vocational education. The logic of industrialism called for
one along with the other. Spokesmen from all groups concerned with
vocationalism reiterated a similar description of the educational
predicament: the need for more skills in industry; the lack of training
programs as apprenticeship broke down; the early and heavy dropout
rate; the floundering of youth who did leave school—their tendencies
to drift into trouble, despair, or dead-end jobs; the waste to industry
resulting from rapid job turnover and a backlog of undereducated
workers incapable of being retrained for rapid technological change;
the fear that America's prosperity would be eroded if appropriate work
skills were not created.

A common conclusion of concerned people was that more programs of vocational training at public expense were required. That was
what "the movement" was all about. At the same time, some people felt
that a system was needed to lead individuals to training programs and
to mesh the job interests and skills of individuals with the needs of
industry. This meant some system of guidance.

Orators endlessly repeated their conclusion that traditional secondary schools and colleges were doing a relatively adequate job of educating persons for professional and managerial roles.[1] the schools were

---

[1]The universities were also feeling new pressures to transform their programs along
utilitarian lines. Lincoln Steffens caught the new mood in his description of the role of

most inadequate, they insisted, in preparing those who would work in the lower and middle level positions in industry. Complaints were aimed particularly at the upper grades of the grammer school, the point at which many students left school or had to make educational choices which affected their futures.

If vocational guidance was a necessity, someone had to think about where, when, and how it should be provided and about who would provide it. There was considerable appeal to the idea that the aim of guidance should be "to fit the boy to the job." This reflected the wish of many in industry to see the school system redesigned to mirror effectively the job requirements of American business and manufacturing. According to this idea, the school levels would be geared to the lower, middle, and higher skill needs of industry. If a proper sequence of skill training programs could be established, along with an efficient system for sorting out youths with skills appropriate for the various slots in the system, then industrialists could look forward with confidence to "overtaking and passing" the Germans. Many were saying that no better approach could be taken than to look to the German system itself. It was a model of an efficient, hierarchical school structure supporting a level of economic productivity which had become the marvel of the new era.

1. Charles Eliot and Guidance According to "Probable Destiny"

The call for a system of school guidance which would fit such a model came from no less a figure than Charles Eliot, who was just about to terminate his illustrious, forty-year career as President of Harvard University. His address to the 1908 NSPIE convention was entitled "Industrial Education as an Essential Factor in our National Prosperity."[2] He made a plea for the introduction of industrial education into the public school system. In order to avoid confusion about what the term meant, Eliot said, it "ought to mean trade schools, and nothing but trade schools; that is, schools directed primarily and expressly to the preparation of young men and women for trades"[3]—either full or part

---

the State University in Wisconsin. In his article, "Sending a State to College," Steffens described the University of Wisconsin as being willing "to teach anybody—anything—anywhere." He listed as examples of a grass roots utility orientation the University's machine shops, model dairy farms, Housekeepers Conferences, etc. For a fuller account of such developments at the university level, see Laurence R. Veysey, *The Emergence of the American University* (Chicago: U. of Chicago Press, 1965), Chap. 2, "Utility."

[2]Charles W. Eliot, "Industrial Education as an Essential Factor in Our National Prosperity," NSPIE *Bulletin*, No. 5, 1908, pp. 9–14.

[3]*Ibid.*, p. 9.

time. They should be new schools, separate from the existing public schools, and should have a role quite distinct from the Manual Training or The Mechanics Arts High Schools. Eliot accepted manual training as a welcome addition to either the elementary or the secondary curriculum but said it "is for culture, not for skill." The new Trade Schools "should produce not foremen or managers, except as skilled workmen may grow up to these positions, but actual journeymen for the trades. This is the object of industrial education."[4]

We live in a new world, Eliot proclaimed. "Nothing whatever in our country is now done as it was done fifty years ago." Science has changed the world of work so that a great variety of complicated occupations have come into being which are based on applied science. The results have profound implications for approaches to education and industry. "We must get rid of the notion that some of us were brought up on, that a Yankee can turn his hand to anything. He cannot in this modern world; he positively cannot." Furthermore, we must disabuse ourselves of any misconception that democracy means that children are equal. "There is no such thing among men as equality of natural gifts, of capacity for training, or of intellectual power."[5]

The proper stance, said Eliot, was to recognize that special kinds of education were needed for the different levels of specialized skills required in industrial society. Eliot then raised a question: Suppose we establish trade schools; how are children to be got into them? In the first place, compulsory attendance laws would assure that all children continue in formal schooling, at least on a continuation-school basis, until they were sixteen, or perhaps seventeen or even eighteen.

Eliot then specified a major new function to be carried out by the schools.

> But how shall the decision be made that certain children will go into industrial schools, others into the ordinary high schools, and others again into the mechanic arts high schools? Where is that decision to be made? . . . Here we come upon a new function for the teachers in our elementary schools, and in my judgment they have no function more important. The teachers of the elementary schools ought to sort the pupils and sort them by their evident or probably destinies.

He anticipated that critics might view such thinking as undemocratic and sought to blunt their charges.

> We must conform to nature in regard to the training of our children; we must guide each child into that path in life in which he can be most

[4] *Ibid.*, p. 11.
[5] *Ibid.*, p. 13.

successful and happy; for none of us can be happy in any life-work unless we have the power to achieve something in that work.[6]

Jane Addams was the first to take exception to the implications of Eliot's speech. In a discussion period following the address, she challenged the notion that teachers in the elementary grades could or should sort out children according to their "probable destinies." Eliot soon did in fact pull back from his 1908 position. In 1910 he made a speech to the NEA on the value of the "life-career motive" in education which was much more popular with the schoolmen than his 1908 endorsement of a dual school system.[7] He argued that students in professional and vocational schools were more highly motivated than students in general courses. Educators should sensitize themselves to the life-career aspirations of their students on the principle that active interests secure the cooperation of pupils' minds. He dropped the plan of identifying probable career lines in the elementary grades and funneling prospective workers into separate trade schools. He now suggested that career choice and training should begin at age sixteen or later.

Eliot recommended that the common school program introduce a wider variety of courses including shop and commerical work at the upper elementary grades. Students would be permitted to choose electives which would help them make eventual career choices. This kind of an idea provided the early rationale for the junior high school.

Eliot thus returned in 1910 to his preference for a free elective system. His 1908 speech, favoring prescription according to probably destiny, may be viewed as a temporary aberration.[8] It is more likely that "the two Eliots" reflected contradictory pulls within his own conservative social philosophy. As a serenely confident member of a family in the New England commercial aristocracy, he rejected determinisms and had faith that all would turn out for the best if men could make free choices guided by unrestricted free wills. (Hence the Eliot of the elective system.) But another article of the conservative faith upheld the proposition that there was a natural distribution of talent and ability. From this perspective, Eliot had maintained that the problems of democracy could be solved only when people were taught to recognize the wisdom and authority of experts in public affairs.[9] The well-ordered society would be the one where managerial authority was entrusted to

[6] *Ibid.*, pp. 12–13.

[7] Charles W. Eliot, "The Value During Education of the Life Career Motive," NEA *Proceedings*, July 2–8, 1910, pp. 133–141.

[8] See Edward A. Krug, *The Shaping of the American High School* (New York: Harper, 1964), pp. 224–227.

[9] See Rush Welter, *Popular education and Democratic Thought in America* (New York: Columbia U. Press, 1965 ed.), pp. 194–199.

the natural leaders (aided, no doubt, by appropriate training at Harvard University), while others, following a schooling appropriate to their endowments, would be content to fill more modest roles.

2. Prosser and Scientific Testing as the Basis for Guidance

Schoolmen were relieved to hear Eliot pull away from advocacy of separate vocational schools, but many in the vocational education camp preferred Eliot's original position. Some NAM speakers referred to that early speech with approbation for years to come. And the mainline vocational educators were much attracted to the "probable destiny" idea. Many remained convinced of the virtues of early career selection in the elementary grades.

Charles Prosser, the executive secretary of NSPIE, took a leading role in supporting the new vocational guidance movement. He spoke to the NEA in 1912, arguing that vocational guidance was the hand-maiden of vocational education in "the problem of fitting the great mass of our people for useful employment."[10] He maintained that it was time to establish separate courses—high school preparatory, commercial, practical or industrial arts, and domestic arts—for students in the twelve to age-fourteen group. Children at this age should be guided into the course appropriate for them. Eliot's earlier idea of assigning the task of selection to the general elementary teacher was dropped. New, more scientific means were at hand, Prosser promised.

> More and more, in our theory of the American public school sys-
> tem, we are swinging around to the idea that it is to be the mission of
> the schools of the future to select by testing and training—to adjust
> boys and girls for life by having them undergo varied experiences in
> order to uncover their varied tastes and aptitudes and to direct and to
> train them in the avenues for which they display the most capacity.
> Such a program would require a differentiation of the course of study
> for pupils between twelve and fourteen years of age. [11]

Schoolmen no longer would have to rely on the imperfect, subjec-tive judgments of teachers. New scientific testing instruments would eliminate the guesswork. Prosser could speak with justified confidence, for practitioners of scientific psychology were then creating the new instruments of educational tests and measurements. Binet and Simon had published their measure of general intelligence in 1905, with revi-sions in 1908 and 1911. Edward L. Thorndike's *Theory of Mental and Social Measurements* had appeared in 1904. Hugo Munsterberg, the

[10] Charles Prosser, "Practical Arts and Vocational Guidance," NEA *Proceedings*, July 6–8, 1912, p. 647.
[11] *Ibid.*, p. 650.

Harvard psychologist, was active in 1911 in exploring the applications of psychology to industry. His experiments in job efficiency and tests for job selection provided the groundwork for the practice of industrial psychology.

A bewildering array of instruments for testing intelligence, aptitudes, abilities, and interests were beginning to appear. There was growing excitement over the possibility that new scientific instruments might banish the confusions and uncertainties from educational decision making.

There were perceptive observers, even at the time, who were aware of possible misuses of the new techniques, and of the temptation to become overly fond of impressive-sounding terminology. Alice P. Barrows, director of the Vocational Guidance Bureau in New York, brought a refreshing note of candor and reality to the talk about guidance.

> "Vocations and Guidance" are dangerous words, both because they are vague and because they sound impressive. I have never been able to find a satisfactory definition of vocation, and it certainly does not seem to be a word descriptive of actual conditions. There are "jobs" and there are positions. . . . "Guidance," on the other hand, has an ecclesiastical tang that is particularly dangerous to the cause of democratic education. It is most questionable that anyone has the right to guide children systematically into vocations. Giving guidance is one thing, and giving information so that there will be greater freedom of choice is quite a different thing. At present, we can not give even this information about vocations, because we do not know enough about actual conditions to give it. Yet it sometimes seems as if the whole tendency of vocational guidance at the present time were to give information, any information, because the lack of it is felt so keenly.[12]

An overly hasty impulse to "do something," added Miss Barrows, had led to the establishment of job placement services in some schools which were given the unwarranted titles of "guidance bureaus." These services tended to "guide" untrained fourteen year-old children into "vocations" which consisted of nothing more than jobs which local industries wanted to fill immediately. Miss Barrows warned that the scene was set for "a more subtle and indefinable exploitation of children than the world has ever seen—subtle and indefinable because all would be done in the name of 'the good of society and of the child.'" She added,

[12] American Federation of Labor, Report of the Committee on Industrial Education, Senate Document No. 936, 62nd Cong., 2nd Sess., Vol. 4 (Washington, D.C.: Government Printing Office, 1912), p. 99.

I should say that to arouse the ambition and interest of a child of fourteen by promising him "trade training" the value of which is dubious, and then a job where he can work up, when we have no facts to prove that he can work up, and a distinctly uncomfortable feeling that he can not, is after all even worse than stunting a child by premature labor so that you can not arouse his ambition at all.[13]

Years later Michael Young in *The Rise of the Meritocracy*[14] projected the ends toward which conceptions of technocratic guidance might lead. In the coming "meritocratic society," improved testing instruments will have made it possible to sort out all individuals according to levels of Merit (Merit = IQ plus effort). Merit-rating will provide the definitive means for processing people according to their "probable destinies." Every individual will be guided to his allotted role in the smooth-functioning social machine.

3. The Settlement House Reformers Sponsor Vocational Guidance

Vocational guidance was seen as a necessary companion to vocational education by the proponents of business efficiency. Settlement house workers also took up the cause of vocational guidance, but with distinctly different social goals in mind.

The work of Frank Parsons, founder of the Boston Vocation Bureau and acknowledged father of the guidance movement, is a case in point,[15] Parsons, trained as a civil engineer at Cornell and thrown out of work as a young man by the panic of 1873, knew both the virtues and vices of the industrial system. Like other progressive reformers, he was shocked by the conditions of urban slum dwellers and repelled by the human and economic waste of unbridled capitalism. During the nineties he developed a rationale which attacked the economic roots of social distress. His concern with social philosophy was accompanied by a desire to help individuals find their way in the urban jungle. His analyses led him to view both industrial education and vocational guidance as important instruments of urban reform.

Parsons came to believe that the underlying source of human distress was the control of economic processes by private industrial monopolies. "Oppression by an aristocrary of industrial monopolists," he charged, "is as bad as oppression by an aristocracy of political

[13] *Ibid.*
[14] Michael Young, *The Rise of the Meritocracy, 1870–2033* (Baltimore: Penguin Books, 1958).
[15] I am indebted to the scholarship of W. Richard Stephens of Indiana State University for delineating the relationship of Parsons' work to the broader industrial education movement. I have drawn freely on his work.

monopolists." Parsons saw the city as the place where the crisis of civilization would have to be faced.

> The problem of the city is the problem of the future, and the problem of the city is the problem of monopoly. Diffusion is the ideal of civilization—diffusion of wealth and power, intelligence, culture, and conscience. . . . Combination, integration, union are most excellent if their benefits are justly distributed.[16]

The private monopolies were evil, in Parsons' view, because they did not have "the development of manhood and the progress of civilization as their aim." They selfishly exploited both natural resources and people. Parsons acknowledged that a few "monopolies" paid fair wages and gave fair treatment to their workers; but in most cases, he felt, "workers are no more to them than so many cogs in the machinery of their power house."[17] He concluded that the city could not become a center of civilized life unless its heart, "the industrial machine," was reformed to support human values—a position taken by other Settlement House leaders like Robert Hunter and Jane Addams. Parsons was ready to argue that in the interest of progress toward "a more perfect democracy of self-government," the government must take over "ownership of industrial monopolies" and the "people [must] own the government."[18] In the hard years of 1893–94 Parsons was dismayed by the callous attitude of businessmen toward the plight of the unemployed.[19] After the panic of 1893 he urged that "the unemployed be provided for by public works, making good roads, planting forests, digging canals, building ships, establishing schools, etc."

Parsons' awareness of the misery of the unemployed served to draw his attention to the problem of the urban children. He complained in 1894 that the training of race horses and the care of sheep and chickens had been carried to the highest degree of perfection, while "the education of a child, the choice of his employment are left very largely to the ancient haphazard plan—the struggle for existence and the survival of the fittest."[20] He had become convinced that reform of the city required not only a change in the underlying economic structure, but specific services to help the individual find his way in the ruban maze.

Parsons' worries about slum dwellers were marked by a mixture of compassion and fear that characterized many middle-class reformers as

[16] Frank Parsons, *The City for the People* (Philadelphia: C. F. Taylor, 1901), pp. 9–11.
[17] *Ibid.*, pp. 94–104 *et passim*.
[18] *Ibid.*, pp. 94, 12.
[19] Arthur Mann, *Yankee Reformers in the Urban Age* (Cambridge: Harvard U. Press, 1954), p. 137.
[20] Frank Parsons, *Our Country's Need* (Boston: Arena Publishing, 1894), p. 15.

they contemplated the tides of immigrants from eastern and southern Europe. He expressed the urgent need for the Americanization of immigrants in statements with racist overtones. Further progress in the cities would be impossible, he said, if the "heroic [Anglo-Saxon] blood" of America were diluted by the "foul mixture of serfhood . . . pouring in from Europe."[21] While Parsons felt that masses of uneducated, unassimilated immigrants were a hindrance to social and industrial progress, he also believed that industrial monopolists exacerbated the problem by exploiting newcomers in ways which delayed their development into effective citizens.

Parsons thought the answer lay in adoption of a "philosophy of mutualism" whose basic principle was "the ideal of mutual help which lay at the foundation of family life." Parsons envisioned the evolution of society to a point where "man would labor out of love for society."[22] Thus the "city of the people" would be based on those kindlier virtues which progressives felt had characterized the preindustrial era.

When Parsons came to Boston after the turn of the century, he was attracted to the work of the Civic Service House, located in the North End among Italian, Polish, and Jewish immigrants. The House had been founded in 1901, with the cooperation of Lillian Wald and Meyer Bloomfield, and with the advice of Jane Addams. It became a center where university intellectuals could teach "culture" and "discipline in the art of democratic association" to immigrant workers who worked in the industries of Boston.[23]

a. The Boston Vocation Bureau

Parsons joined the Civic Center House in 1905. He found people and resources to support his growing interest in meeting the vocational needs of immigrants. Parsons taught in the Breadwinners Institute, a vocational-cultural school, at the House. He was in constant communication with Boston reformers who were leading the drive for industrial education: Robert Woods, who became temporary chairman of the Douglas Commission in 1906, and Lincoln Filene, the reform businessman who introduced a profit-sharing plan for his employees and was active in the work of the Douglas Commission and in NSPIE.[24]

Parsons began to have firsthand experiences with the school dropouts Susan Kingsbury had reported on in the Douglas Commission

[21] *Ibid.*, p. 4.
[22] Mann, *op. cit.*, p. 133.
[23] Robert A. Woods and Albert J. Kennedy, *The Settlement Horizon* (New York: Russell Sage Foundation, 1922), pp. 108–112 *et passim.*
[24] Mann, *op. cit.*, p. 130

Report. He reported that such children drifted from "one employment to another in an effort to make a living, running an elevator in one place, marking tags in another, tending a rivet machine, etc., spending years of time and energy in narrow specialization and getting no adequate, comprehensive understanding of any business or industry."[25]

Parsons' personal solution to this problem was to use his formidable energy to create the Boston Vocation Bureau and to support the kind of industrial education favored by social workers.

Three basic features were built into Parsons' program. The first was self-study by the individual job-seeker to help him identify his capacities, interests, resources, and limitations. For this purpose Parsons developed an elaborate questionnaire—"Personal Record and Self-Analysis"—to be completed carefully and reviewed jointly by the applicant and his counselor. The twenty pages of items in the questionnaire reveal that Parsons was influenced by the values of Horatio Alger as well as by utopian reform: "Do you realize that wages depend largely on the efficiency and productive value of workers?" "Do you cultivate smiles and laughter by right methods; not mechanically but at the root, by cultivating the merry moods and friendly feelings that naturally express themselves in smiles?" "Do you shake hands like a steam engine, or a stick, or an icicle, or like a cordial friend?" "Are your collars and cuffs Caucasian?"[26]

The second step in Parsons' program was a systematic accumulation of occupational information. Surveys were made of the job requirements of specific industries, the work traits and skills desired, the conditions of work, and the chances for worker advancement. Parsons and his staff developed files of data on hundreds of occupations, and carried on a heavy correspondence in behalf of clients or referred them to other placement agencies.

The third aspect of the program was the creation of a training program for counselors to make them effective with clients and to inform them about the world of work. Parsons collaborated with the Boston YMCA in the establishment of a school for training vocational counselors. His approach which he repeated in many addresses was: "If you take up a line of work to which you are adapted or can adapt yourself, you are likely to be happy and successful. If a man loves his work and can do it well, he has laid the foundation for a useful and happy life."[27]

[25]Frank Parsons, "The Vocation Bureau," *The Arena*, Vol. 40 (September 1908), pp. 180–181.
[26]Frank Parsons, *Choosing a Vocation* (Boston: Houghton Mifflin, 1909), pp. 24–46 *et passim*.
[27]Frank Parsons, *The Arena* (July 1908), p. 9.

Parsons believed that with the aid of this self-study program and the help of a vocational counselor, the individual could make a rational choice about his work, or the kind of additional education he needed. The faith of progressive reformers that science held the key to progress would be confirmed by the substitution of "a scientific method of choosing a vocation" for irrational and wasteful procedures.

Meyer Bloomfield, who became director of the Boston Vocation Bureau when Parsons died in 1908, was willing to extend the social reconstruction of Parsons' work. He made the startling recommendation that guidance include an evaluation of the human satisfactions that could be found in various jobs.

> While the authorities are given increasing resources to train their charges for the demands of modern vocational life, should they not be likewise empowered to deal with abuse and misapplication of society's expensively trained product? A searching evaluation of occupations must surely be undertaken. . . . The job, too, should be made to give an account of itself. The desirable occupations must be studied and better prepared for; the dull and deadly being classified in a rogue's gallery of their own. Then only can reciprocal purpose mark the relation between employer and employee.[28]

This radical suggestion did not get far. Jesse Davis, a young pioneer of vocational guidance in Michigan, set out to determine the suitability of jobs for his young clients. He knew that factory inspectors filed reports at the state capital which included information on items like hours of work, accident records, etc. He reported that, "In my ignorance, I went to Lansing and as a citizen of the state asked to see the inspectors' reports on industries in Grand Rapids. I was refused, as these reports were held strictly confidential."[29] By a bit of finagling with his friend the Governor, Davis eventually attained access to the records; but the general idea that jobs should be worthy of people seemed too preposterous to be taken seriously.

The Vocation Bureau became reality shortly before Parsons' death. The flexible rhetoric of progressivism was useful in winning broad-based community cooperation. Terms like "waste" and "efficiency" were emphasized, with the knowledge that such words carried nuances of meaning that suited the divergent persuasions of social reformers and business leaders alike.

In seeking support from the business community, Parsons described the purpose of the Bureau as aimed at reducing

---

[28]Meyer Bloomfield, *The Vocational Guidance of Youth* (Boston: Houghton Mifflin, 1911), pp. 23–24.

[29]Jesse B. Davis, *The Saga of a Schoolmaster* (Boston: Boston U., 1956), p. 183.

the percentage of inefficiency and change you may experience in your working force, and the care it entails in employment expense, waste of training and low grade service . . . due to the haphazard way by which young men and women drift into this or that employment, with little or no regard to adaptability, and without adequate preparation.[30]

The membership of his board reflected the wide range of support that marked the industrial education movement itself. Lincoln Filene was one of the enthusiastic supporters. Joining him were J. Z. Richards, president of Boston Consolidated Gas Company; Paul Hanus of Harvard, chairman of the Douglas Commission; F. P. Speare, educational director of the YMCA; Mrs. Mary Morton Kehew, president of the Women's Educational and Industrial Union; and John F. Tobin, president of the Boot and Shoe Workers Union. Parsons' work, incidentally, won early support from labor. The 1910 Mitchell Report described "vocational guidance as the newest development in connection with industrial education" and said:

> No more far-reaching piece of work has been done to provide an insight into an intelligent interest in trades than that accomplished by the Vocation Bureau of Boston. The research studies by the Bureau on vocations, published in bulletin form (on "The Machinist," "The Grocer," "The Baker," etc.) supplies those interested with a pen picture of the trades never before attempted.[31]

Gradually leaders of the guidance movement saw that the problems of the slums were too enormous to be handled by private means. The year after Parsons died, the Boston School Committee asked the Vocation Bureau for help in drawing up a plan for a program of vocational guidance for public school students.

Parsons shared the conviction of Jane Addams that it would not be enough merely to add vocational guidance to standard school programs. He argued that urban children were experiencing the evils of specialization that marked the industrial society: specialization either in the form of boring, irrelevant "book work" in school, or in the narrowly specialized, routine work of industry. Both experiences were mind-killing. What was needed was a reform of urban schooling: Parsons wanted a new approach

> Book work should be balanced with industrial education; and working children should spend part time in culture classes and industrial science. Society should make it possible for every boy and girl to secure

[30]Parsons, *Choosing a Vocation*, p. 4.

[31]American Federation of Labor, Report of the Committee on Industrial Education, *Senate Document* No. 936, 62nd Cong., 2nd Sess., Vol. 4 (Washington, D.C.: Government Printing Office, 1912), pp. 98, 100.

at least a high-school education and an industrial training at the same time.[32]

He argued for greatly extended work-study opportunities for all high school students. Some should have chances to work in the public water works, lighting, or transportation, or other public services; others should work with private employers on the basis of agreements established between the schools and merchants and manufacturers, "so that no boy or girl shall be debarred from the training of mind and hand, which is the rightful heritage of every child society allows to be born into this complex and difficult world."[33]

Beyond that, Parsons argued for the modification of general methods of education. Schooling centered on passing examinations, he said, cheats youth of adequate preparation for life and work—"the principal test should be the successful performance of things that have to be done in daily life." Schools as presently organized, he argued, produce "good bookworms, sponges, absorbing machines, but they do not know how to do things." Urban children needed, rather, "the powers of thought and verbal expression that come with general culture," plus the chance to test their powers and expand their interests through real work in the institutions of their communities.

The problem of designing education that urban youth can find meaningful has remained a dilemma. Frank Parsons might not be surprised to observe educators, more than a half century later, discovering merit in his kinds of ideas.

B. NSPIE AND VOCATIONAL GUIDANCE

By the early 1900's, a number of educators had joined the attack on "bookish education." As we have seen, however, the drive to vocationalize schools came chiefly from outside the ranks of educators; and the major instrument for coordinating pressures on the schools was the National Society for the Promotion of Industrial Education. The Society's style is revealed in the role it played in advancing the cause of vocational guidance.

The first convention opened a harsh debate within NSPIE over whether to sponsor the dual school plan, or to work to include vocationalism within the public school system. The latter course of action gradually won majority support; and the first formal move to induce public schools to offer vocational guidance to students came at the 1910 convention in Boston. Three powerful members of NSPIE—David Sned-

[32]Parsons, *Choosing a Vocation*, pp. 161–162.
[33]*Ibid.*, p. 162.

den, Massachusetts. Commissioner of Education, Bernard J. Rothwell, President of the Boston Chamber of Commerce, and Frank Thompson, Superintendent of the Boston Public Schools—met with Meyer Bloomfield of the Boston Vocation Bureau to plan the first National Conference on Vocational Guidance.

The conference was called for the three days prior to the NSPIE meetings and the roster of people who spoke reads like a Who's Who of NSPIE.[34] The speeches were cast in NSPIE-style rhetoric and could have been recorded for replay at the convention that was to follow immediately. There was a consensus that vocational guidance and industrial education were related facets of public school reform. A planning committee was established, and a second Vocational Guidance conference was held in New York in 1912.

New York had been an active center of agitation for industrial education. The Public Education Association had hired Alice Barrows in 1912 to conduct a Vocational Education-Guidance Survey for New York City. This, together with the famous Hanus survey of 1911–12 which charged New York schools with financial inefficiency, provided the base for the Public Education Association's drive to introduce the Gary Plan into the public schools of the city. Alice Barrows reported to the second Vocational Guidance conference that what children wanted was not guidance into jobs but guidance into training programs. "The kernel of truth in this popular movement for vocational guidance is the need for vocational training for children."[35]

A reporter for *Survey* wrote that the great service of the conference was that it brought into the open two conflicting views of how to handle the massive numbers of school dropouts who were drifting from job to job. One group urged the establishment of "placement bureaus"; the other argued that the need was to "reconstruct our system of education so that it will fit youth for the work it will have to do." The *Survey* reporter judged that the second method elicited "wide-agreement," while "placement" was viewed primarily as a useful way to get at "the desired facts about industry."[36] Richard Stephens, the historian of vocational guidance, comments: "Since it was the second method that the

[34]W. Richard Stephens of Indiana State University has been the first to document this close connection between NSPIE and the NVGA. The account which follows relies heavily on his work. Addresses were made by three of the organizers of the conference, Snedden, Rothwell, and Bloomfield; and by others such as Paul Hanus of Harvard, Susan Kingsbury, Robert A. Woods of the South End House, Felix Adler of the Ethical Culture School, Professor Charles Richards, Owen Lovejoy of the National Child Labor Committee, Frederick Fish, Boston businessman and President of the Massachusetts Board of Education, and, as to be expected, President Eliot of Harvard.

[35]Sol Cohen, *Progressive and Urban School Reform*, (New York: Bureau of Publications, Teachers College, Columbia University, 1964) p. 74.

[36]Winthrop Lane, *Survey* (November 1912), pp. 225–226.

powerful NSPIE was thumping, it was no surprise to see it win out eventually at the Grand Rapids meeting the next fall, 1913."[37]

An organizing committee of the Conference on Vocational Guidance decided to accept Prosser's invitation to launch a guidance organization in conjunction with the 1913 NSPIE meetings in Grand Rapids. There was much optimism at the 1912 meetings. Prosser was elated because eight states had recently enacted vocational education laws. NSPIE leaders rejoiced, too, in the victory of Woodrow Wilson and his promise of the "New Freedom." New sources of support were foreseen; and the possibility of coordinating vocational guidance with industrial education, a long-time hope of vocational leaders, seemed within reach.

At the guidance wing of the 1913 meetings, some delegates wanted the new Vocational Guidance Association to affiliate directly with NSPIE or the NEA. They were overruled, however, and the decision was made to start a separate organization.

This resistance to direct affiliation with established organizations reflected the fact that the vocational guidance movement contained perhaps even greater diversity of support than did NSPIE. A group whose major allegiance was to the NEA was sceptical about being tied too closely to NSPIE. Still others in the guidance movement came from within the ranks of industry and stressed the placement aspect of guidance.

There was a sizable group of noneducators among the speakers at the joint meeting of NSPIE and the National Vocational Guidance Association at Grand Rapids in 1913. A number of the prominent speakers, for instance, represented the humanitarian wing of progressivism. Ida Tarbell, queen of the muckrakers, told the joint convention of the "average girl's" need for industrial training—"training in the domestic industries." She forcefully argued the case for including girls in the industrial education movement. Prior to industrialism, she said, "home industry" (canning, sewing, textile work, gardening, etc.) had been an important aspect of the American economy. When families moved to the cities, however, new complexities in handling health and child rearing arose. Also many women were taking employment in industry, where they were often exploited more than any other group. Ida Tarbell pointed out that forty-five million women "do housekeeping," maintain a family, and conduct financial transactions. She argued that the role of housewife was a "scientific business for which one can be trained as for any other business." NSPIE, she said, could "do no greater service to women . . . than to throw all its influence to dignifying and elevating the domestic industries."[38] Her

[37]Richard Stephens, *Social Reform and the Dawn of Guidance* (Terre Haute: Indiana State University, 1968), p. 52.

[38]Ida Tarbell, "What Industrial Training Should We Give the Average Girl," NSPIE *Proceedings*, 1915, pp. 132–135.

words and those of her women colleagues did not fall on deaf ears. The introduction and expansion of home economics and domestic science was included within the industrial education reform movement.

Owen R. Lovejoy, Secretary of the National Child Labor Committee, told the convention that both industries and schools needed to be reformed before children could experience the "Promise of America" of which Herbert Croly had written. He said that schools needed to introduce programs of vocational guidance which would "analyze our industries and train our youth to distinguish between a 'vocation' and a 'job'." He criticized the "captains of industry" who said " 'Here are the jobs: what kind of children have you to offer.' " Educators and guidance personnel must reverse the inquiry, said Lovejoy, and ask, " 'Here are your children; what kind of industry have you to offer.' "[39] He recognized also that schools needed to provide each child with a "conception of his industrial obligations and opportunities," a change which would infuse the entire curriculum "through and through with the meaning, the history, the possibilities of vocation."[40]

This latter theme was repeated by George Herbert Mead of the Chicago reform group. He interpreted the demands for vocational education and guidance as evidence of a general trend to relate the work of the schools more directly to the family, community, and industry. This new trend might help schools to overcome their tendency to retreat into academism. Mead's test of a vital education was whether it helped students cope effectively with urban-industrial realities. He joined John Dewey at the 1913 meetings in opposing the temptation to establish separate vocational school systems. The real issue, as Dewey and Mead saw it, was whether vocational-technological studies could be added to public education in such a form as to provide insight into the realities and value issues of the industrial society, or whether vocational studies would merely become training programs to serve industry. "A democratic education must hold together the boys and girls of the whole community; it must give them the common education that all should receive, so diversifying its work that the needs of each group may be met within the institution whose care and generous ideals shall permeate the specialized courses, while the more academic schooling may be vivified by the vocational motive that gives needed impulse to study which may be otherwise, or even deadening."[41]

[39]Owen R. Lovejoy, "Vocational Guidance and Child Labor," U.S. Bureau of Education *Bulletin* No. 14, (Washington, D.C.: Government Priniting Office, 1914), p. 13.
[40]*Ibid.*
[41]George Herbert Mead, "The Larger Educational Bearings of Vocational Guidance, "U.S. Bureau of Education *Bulletin*, No. 14 (Washington, D.C.: Government Printing Office, 1914), p. 17.

Professor Frank Leavitt of the University of Chicago, who was to become the first President of the NVGA, restated the value choice which had to be confronted. It is possible, said Leavitt, to think of vocational education as having for its purpose "the salvation of our industrial system and the maintenance of our commercial supremacy," while vocational guidance may have as its chief purpose "the salvation of lives and the ideals of the nation's workers." Although the two are not necessarily antagonistic, he continued, the differences in emphasis may be very real. He supported Lovejoy's argument that vocational guidance workers needed to study industries from the point of view of whether or not they were "good for children." Such studies, "if carried out in a comprehensive, purposeful and scientific way, may force upon industry many modifications which will be good not only for the children but equally for the industry." Vocational guidance will not hesitate to make such demands just because an industry is rich and powerful, Leavitt added. "Why should we hesitate to lay hands on industry in the name of education when we have already laid hands on the school in the name of industry?"[42]

The "Chicago school"—Mead, Dewey, and Leavitt—brought the perspective of democratic philosophy to the discussion of vocational guidance. Leonard P. Ayres, Director of the Educational Division of the Russel Sage Foundation, rejected such ideological talk and insisted that guidance programs should derive their goals from a study of the objective facts about American schools and industries.

Ayres reported on a series of studies he had conducted with "the object of finding a fact basis of some of our thinking." His facts revealed such items as: (1) Thirteen-year-old boys were distributed over many grades, including second and third grades. Educators should talk more about level of educational accomplishment than about the ages of children when deciding who was ready for work. (2) Only one family in six was living in the city where the child was born, a fact which pointed to the mobility of families in industrial society. Ayres said this raised questions about the justifiability of planning vocational programs in terms of the needs of local industries. American problems, he pointed out, were becoming more and more national in scope. This fact was not lost on NSPIE leaders as they began their serious drive for federal support. (3) Industries could be divided into different categories for purposes of planning vocational education and guidance programs. Ayres reported that certain "constant occupations" could be found in

[42]Frank M. Leavitt, "How Shall We Study the Industries for the Purposes of Vocation Guidance," U.S. Bureau of Education *Bulletin* No. 14 (Washington, D.C.: Government Printing Office, 1914), pp. 79–81.

every community. Every town needs barbers, for example; and Ayres found that in the average city of 50,000, 150 barbers would be needed. (4) The working conditions of industries could and should be ascertained. Thus Ayres reported on wage rates, annual unemployment, and death rates for various occupations. Ayres drove home his point: "If we are to engage in vocational guidance, our first and greatest need is a basis of fact for our own guidance."[43]

It is clear that NSPIE took a leading part in working for the inclusion of guidance programs in the public school system. It is clear, too, that the question of whether guidance should be envisaged primarily as an efficient aid to industry, or whether it should be viewed as a force for reform of both industry and education reflected the differences in value orientation within the larger industrial education movement.

C. VOCATIONAL GUIDANCE IN INDUSTRY: THE EMPLOYMENT MANAGERS ASSOCIATION AND THE NATIONAL ASSOCIATION OF CORPORATION SCHOOLS

The NVGA committed itself to promoting guidance programs in the public schools, but it had important relations with industry, too. Industrialists had interests which bore little relation to the "reform of work" cherished by humanitarian progressives. In order to understand how guidance was related to the needs of industry and education we shall have to look briefly at the rise of two new organizations: The Employment Managers Association (EMA) and the National Association of Corporation Schools (NACS).[44]

1. The Employment Managers Association

When Meyer Bloomfield took over the Boston Vocation Bureau in 1909, he was instrumental in having a study made of two hundred leading establishments in business, industry, and professional services.[45]

Lincoln Filene said that the results of the study showed that the best efforts of the Bureau and the schools were being undermined because employers did "not recognize the underlying principles of fair condi-

---

[43]Leonard P. Ayres, "Studies in Occupations," U.S. Bureau of Education *Bulletin*, No. 14 (Washington, D.C.: Government Printing Office, 1914), pp. 27–30.

[44]For a general account of these organizations, see W. Richard Stephens, *Social Reform and the Dawn of Guidance* (Terre Haute: Indiana State University, 1968), pp. 61–66.

[45]Meyer Bloomfield, "The New Profession of Handling Men," Daniel Bloomfield (ed.), *Selected Articles on Employment Management* (New York: H. W. Wilson, 1920), p. 33.

tions of employment," nor did they know how to give training and guidance to help individuals to better jobs. It was necessary, then, to attempt reforms through organizing the employment managers.[46]

In 1913, the year the NVGA was formed, Meyer Bloomfield called the founding meeting of the Employment Managers Association. Bloomfield saw this organization as the third phase of the vocational reform movement:

> In the creation of the EMA, a new agency for vocational help has come into being and it is of the utmost importance to workers in the field of vocational education (NSPIE) and vocational guidance (NVGA) to watch the activities of the employment officials (EMA) and enlist them in the common task of starting young people in the work they should be doing under conditions that will make employment mean growth as well as wages.[47]

At the founding convention, apart from employment managers from various American businesses, the speakers included the usual vocationalists: Charles Prosser, William Redfield, former President of NSPIE and now Secretary of Commerce, Lincoln Filene, and Meyer Bloomfield.

The speeches of employment managers reflected their awareness of the growing complexity of the hiring, training, and promoting of personnel, and a new level of interest in the discontents of workers. As Bloomfield put it, "we must go to school again . . . to find out what the workingman in the twentieth century is going to demand as his price for being efficient, for being loyal; to find out what the community is going to demand, before it bestows success on an enterprise."[48] Some of the speakers agreed with the Bloomfield-Filene position that employers needed to coordinate their hiring, training, and promotion policies with the efforts of the schools, and that enlightened self interest now required employers to think seriously about worker satisfaction. As Meyer Bloomfield put it, to get "team play" in industry requires "the same scientific study that has so far been given to cost keeping, factory management, and the other devices which have dealt with machines, with management, and, too, incidentally, with men."[49]

When Mr. George Bundy, employment manager of the Ford Motor

[46] *Vocational Guidance Magazine.* Bureau of Vocational Guidance: Harvard University, December 1925, pp. 121–122.
[47] *Vocational Guidance Bulletin,* October 1916, p. 2.
[48] Meyer Bloomfield, "The Aim and Work of Employment Managers Associations," NSPIE *Proceedings,* 1916, Appendix: *Proceedings* of Employment Managers Conference, p. 44.
[49] *Ibid.*

Company, got up to speak he wasted no words on altruistic motivations but spoke enthusiastically about new techniques and cost-cutting techniques in employee relations. He reported that the Ford Company had at one time conducted personal interviews with every applicant. Recently, however, the number of job seekers had "got so large that we had to turn the hose on them to keep the crowd from breaking in one side of the building."[50] To avoid such embarrassments, the company had decided to do all hiring through form applications. Bundy's speech consisted of an elaborate description of the variety of forms which had been developed, together with an exposition of the suitability of the form system to the needs of the plant. Something of the new style of employer-employee relations was reflected in the postal card which was sent automatically to each applicant. "In repsonse to your recent inquiry, we regret to advise that we can offer you no encouragement, as there are no vacancies in our factory at present, but will file your application and notify you later should we have a position to offer you."[51] This card dampened anticipations, Bundy said, and served to avoid disappointments.

The war disrupted Bloomfield's efforts to sponsor close working relations between the EMA and the National Vocational Guidance Association. After the war, the NVGA seems to have lost active contact with its EMA colleagues and returned to its focus on guidance in the schools.

2. The National Association of Corporation Schools (NACS)

While the vocational education and guidance reform groups were building a network of collaborations between the schools and industries, another organization appeared which was designed specifically to promote training and guidance in the interests of the largest corporations. A number of very large industries had begun to establish their own training schools after about 1905. In 1913 several of them came together to form the National Association of Corporation Schools. Companies such as the New York Edison, National Cash Register, Tide-Water Oil, Westinghouse, General Electric, and the Pennsylvania Railroad, expressed disenchantment with the efforts to have "our educational system . . . brought into some correlation with the business world." The people best qualified to effect a relationship between train-

---

[50]George Bundy, "Work of the Employment Department of the Ford Motor Co.," NSPIE *Proceedings*, 1916, Appendix, p. 63.

[51] *Ibid.*

ing and industry, they decided, were the industrialists themselves.[52] The corporation school, argued one spokesman for big business, would take the education of the workmen out of the "hands of the trade unions, the hands of the Industrial Workers of the World, and the Socialist Party," and put it into the hands of industry, thus yielding "the highest kind of insurance that any industrial corporation can have. . . . " Corporation schools could play a role in the "gradual democratization of industry," by educating men "so that they can handle the privileges which are to come to them through this idea of democracy." Schools run by corporations would know best how to teach workers their responsibilities in a democracy. Industry, he said, knew how such education could be "handled with the proper conservatism and power, and correct point of view, better than it [could] be done from any other source."[53]

The members of NACS had many interests in education and were developing sophisticated training programs. Programs at one level were designed to prepare college graduates and the most skilled technical workers for managerial positions: industrial theory was combined with guided experiences in the shops. At another level, apprenticeship schools were established in which students were taught basic subjects related to the mechanical skills needed in the factory. Finally, basic education programs were established for immigrants and the growing number of uneducated blacks from the south. Literacy training was combined with instruction related to health, safety, and work procedures. For the immigrants, a heavy stress was placed on Americanization to offset "possible menaces to the factory and national security."[54]

Generally, NACS remained uninvolved in attempts to incorporate industrial training into the public schools and paid little attention even to the efforts to enact Smith-Hughes. The attitude of these industrial giants reflected both supreme confidence in their own ability to handle their training needs, and skepticism about public school capabilities. Thomas E. Donnelly of the Lakeside Press of Chicago, for example, argued for private rather than public school industrial education. His company took boys at fourteen and put them into apprenticeship instruction for six and one half years. Donnelly maintained that all the talk of NSPIE-type vocationalists was only a "dream of the schoolmaster and

[52]National Association of Corporation Schools. *Proceedings*, 1914, pp. 341–344. Minutes of the Meeting for Organizing NACS, held at New York University, January 24, 1913.
[53]NACS *Proceedings*, 1914, pp. 350–352.
[54]Albert James Beatty, *Corporation Schools* (Bloomington: Indiana U., 1918), pp. 44 ff.

the professional or dilettante social reformer."[55] The American school system, unlike that of Germany, was "democratic" and therefore "politics ridden," subject to pressures from groups like organized labor. Corporations would be better off, said Donnelly, running their own schools tailored to their own needs. Some NACS members supported public school vocationalism but the largest corporations, wealthy enough to bypass the public schools, felt there were advantages to taking fourteen-year-old workers and training them in company schools which served their specific needs. As Donnelly put it, "We look upon our school as a means of training our future factory organization."

Corporation training programs thus became an important element in the total educational effort to make the industrial system function. In concept, these programs reflected the ideas of early NAM leaders who supported private schools run by industrialists. The dramatic expansion of such schools waited until the demands of World War II forced industries to reexamine training programs. Corporation training programs have been expanding rapidly ever since, although they remain a relatively unstudied aspect of the American educational effort.[56]

[55]Thomas E. Donnelly, "Some Problems of Apprenticeship Schools," NACS *Papers*, I, 1913, p. 131. See also Berenice Fisher, *Industrial Education*, pp. 110–114.
[56]See Harold F. Clark and Harold S. Sloan, *Classrooms in the Factories* (Rutherford, N.J.: Institute of Research, Fairleigh Dickinson University, 1958).

6/ The National Education Association Takes a Position

The National Education Association was forced to stir under the pressure of the vocationalists. It made a direct response by appointing two major committees: the Committee on Vocational Education and Vocational Guidance (1912), and its more famous Commission on the Reorganization of Secondary Education (CRSE) in 1913. These steps signalled the end of the NEA's first round of efforts (begun in the nineties) to make the school system answer the needs of urban America. The expansion of industrialism called now for common school change of a different order.

In retrospect we can see that the earlier reforms had served primarily the needs of those who would assume technical and administrative roles in the corporate bureaucracies. This was accomplished by instituting measures to assure to the ambitious an easier transition from the public schools to the rapidly growing colleges and universities. This move bore with it the happy assumption that what would best serve those who aspired to higher education would automatically serve all others as well.

The free public high school had been a relatively rare phenomenon before the Civil War; yet by 1890, after a forceful secondary school expansion in the eighties, the U.S. Commissioner of Education reported a count of 2,556 high schools. The phenomenon of at least a doubling of the high school population each decade had begun. A concomitant development, with acceleration in the nineties, was the proliferation of professional training programs in American universities into such areas as agriculture, forestry, engineering, commerce, social work, and education.

The means to educate those who would lead and manage more complex institutions were being created. The problem, clearly identified by Harvard's President Charles Eliot in an address to the NEA in 1890, was that the pell-mell growth of the public schools was occurring in the absence of any orderly system of education. In the absence of rational coordination of the different school levels, expansion was leading to chaos rather than to progress. The NEA responded to this situation in 1892 by appointing its "Committee of Ten," headed by Eliot, to explore the problem of the articulation of high schools and colleges. The classical tradition, with its simple assumption that the proper task of secondary schools was to teach Latin and Greek to young gentlemen headed for the colleges, was in disarray. The high schools, yielding to demands of its urban clientele, were adding a variety of new courses— natural sciences, "scientific engineering," modern languages, "commercial English," manual training. The colleges and universities, caught between a tendency to cling to old norms and the inclination to add new programs, were unsure about proper admissions procedures. Both high school and college officials were bewildered about college preparatory programs.

As the nineteenth century drew to a close, a series of steps were taken in an attempt to end this confusion. Eliot's Committee of Ten recommended first that nine high school courses should be considered as equivalent in value for college admission: Latin, Greek, English, modern foreign languages, mathematics, physical science, natural history, history, and geography. Colleges were urged to admit students who had followed programs based on some combination of these nine subjects. With college admission as the prize, high schools were thus encouraged to restrict their programs to these nine subject areas.

Ordering of the system progressed further with the establishment of the College Entrance Examination Board (CEEB) in 1900 and of the "Carnegie Unit" method of educational bookkeeping in 1909. The College Entrance Examination Board was instituted through the leadership of Nicholas Murray Butler, the energetic President of Columbia University. In consultation with Eliot, the CEEB created a series of standard tests on subjects very similar to those that had been recommended by the Committee of Ten. The Carnegie Foundation gave additional support to the Credit structure when, in 1909, it agreed to institute pension plans to Colleges which met standards specified by the Foundation. One of these was that colleges should admit only those students who had finished a standard high school course. Such a course was defined as one which consisted of sixteen units of 120 class hours in one subject each. The Foundation Trustees, furthermore, indicated their approval of the subjects for which the CEEB had prepared examinations. The high schools quickly responded to pressures from the colleges by agreeing to measure the work of their students in terms of "Carnegie Units."

The aim of these weighty efforts had been to provide a blueprint for American high school programs. The initiative had been taken by leaders of higher education who assumed that measures which would efficiently coordinate high schools with colleges would *ipso facto* result in the right programs for all high school students. Yet, as Henry Perkinson pointed out, ". . . in spite of all that prestige and power—by 1920 only a minority of high school students followed the program of studies proposed by the Committee of Ten."[1]

The actions taken had reduced confusion and had created opportunities for those who wished to prepare for both the old and the new professions. The Committee of Ten rationale, however, lacked relevance for the mass of students who were preparing to enter business and industry directly from school. Both these students and their employers began to sense that the educational system was offering training that furthered economic opportunity for technicians and administrators but was failing to provide comparable programs for people below those levels. Such feelings brought businessmen together with laborers in a common complaint against "bookish education" and outdated, impractical school masters.

Faced with these criticisms, the educators could either stand pat, engage in a thoroughgoing vocationalizing of the school system, or try to find a compromise. The majority probably would have preferred to maintain the status quo. The pain of institutional change is not eagerly embraced. Events, however, ruled out inaction as a real choice. Other educators were ready to accept the gospel of vocationalism according to NSPIE. They sensed that America had become a corporate-bureaucratic society and that people had to find their places in a hierarchically ordered system. Charles Eliot phrased the point aptly: "We must get rid of the notion that some of us were brought up on, that a Yankee can turn his hand to anything. He cannot in this modern world; he positively cannot."[2]

Advocates of the social efficiency philosophy wanted simply to tool up the system for effective performance at all levels. If each individual made his little corner hum, everyone would benefit from a higher standard of living. The obvious model to copy was the German one, in which a hierarchy of schools had been designed to serve the needs of the economic system. Some were willing to follow NSPIE where its logic pointed: the creation of a dual educational system and an efficient career-sorting arrangement based upon scientific vocational guidance programs.

[1]Henry J. Perkinson, *The Imperfect Panacea: American Faith in Education, 1865–1965* (New York: Random House, 1968), p. 137. See Chapter 4 for an insightful account.
[2]NSPIE *Proceedings*, 1908, Part I, Bulletin No. 5, p. 9.

For most educators, however, such a medicine was too strong to swallow. For one thing, it seemed outrageously at odds with the common school ideal, with its promise of producing socially mobile, self-reliant, involved citizens rather than compliant hired hands.

The move then was toward compromise, one which would reconcile the conflicting desires for efficiency and economic welfare with those for self-realization and democratic citizenship. In the work of the two committees appointed by the NEA in 1912, one can see both the conflicts and attempts to resolve them.

A. THE NEA COMMITTEE ON VOCATIONAL EDUCATION AND VOCATIONAL GUIDANCE

The Committee on Vocational Education and Vocational Guidance clearly bore the marks of the influence of NSPIE. Its ten members included Charles Prosser, Executive Director and chief lobbyist of NSPIE, David Snedden, Lincoln Filene, and Owen Lovejoy. The Chairman was Frank Leavitt, who had been first President of the National Vocational Guidance Association. The Committee took its job to be one of selling the virtues of vocational guidance programs to the city school systems. It issued its major report in 1916. The Committee attended joint meetings of NSPIE and NVGA in 1913 and 1914; and in 1915, it was invited to present a report to the influential NEA Department of Superintendence.[3] The general conversion of NEA leaders between 1910 and 1915 to the doctrines of business efficiency in administration made them receptive to the case for vocational guidance. The relationship was not harmed by the appearance in 1915 of a NSPIE survey on Minneapolis schools where the Superintendent was the powerful Frank Spaulding. Spaulding's Department of Attendance and Vocational Guidance was awarded special commendation. Bloomfield of the NSPIE survey team called it a "wonderful example of complete community cooperation" and an exemplary "scheme of guidance, training, employment, and starting in life."[4]

In the NEA Committee's 1916 final report,[5] David Snedden wrote a chapter which defined vocational education and guidance with examples from school practice; Charles Prosser told how NSPIE had used school surveys to produce vocational reforms; and Bloomfield wrote a

[3]See *Vocational Guidance Bulletin*, March, 1916, p. 1. For a general account of these relationships, see Richard Stephens, *Social Reform and the Dawn of Guidance* (Terre Haute: Indiana State University, 1968).
[4]NSPIE *Proceedings*, 1917, Appendix, p. 43.
[5]U.S. Bureau of Education, *Bulletin*, "Vocational Secondary Education," 1916, No. 21.

chapter which outlined a rationale to justify guidance programs. He noted the importance of the criterion of "efficiency" and described how vocational education and guidance were directly concerned with conserving natural and human resources. They were aimed at reducing that most costly waste, the "drifting from school to work, and from job to job." The way to reduce the waste, Bloomfield said, was to introduce vocational training opportunities, especially in "prevocational schools (Junior High Schools), which . . . will become self-discovery schools, and as such afford young people and their teachers a most important basis for vocational guidance." He concluded by saying that "efficiency in living life as a whole, as well as efficiency at work, is the goal of the vocational education movement in education." Returning to the theme of his mentor, Frank Parsons, Bloomfield added, "vocational guidance aims to lay down the specifications for a life career, vocational education, to supply the best methods for working them out; and if the messages of these enterprises is heeded in the occupations, we may expect employment to be a period of consummating the labors of the school."[6] The new system might, after all, become the means for realizing an old dream.

B. THE NEA COMMISSION ON REORGANIZING SECONDARY EDUCATION

The major NEA effort to rethink the program of the public schools was represented in its Committee on Reorganizing Secondary Education (CRSE), which produced the famous "Cardinal Principles of Secondary Education" statement in 1918.[7] The Committee's chairman was Clarence Kingsley, who in 1912 had just been selected by David Snedden, Massachusetts Commissioner of Education, to be the High School Agent of the State. Snedden was looking for someone to help Prosser and himself reorganize the high schools along vocational lines.[8]

Kingsley and his Committee, to the dismay of Dr. Snedden, backed away from seizing the opportunity of his NEA appointment to win a national victory for vocationalism. Instead, the Final Report extrapolated themes from the old common school ideal and recommended them as the basis for a new universal secondary school for "all the people." The keynote of the Report was a contention that the high

[6]Meyer Bloomfield, in U.S. Bureau of Education *Bulletin* (1916), pp. 118–129 *et passim.*

[7]*Cardinal Principles of Secondary Education: A Report of the Commission on the Reorganization of Secondary Education,* NEA, U.S. Bureau of Education, 1918, No. 35.

[8]See Walter H. Drost, *David Snedden and Education for Social Efficiency* (Madison: U. of Wisconsin Press, 1967), pp. 120–126.

school should abandon its traditional attachment to the colleges and become a secondary extension of the elementary common school. Its programs should meet the "real life" needs of all youth rather than cater to the minority that was college-bound. America's high schools should be rededicated to the old ideal of equalizing opportunities and of instilling common loyalties and commitments in young Americans from all backgrounds. The Report was an example of the progressive yearning to sustain values of democracy and community under conditions of corporatism and megalopolitan living.

The means for reconstituting the high schools was to be found in a new principle for planning the curriculum. Instead of following the academic disciplines so favored by the colleges, the new high schools should offer studies designed to help the great majority face the problems of living. The "seven cardinal principles" identified the goals for survival and social adjustment which should provide the common core of study for all: (1) health, (2) command of fundamental processes, (3) worthy home membership, (4) vocation, (5) citizenship, (6) worthy use of leisure time, and (7) ethical character. Thus the schoolmen repudiated their earlier preoccupation with articulation of lower school work to the demands of the universities—the main concern of the Committee of Ten. Now they were advocating an education that would help the young adjust to life.

The cardinal principles coincided to a remarkable degree with Herbert Spencer's advice (1860), that a social utilitarian education be created as an alternative to classical studies.[9] Spencer had answered his own question of "what knowledge is most worth?" by insisting that defensible studies would be those which equip men for self-preservation: knowledge required for health; for facilitating the gaining of a livelihood; for effective child rearing; for effective citizenship and moral living; and for worthy use of leisure time. We point out in the next chapter that leaders of the vocational education movement like Snedden and Prosser were attracted to Spencer's concept of schooling. In the early 1900's many urban educators were drawn to the utilitarian rationale expressed by Spencer—due, no doubt, more to the fact that "life-adjustment" principles related to the harsh problems of urban living than to any special intellectual power of Spencer's argument. The muckrakers, for example, were exposing the hazards for Americans in the industrial society: health hazards such as food and drug impurities, and lack of bathing and sanitary facilities for the urban poor; the weakening of family life and the neglect of children in tenement living

[9]Herbert Spencer, *Education: Intellectual, Moral and Physical* (New York: Appleton, 1860).

where both parents were forced to work and young children were put into factories; the economic vulnerability of immigrants who lacked the "fundamentals" of English and arithmetic as well as marketable work skills. In addition, there were the anxieties of national-type progressives who had doubts about the moral and civic reliability of the foreign newcomers—"the great unwashed."

The CRSE Report recommended that American communities establish *comprehensive* secondary schools. The goal of the vocationalists —to create separate types of high schools—was repudiated. Instead, the CRSE Commission promised that class divisiveness would be countered by bringing together the young from all classes under the roof of one high school. Teachers would be committed to the goals of the seven cardinal principles in the total school program. These principles would pervade the various subjects, especially certain common studies like English and social studies. All students would participate in common activities such as sports, assembly programs, and student government. The result would be that students would "become friendly with pupils pursuing other curriculums and having educational goals widely different from their own."[10]

The comprehensive high school idea was an effort to secure the best of two worlds. On the one hand, it recommended a program of common learnings based on the cardinal principles to assure democratic "equality" and "cultural unity"; on the other hand, it promised separate courses—college preparatory, vocational, and general—to meet the economic needs of skill training and career sorting.

It was an ingenious rationale, but it turned out to be easier to verbalize the objectives than to implement them. In time, the comprehensive high school idea became a disappointment both to the vocationalists and to those who hoped for schools which would provide authentic educative experiences for all.

The vocationalists had their doubts about the *comprehensive* idea from the beginning. The CRSE Report had little to say about specific trade training programs so close to the hearts of the vocational educators. "Vocation" had been placed on a par with six other cardinal principles. Observing these developments, David Snedden felt impelled to remark that "in spite of its insistence to the contrary, it is hard to believe that the Committee (CRSE) is genuinely interested in any vocational education that can meet the economic tests of our times."[11] Kingsley "replied with vigor" to the misgivings of his erstwhile boss. He main-

[10]For an insightful account of the work of the CRSE Commission and related developments, see Perkinson, *op. cit.*, Chap. 3, "Economic Opportunities and the Schools."
[11]See Edward A. Krug, *The Shaping of the American High School* (New York: Harper, 1964), p. 395.

tained that the new comprehensive high schools would be prepared to
give real vocational education, according to community needs, in addition to academic programs. But Snedden's instincts were sound. There
were basic differences in orientation between "true vocationalists" and
advocates of the comprehensive high school. After World War I the split
widened and the two groups moved off in separate directions more
often than not.

It also turned out to be an illusion to think that educators alone
could create genuine and vital comprehensive high schools. The vision
of a democratic, humanistic education for all would be destroyed as
opposing forces from the larger society pressed in. Social class and race
divisiveness, and the hierarchical skill and status differentiations of the
corporate bureaucracies exerted powerful counter effects upon the
schools.

Fifty years after the release of the CRSE Report it had become clear
what kinds of communities the American people would create in the
century of technology and urbanism. The configurations of megalopolitan society, in the main, made a mockery of the hope of realizing the
comprehensive school ideal.

Studies of several generations of class structure in American communities showed that housing patterns roughly reflected status in the
income-job structure of the corporate economy. The picture has become thoroughly familiar: blacks concentrated in the decaying inner-
city ghettos, together with poor whites from submarginal farm areas
and aged pensioners; beyond the city boundaries, the white suburban
housing developments—frame box, Cape Cod, ranch style, split level,
and exurban manors. When these housing patterns were combined
with the neighborhood school heritage, a basic assumption of the comprehensive school—that children from all backgrounds would study
together—was vitiated.

While the comprehensive school ideal received increasing attention between 1910 and 1920, many administrators were willing to accept the fact that neighborhoods tended to be inhabited by people of
similar social rank. Ellwood Cubberly, for example, advocated that the
programs of neighborhood elementary schools should be tailored to fit
the socioeconomic status of the area. One of the earliest and most
candid arguments for this idea was made by Superintendent Elson of
Cleveland in 1910.

> It is obvious that the educational needs of children in a district where
> the streets are well paved and clean, where the homes are spacious and
> surrounded by lawns and trees, where the language of the child's
> playfellows is pure, and where life in general is permeated with the

spirit and ideals of America—it is obvious that the educational needs
of such a child are radically different from those of a child who lives
in a foreign and tenement section.[12]

The congruence between social class and the quality of school experience became a dominant fact.

There were still, however, the small towns, middle-sized cities, and
border areas of the big cities and suburbias where socially mixed living
patterns were in effect. In such areas the conditions for comprehensive
schools existed, as children from different backgrounds met daily in
schools. Processes operated even in these schools, however, to assure
social class divisions. The system of ability tracking and differentiated
courses—general, commercial, trade, and "college prep"—was supple-
mented by school counseling to keep most children in the same track
their parents had been in. Henry Perkinson, in *The Imperfect Panacea*,
summed up the findings of decades of research on American communities.

> Study after study of the American schools revealed that they failed to
> equalize; they merely sorted and selected students for different ca-
> reers, different ways of life. In their study of a typical town first in the
> twenties and then again in the thirties, Robert and Helen Lynd re-
> ported that the school system of Middletown sorted out children for
> different careers. . . . In the fifties, Patricia Sexton found that the
> schools still failed to equalize children. Focusing on "Big City," a large
> midwestern city, she charted the "inequalities of opportunity in the
> public schools." She discovered that in the high schools the children
> from low-income families were almost completely separated from chil-
> dren from high-income families. Children from each group tended to
> take different programs. When they took the same courses, the upper
> income students were sorted into the higher ability sections of these
> courses.[13]

The truth is not served by oversimplification. The tremendously
productive business and industrial system did raise the general standards of living for most Americans. Comprehensive schools did function,
and many young people had experiences in school which enabled them
to realize their potential and improve their social standing. The
majority in the United States were able to enjoy the creature comforts
of middle-class life by 1970—only to discover, ironically, that they
might be poisoned by the pollution engendered in producing the ple-
thora of goods. Meanwhile, racism and poverty which shut out millions

[12]W.H. Elson and R. Backman, *Educational Review*, Vol. 39, pp. 357–359, quoted
in Sol Cohen, "The Industrial Education Movement, 1906–1917," *The American Quarterly*, Spring 1968, pp. 95–110.
[13]Perkinson, *op. cit.*, pp. 149–150.

from the general prosperity became more shameful as they became less excusable. The price paid was the burning of American cities in the sixties.

American teachers were reluctant to admit that schools had assumed a critical career-sorting function. The educational literature continued to speak of the common school as a "great equalizer" even though daily practice belied it.

Only as American society has threatened to disintegrate under the stresses of population explosion, pollution, racism, and overseas adventurism, has it become apparent how much we have lost of the substance of democratic, humanistic values. We are now in the testing time to find out if they can be recovered at all under the circumstances of twentieth-century life. The debate over the creation of the comprehensive school reveals the tension between the drives for democratic processes and the career-sorting, efficiency demands of technocracy.[14]

C. COMPREHENSIVE JUNIOR AND SENIOR HIGH SCHOOLS

The Cardinal Principles Report began by saying, "It is the ideal of democracy that the individual and society may find fulfillment each in the other. Democracy sanctions neither the exploitation of the individual by society nor the disregard of the interests of the society by the individual."[15] "This ideal," the report added, "demands . . . a high level of efficiency; . . . and those forms of social service in which the individual's personality may develop and become more effective."[16] Vocational studies were placed under the aegis of the public high school.

> It is only as the pupil sees his vocation in relation to his citizenship and his citizenship in the light of his vocation that he will be prepared for effective membership in an industrial democracy. Consequently, this commission enters its protest against any and all plans, however well intended, which are in danger of divorcing vocation and social-civic education. It stands squarely for the infusion of vocation with the spirit of service and for the vitalization of culture by genuine contact with the world of work.[17]

[14]Jacques Ellul, *The Technological Society* (New York: Vintage, Random House, 1967) underscores the forces of the system on all advanced societies whether they be capitalist, socialist or communist.

[15]NEA, *Cardinal Principles of Secondary Education:* A Report of the Commission on the Reorganization of Secondary Education, U.S. Bureau of Education *Bulletin*, 1918, No. 35, p. 9.

[16]*Ibid.*

[17]*Ibid.*, p. 16.

The educational structure that the Committee on Reorganizing Secondary Education recommended was a six-year elementary school followed by a three-year junior high school acting as the vestibule to a three-year comprehensive high school. Neither the junior high school nor the comprehensive-type high school existed in 1900. Edward A. Krug, in *The Shaping of the American High School*,[18] has begun to unravel the complex events which led to the creation of these two new educational institutions.

As Krug points out, intermediate or junior high schools were being established here and there across the country by 1910. There is still lack of clarity about all of the factors responsible for their appearance. Krug says, "Nobody quite knew where this junior high school had come from but there it was."[19]

It seems clear, however, that one major factor in the creation of the junior high school was the industrial education movement. The various interest groups which came together in NSPIE shared the conviction that a major failure of the public schools was the lack of adequate offerings for students in the early teen years. They called attention to the fact that alarming numbers of America's children were leaving the school system before the seventh grade; and this at a time when technology and complex city life demanded a more highly educated work force.

It is not surprising, then, that new calls for change were heard. A slogan appeared which expressed the mood of the period 1905–15: "Education for Social Efficiency."[20] William C. Bagley, then a young professor in a Montana Normal School, announced unabashedly in 1905 that "social efficiency is the standard by which the forces of education must select the experiences that are impressed upon the individual. Every subject of instruction, every item of knowledge, every form of reaction, every detail of habit, must be measured by this yardstick."[21] By 1909, an orator at the Oregon State Teachers Association could announce that the trend was to introduce subjects "better suited to the economic and social needs of the pupils, meaning increased social efficiency of all future citizens who attend school."[22]

When attention turned to the question of what to do for the thirteen-to-sixteen-year-olds, where the problem seemed most acute, a few influential educators began to lead a move to establish a separate set of

---

[18]Edward A. Krug, *The Shaping of the American High School* (New York: Harper, 1964).

[19]*Ibid.*, p. 327.

[20]See Krug, *op. cit.*, pp. 273–278.

[21]William C. Bagley, *The Educative Process* (New York: Macmillan, 1905), p. 60.

[22]Krug, *op. cit.*, p. 275.

trade schools in line with the demands of a major segment of NSPIE. Andrew S. Draper, Commissioner of Education of the State of New York, made such a plea to the NEA in 1908. He argued that school programs were needed to meet particular needs, whether those needs are high or low, academic, professional, commercial, agricultural, or manufacturing.[23] In another address to the same convention, he argued for separate public trade schools: " 'a new order of schools' because the new schools ought to be sharply distinguished from any schools that are known in America." They were to be quite different from manual training schools. Their aim, he said, should not be "to quicken the mentality nor to develop culture. . . . The 'culturists' are not to appropriate these new schools." Furthermore, they should not be designed to develop engineers or foremen. "The new schools," Draper insisted, "are to contain nothing which naturally leads away from the shop. *They are to train workmen to do better work that they may earn more bread and butter.*"[24] Draper wanted additional specialization even within the new system: one class of schools to train all-around mechanics for the new factories where each workman is "part of an organization, and where much machinery is used," to be called "factory schools"; another class of schools to train mechanics who worked independently with their own tools, to be called "trade schools." Technocratic doctrine had found a convert in the New York Commissioner of Education.

Opposition to Draper's kind of proposal appeared at once. Dean Eugene Davenport of the University of Illinois, speaking before the Society for the Promotion of Agricultural Science, accepted the legitimacy of the popular demand for agricultural education but argued against special agricultural high schools. He urged that one quarter of the class time in unified or comprehensive high schools be devoted to vocational studies. "In this way, we should have a single system of education under a single management, but giving to all young men and women really two educations; one that is vocational, fitting them to be self-supporting and useful, the other nonvocational and looking to their development."[25]

Agreement about the need for some new kind of intermediate school was growing rapidly; and reference to it was made in terminology reflecting the influence of vocational educators—"intermedi-

[23]Andrew S. Draper, "Desirable Uniformity and Diversity in American Education," NEA, *Addresses and Proceedings*, 1908, p. 224.
[24]Andrew S. Draper, "The Adaptation of the Schools to Industry and Efficiency," NEA, *Addresses and Proceedings*, 1908, pp. 74–75.
[25]Eugene Davenport, "Industrial Education a Phase of the Problem of Universal Education," NEA, *Addresses and Proceedings*, 1909, pp. 277–288.

ate industrial schools," "schools of mechanical industries," or "junior industrial high schools."[26]

A school often referred to as the first junior high school in America was the "introductory high school" of Berkeley, California. Superintendent Frank Bunker established the new school for grades seven through nine in 1910. He justified it, in part by contending that it was designed to meet the special needs of early adolescents. He made it clear, however, that his move was based upon more than psychological arguments. Adolescents, he said, need a more gradual transition from school to the "world of work." Bunker's ideas reflected the tendency in 1910 to regard the junior high school as a terminal school, a more efficient vehicle for bringing the average fourteen to sixteen-year-olds to jobs. Bunker relied heavily on the studies of retardation and dropouts made by Ayres, Strayer, and Thorndike. Berkeley students dropped out, he said, because of an overly academic curriculum. Nothing less than a radical change in the nature and content of the accepted courses of study would serve to remedy the situation. He described in detail the new vocational emphasis in his junior high school. Special courses such as typewriting, commercial law, domestic science, bookkeeping, and manual training were being added; and some academic courses were being translated into "business arithmetic," "business English," and the like.[27] Bunker reflected also the current interest in business efficiency by pointing out that dropouts were "wasteful." He argued that the reorganization of the "upper grades of the grammar schools" was the "only arrangement that could be made within "reasonable limits of expense."[28]

Within the next three or four years, over one hundred and fifty city school systems joined the movement to establish junior high schools. By 1922, 456 cities reported a total of 733 such schools.[29]

W. Richard Stephens has clarified the role of NSPIE in urging that the goals of social and economic efficiency be brought into the emerging junior high school.

> NSPIE not only propagandized the nation into an awareness of its "needs" for vocationalizing its public schools. It also became directly involved in reorganizing them. The specific mechanism by which the

[26]See Paul Hanus, "Industrial Education," *Atlantic Monthly* (January, 1908), p. 66; and Charles De Garmo, "Relation of Industrial to General Education," *The School Review* (March 1909), pp. 145–153.

[27]Frank F. Bunker, *Reorganizing the Public School System*, Bureau of Education Bulletin No. 8, 1916, pp. 105–115.

[28]*Ibid.*

[29]W. Richard Stephens, *The Junior High School, A Product of Reform Values, 1890–1920* (Terre Haute: Indiana State University, 1968), pp. 17, 23, citing *Report of the Commissioner of Education*, 1912, Vol. 1, p. 155.

society became involved was the school and industrial survey. In 1914, Leonard Ayres directed the first survey sponsored by NSPIE for the schools and industries of Richmond, Virginia. Ayres focused on the fourteen to sixteen-year-old drop-outs and the relation of the curriculum of the schools to the needs of local industries. The pattern of conducting the Richmond survey was followed by Charles Prosser as he directed the Minneapolis survey in 1915: Superintendent of Schools Frank Spaulding, who was also an active member of NSPIE, had requested the Society's sponsorship of the survey in April, 1915. In both of these surveys the Society recommended that the curriculum of the schools, especially for the grammar grades, be "industrialized" to prepare the fourteen to sixteen-year-old youth for employment.[30]

The kind of role which NSPIE played may be clarified further by noting the nature of its work in its "Indiana Surveys" of 1915–16 in Richmond, Evansville, and Indianapolis. In 1913 Indiana passed a Vocational Education Law. Its author was John A. Lapp, a NSPIE leader and chairman of the State Commission of Industrial and Agricultural Education. In 1915 C. R. Richards and Charles Prosser were appointed to the Indiana State Survey Committee, with Prosser as Chairman. The inclinations of this committee were revealed in the work undertaken in Richmond, Indiana.[31]

A Local Survey Committee was divided into subcommittees with members representing all phases of industrial, business, domestic and agricultural activity. Each subcommittee applied the principles of scientific management to analyze in minute detail the tasks performed by each occupational group. The Metal Working Committee, for example, recommended that Richmond schools offer night courses in machine operating; the Printing Committee proposed a "finding course" in printing for the junior high school, to be followed by a "trade preparatory" printing course in the senior high school; the Commercial Employment Committee wanted a junior high course to emphasize the importance of sales "to the entire community." In its final report, the Local Survey Committee commended the Richmond schools for adopting the "life career" plan which called for vocationalizing the curriculum for all pupils "regardless of sex and future vocation." It urged the new Garfield Junior High School to introduce required courses that would be "of general value" to all occupations, as well as "providing some elements that make for practical efficiency." Finally, where general studies were concerned, the committee recommended that civics

---

[30] *Ibid.*, p. 17. The material on NSPIE and the Junior High Schools is based on Stephens' study, pp. 15–25 *et passim.*

[31] Robert J. Leonard, *Richmond Survey for Vocational Education* (Indianapolis: Indiana State Board of Education, 1916), p. ix.

deal with the practical "everyday problems of community life"; that science be approached "from situations having immediate, appreciable problems"; and that mathematics be "largely practical or economic arithmetic," emphasizing problems growing out of the practical arts, or from "the standpoint of the consumer."[32]

It is clear that NSPIE's vocational emphasis played a powerful role in the beginnings of the junior high school movement. Two of the aspirations of the vocationalists, however, were to remain unrealized. The early expectation that the "intermediate industrial school" would be the terminal school for the great majority of fourteen-to-sixteen-year-olds was bypassed in fast-moving events. It soon became apparent that an education concluded at the ninth-grade level would be inadequate in the industrial era in terms both of societal needs and of personal ambitions. Even while the junior high school was being established, a majority was planning to stay in school beyond that level. The senior high school was to become the capstone of the public school system until the 1960's when the need for "middle level" technicians led to the addition of Junior Colleges to the common school system. As the high school expanded, the junior high school provided the transition between the elementary and senior high components of the system. This forced it to redefine its purposes all over again. Instead of acting as a gateway to work, it took on the function of the initial career-sorting agency which guided students into differentiated courses at the senior high level.

The emergence of the comprehensive school at the junior and senior high levels served also to thwart the vocationalists from creating a massive, separate vocational school system. Ben W. Johnson, Director of The Manual Training Schools in Seattle, enunciated the idea in 1910 which eventually was to win the day.[33] Johnson said there had been a growing realization of the wide differences among children, in physical condition, mental alertness and attitude, interest, vocational aim, and environmental background. The belief was growing, he said, that the elementary school should end at about age twelve or at the end of the sixth grade. This stage should be followed by an intermediate school consisting of the seventh and eighth grades plus the first or second year of high school. The seventh and eighth grades would duplicate neither the elementary nor the high school settings, but would institute programs to meet the specific needs of children in the age thirteen-to-sixteen group. Subjects would be planned and studied "from the stand-

[32]Stephens, op. cit., pp. 19–21.
[33]Ben W. Johnson, "Children Differ in Vocational Aims: Industrial Education in the Elementary School," NEA Proceedings, 1910, pp. 253–260.

point of social need and not as separate subjects." Children would have
an opportunity to elect courses from either the "industrial culture line"
of work or from the "academic culture." Johnson rejected the idea of
offering these courses in separate schools. The intermediate school
would offer both prevocational and academic studies within the same
school unit. The plan would differ from the German system, Johnson
said, because it would be "democratic, 'open at the top' to further
education or training." He quoted with approval a statement by Leonard Ayres: "The courses of study of our city school systems are adjusted
to the powers of the brightest pupils. They are beyond the powers of
the average pupil, and far beyond those of the slower ones." As Johnson
envisaged it, the obligation of schools in a democratic society was to
create a variety of experiences appropriate to the tastes and abilities of
all children. The "culturists" had no right to dominate the whole program.[34]

It was a time for far-reaching educational change, and pulls and
counter-pulls were at work in NEA conventions. There were still a few
"classicists" who resisted the move toward practical or vocational additions to the curriculum. Vocational educators who emphasized business
efficiency were active alongside progressive educators who wanted to
stress school programs which would support democratic values. All
groups employed a common rhetoric in their condemnation of the
sterile quality of traditional schooling, and in their call for an education
relevant to new socioeconomic conditions. They were often unaware of
the divergencies inherent in their basic value preferences, despite surface verbal agreements. It is not surprising to find schoolmen being
pulled this way and that in the whirl of contention.

One critical issue was whether school programs should be tied to
the needs of industry, or whether the main obligation was to take
advantage of the multisensory and field experience dimensions of industrial education to vitalize the general education of all children.
When educators like Ben Johnson talked about including "industrial-
cultural" courses in the new intermediate schools, he made vocationalists like Charles Prosser deeply suspicious. Johnson wrestled with the
question of how to avoid fragmented, specialized school courses that
tended to reflect the nature of the technological system itself. He talked
about curriculum experiments which would help students understand

---

[34]Articles in popular journals took up the cry about the domination of the high school
by the "culturists" and the colleges. They demanded a new kind of curriculum for a high
school that had finally become "the people's college." It should meet the needs of all the
students. See, for example, W. Hughes Mearns, "Our Medieval High Schools," *Saturday
Evening Post*, March 2, 1912, and W. D. Lewis, "The High School and the Boy," *Saturday
Evening Post*, April 6, 1912.

the interrelationships of industrial society and to see the relation between theoretical studies and new techniques and processes of industry. He recommended units which centered on the study of industries.
Manual arts would be broadened to include topics like power (wind,
water, steam, gas, electric), transportation, and shelter. In such units,
students would study scientific concepts while having the opportunity
to conduct experiments and manipulate materials and tools in the
manual arts workshops. The historical evolution of industries would be
studied, and questions would be raised about the social and aesthetic
consequences of technological changes.[35]

A vocational educator like Charles Prosser was in agreement with
Johnson about the need for "industrial education" and yet sceptical
about approaches which promised to integrate industrial studies with
general education experiences. Prosser advocated a simple forthright
task for the schools: "to *direct* and *train* all the children of all the people
for useful service." He stood with those who judged the public schools
in terms of efficiency criteria and found them to be failures.

> Misfits in all vocations confront us everywhere. Many workers are
> inefficient because they are not adapted to the work they are doing and
> some because they have not been properly prepared for it. This lack
> of efficiency constitutes a permanent handicap not only to the worker
> but to the calling which he follows. It means lessened wage, uncertain
> employment, failure of promotion, economic struggle, waste in the use
> of material, poor workmanship, reduced output, and the lowering of
> the standards of skill and workmanship of American industries. [36]

For Prosser, the remedy was clear-cut and obvious: identify the
aptitudes of children as early as possible; find out the needs of local
industry; group children with likely career lines; give the specific training to make them efficient in their work. Prosser recommended that the
intermediate school offer differentiated courses of study for pupils between twelve and fourteen. The seventh and eighth grades ought typi-

[35]Johnson's idea for utilizing the nature of industrial processes and features of the
technological society as a basis for integrating studies and giving insights into the twentieth century human condition was a much more sophisticated concept than the flabby
"cardinal principles" proposals for "life-adjustment." It was similar to John Dewey's
recommendations, described in Part IV. It was much easier to talk about meeting "real
life" needs than to take on the intellectually demanding task required to implement a
plan like Johnson's. This idea was revived in the 1960's when imaginative efforts were
made to transform traditional industrial arts programs into "Studies of American Industry." See for example the Ohio State University Industrial Arts Curriculum Project and
American Industry Project of Stout State University, Menomie, Wisconsin, described in
the last chapter.

[36]Charles A. Prosser, "Practical Arts and Vocational Guidance," NEA *Proceedings*,
1912, pp. 646–647. (Italics added.)

cally to offer a high school preparatory course, a commercial course, a household arts course for girls and a practical arts course for boys headed for a trade school. Johnson's kind of talk, concerning the study of industries and industrial processes as part of a general education, was proof to Prosser of the kind of perversion of trade training that invariably followed when general schoolmen got their hands on it. The differences between the two men reflect basic value differences. We shall return to these issues in Part II where the educational philosophies of Charles Prosser and David Snedden will be compared with that of John Dewey.

The problem of who would control vocational education programs remained a thorny one. At the same 1918 convention which approved the "Cardinal Principles" statement, the NEA also adopted a resolution that "the association favors amending the Smith-Hughes Act to prevent the possibility of establishing a dual system of schools in any state." The general educators were never very happy with Smith-Hughes. They were willing to accept the need for vocational education but were critical of federal aid for "special forms" of education. The attitude of the NEA was revaled in a resolution passed at the 1919 convention in Milwaukee: "A National Policy of Vocational Education." The tortured language of the statement probably reflected the state of mind of the educators on the subject.

> A high standard of intelligence, general vocational efficiency, physical and moral fitness and civic devotion are not only dependent upon an efficient system of public education of all our youth, but also upon the reaction upon human values of the occupations in which the people of the nation engage. If we are to be a homogeneous people generally, happy and prosperous, generally living full, rich, contributive lives, the work which we must do must continue through our lives, the development begun in the earlier years, devoted to specific and formal schooling. To this end, industry in this country must be reorganized. All industry must become educational to those who engage in it. The workers must find in their work an opportunity for self-expression and self-development. Human—not commercial—value must be placed first in our great industrial establishments. The rank and file of those who produce the wealth must, through their organization, share in the control of the policy of the institutions for whom they work. They must find an educative realization of their life's purposes in the output of their daily toil and in the sharing in the direction of the policy guiding its production.
>
> Vocational education must have as its purpose educational industry. Inasmuch as the general policy of Vocational Education in this country is directed by those responsible for the administration of the Smith-Hughes Law, we urge those thus responsible to adopt such a

policy in interpreting and administering this law that the above named ends may be furthered by the system of vocational education now developing under this law; namely (that students) in the schools and departments organized under the Smith-Hughes Law shall be made competent as far as humanly possible for sharing in the control of the policy of the institutions in which they may afterward be employed and that they shall be inspired, so far as is humanly possible, with an impulse to continue their education through the instrumentality of the occupation for which they may be trained, and in which they may be afterward engaged.[37]

This bold appeal that vocational education become an instrument for the reform of industry smacked of the tradition of Frank Parsons and the philosophical arguments of John Dewey. Its prophetic tone differed from the typical staid prose of the NEA. In any case, the Resolution received a vitriolic blast from vocational educators. They maintained that it was ill-advised, incorrect, inconsistent, and most certainly astonishing.[38] The fact that authors of the resolution had consulted no vocational educators, not even people from the NEA's own feeble Department of Vocational Education, reflected the growing schism between the two groups of educators. The most charitable response from vocationalists came from Clarence C. Howell, Supervisor of Industrial Arts, Lincoln, Nebraska: "We co-called vocational men need to get our heads above the sphere of our own little world now and then. We are cock of the walk just now, but it may not always be so—there are others in the educational planet who are still worth listening to on the big problems ahead."[39]

Vocational educators were drawn overwhelmingly to the ranks of the American Vocational Association, which became a powerful organization through the merger of several regional associations in 1926.[40] After that time, the NEA's Department of Vocational Education became relatively inactive. There have continued to be tensions, how-

[37]"Vocational Education at the NEA, *Industrial Arts Magazine*, Vol. 8, No. 9 (September 1919), p. 369.

[38]Arthur F. Payne, "The NEA Adopts a So-Called National Policy of Vocational Education," *Industrial Arts Magazine*, Vol. 8, No. 9 (September 1919), pp. 364–365.

[39]Clarence E. Howell, "Commending the N.E.A. Resolution on Vocational Education," *Industrial Arts Magazine*, Vol. 8, No. 10 (October 1919), p. 425. See also Barlow, *op. cit.*, Chap. 4, "Professional Associations."

[40]The American Vocational Association was formed in 1926 with a deliberate decision to remain separate from the NEA. It has its own journal, *The American Vocational Journal.* The American Industrial Arts Association was organized in 1939 during the annual convention of the American Association of School Administrators, and has been a department of NEA since 1942. It publishes *The Journal of Industrial Arts Education.* (Recently changed to *Man/Society/Technology.*) See Melvin L. Barlow, *History of Industrial Education in the United States* (Peoria: Charles A. Bennett, 1967), Chap. 3.

ever, within the broad vocational education area. Industrial arts educators have continued to see their work as general education and prevocational in nature. Their strength has been at the junior high school level. In many cases, these programs deteriorated into unimaginative shop courses in woodworking, metalworking, and electricity; but there have been periodic efforts to create curricula in which manual activities would be related to other subject matter areas along the lines that Ben Johnson recommended in 1910.

Industrial arts educators remained sensitive to the need to communicate with general educators. The American Industrial Arts Association was organized during the Annual Conference of the American Association of School Administrators in 1939. In 1942, the AIAA became a department of the NEA. It publishes its own journal, *Man/Society/Technology,* and holds its own national convention. It has become a thriving organization in its own right; and several of the most creative curriculum projects produced by American educators in recent years have come from its ranks.[41]

In the early 1900's a variety of people had hoped that the introduction of a vocational component into education might help to overcome the isolation of the school from life. The question of just what response the schools should make to the realities of industrial society was not adequately resolved in the narrow job-training approach. There were those debating the vocational issue who recognized that more was in question than narrow pedagogical concerns—matters of life style and human values in the technological society were involved. We turn next to those who chose to face the philosophical issues.

[41]See Chapter 12.

part IV

Philosophical Issues:
Education and the
Industrial State

INTRODUCTION

It was inevitable that a basic rethinking of the relationship between education and industrialism would occur. The root question was how the schools ought to relate their values and programs to new socioeconomic realities. In order to probe the philosophical issues, we shall compare the positions taken by David Snedden and Charles Prosser, two outstanding leaders of the vocational movement, with the ideas of John Dewey, whose classic *Democracy and Education* (1916) expressed his deep concern about the meaning of the scientific-industrial era for American institutions.

Snedden, Prosser, and Dewey all saw themselves as part of an educational reform movement which assumed that traditional schooling would have to give way to approaches more relevant to changing socioeconomic conditions. On the surface, there were many points of agreement among the three. They all condemned "sterile, exclusively bookish" education and a passive, rote-recitation kind of methodology. All were convinced that the traditional school, in ignoring the needs and interests of the mass of urban and rural children, was failing to meet its obligation to the majority. All three wanted to broaden the curriculum by including studies more appropriate to a scientific-technological era.

Just below the surface, however, there were profound differences which eventually flared into the open and which reflected value tensions characteristic of twentieth-century American life. Large-scale, rationalized modes of production had to be serviced efficiently if the country was to have its rising prosperity—a standard of living which

141

many equated with the American way of life itself. There was some question, however, as to whether an all-out commitment to material prosperity might lead to the loss of those humane and democratic values which the nation also cherished. The problem of the twentieth century was to discover whether the needs of the industrial system and the values of democracy could be accommodated within the same social order.

While the Great Commoner William Jennings Bryan was campaigning against Taft in 1908 on "whether the government shall remain a mere business asset of favor-seeking corporations" or be "returned to the people," Frank Tracy Carlton spoke with equal force about the relevance of the same issue to education. American education, said Carlton, was entering a "factory stage," in which students were turned out by the educational machinery to fit pre-determined roles in a mass production system.[1]

Commercial interests were putting pressures on schools to function according to "business principles."[2] The goal was to obtain from education the same efficiency which had increased production and cut costs in industry. The implied analogy, Carlton said, was false and disastrous on both economic and psychological grounds. Education and commerce were quite different enterprises, and to equate them would pervert the task of educating human beings.

> Children are not pots and pans to be shaped by patterns sent down from a central office. Teachers are not drudges to be ordered about by a master mechanic. Education is an artistic form of industry; its normal product leads to imperfect output. The teacher is a skilled workman, or more accurately, an artist. Methods must vary with teachers; crowded classrooms, systematic and numerous reports bound up in red tape, clock-like precision and central office management convert the school into a factory. Commercialization of the schools hampers and drives out the efficient teacher and spoils the child.[3]

The school, he said, needed to become a "studio, rather than a factory."

The conflicts between Snedden, Prosser, and Dewey illustrate the differences between the social efficiency and the democratic-reform branches of progressivism; yet to state the problem that way is both to tell the truth and to indulge in oversimplification. We shall try to clarify the point as we get into the story.

[1]Frank Tracy Carlton, *Education and Industrial Evolution* (New York: Macmillan, 1908), p. 76.
[2]*Ibid.*, p. 309.
[3]*Ibid.*, pp. 309–310.

7/ Education for Social Efficiency: David Snedden and Charles Prosser

David Snedden was a forty year-old Professor of Educational Administration at Teachers College, Columbia University when, as his biographer reports,

> One evening early in November, 1909, he received an unusual telephone call at his New York apartment. The caller asked to visit him to talk over the school situation in Massachusetts. . . . The mysterious visitor turned out to be Frederick Perry Fish, a famous corporation lawyer from Boston whose major achievement to date had been a series of corporate consolidations creating the American Telephone and Telegraph Company. Fish had recently been called upon to serve as chairman of the newly organized State Board of Education. He came to offer Snedden the position of Commissioner of Education for Massachusetts.[1]

We recall that Governor Douglas had established a Commission on Industrial and Technical Education which reported to him in 1906 a growing feeling of the "inadequacy of the existing public school system to meet fully the need of modern industrial and social conditions." The Douglas Commission had attributed this inadequacy to "an educational fare too exclusively literary in . . . spirit, scope, and methods." The answer, they felt, was to align schools with "the broader-minded students of education, men who look at their own work in the light of all its relations to society." These men were said to be impatient with old-fashioned schooling and preferred industrial education approaches which would familiarize the child with all the activities of the community. Students would be "producing as well as consuming, doing as well as learning." The Commission reported that this kind of education had been "used in the education of the feeble-minded, in the reformation

---

[1] Walter H. Drost, *David Snedden and Education for Social Efficiency* (Madison: U. of Wisconsin Press, 1967), p. 96. This carefully prepared biography provides a definitive account of Snedden's work and philosophy.

of wayward and vicious children at reform and truant schools, and . . . to elevate the colored race in the south." They felt it might be "equally efficient in stimulating and directing the higher orders of the mind, in preventing as well as curing juvenile delinquency, and in improving the social conditions of white as well as black children."[2]

David Snedden had finished his doctoral dissertation at Teachers College, Columbia University in 1906 on the topic, "Administration and Educational Work of American Juvenile Reform Schools." He was co-author with Samuel J. Dutton of *The Administration of Public Education in the United States* (1908). In both of these studies, Snedden had directed his attention to the plight of children twelve to sixteen years old and had championed vocational education as a needed reform. Snedden clearly would find an agreeable climate in Massachusetts among the champions of industrial education. He was Commissioner of Education from 1909 until 1916, during years that were critical to the expansion of industrial education; and he continued to be a leader among those who favored "real vocational education" well into the 1920's, when he became the first editor of the *Vocational Education Magazine*. Snedden became one of the founders of the National Society for the Study of Educational Sociology (1923) and is recognized as a pioneer in that field.[3]

While chief school officer in Massachusetts, he appointed his Columbia colleague Charles A. Prosser as Deputy Commissioner for Industrial Education. Prosser later became Executive Secretary for NSPIE, de facto author of the Smith-Hughes Bill, and director of the famous Dunwoody Institute for Vocational Study in Minneapolis. Prosser-Snedden ideas for *general* education were represented in the famous Prosser Life Adjustment Resolution of 1945, which launched the ill-fated movement bearing that name.

A. DAVID SNEDDEN—THE MAN AND HIS CAREER

David Snedden's life was a testimony to the "rags to riches" American success story. His father, Samuel, had been lured to California by the promises of the Gold Rush of the fifties. Like the great majority of

[2]Commonwealth of Massachusetts, *Report of the Commission on Industrial and Technical Education* (New York: Teachers College Educational Reprints, No. 1, 1906), pp. 3–4.

[3]Drost points out that in his day Snedden was accorded the same attention given to John Dewey and E. L. Thorndike. When Charles Judd, Edward Elliott, and Leonard Ayres organized the exclusive Cleveland Conference, in 1916, Snedden was chosen as a charter member along with Paul Hanus, Thorndike, George Strayer and Ellwood Cubberley as part of a select group of twenty. Norman Woelfel included Snedden among seventeen leaders of American education in his *Molders of the American Mind* (New York: Columbia U. Press, 1933).

prospectors, he failed to make the strike. Eventually he married an Irish girl, Anna O'Keefe, and turned to stock raising in the mountain meadows of Ventura County, California. David, the first of five children, was born in a cabin on Kelso Creek on November 19, 1868. From their earliest years, the children took hard work for granted. By age seven David was riding herd and aiding in harvesting alfalfa, in addition to his regular chores of gathering wood, helping to dig irrigation ditches, and constructing fences.

David's mother, Anna, in addition to making clothes, repairing shoes, canning food, and handling a host of other duties, was the children's teacher. There were a few books in the cabin; and by age eight, David had begun his reading and rereading of old McGuffey readers, *The Vicar of Wakefield*, and *Pilgrim's Progress*. He absorbed the Puritan ethic in deed and word. David's mother led a move to create the Alamo School District to serve the valley; his father helped haul the logs to build the one-room schoolhouse. David was fourteen when he enrolled for the first time in a "real school." He was so quick that he was put into the eighth grade at once. He spent the next two years picking up what he could from a teacher of the most modest ability. After that, an aunt, who had begun to make some money in real estate, provided financial resources for David to attend St. Vincent's College in Los Angeles.[4]

David was an outstanding student in classics, mathematics, and forensics, and graduated with honors in 1890. A cousin introduced him to the works of Huxley, Darwin, and Spencer; and these extracurricular readings and discussions proved more significant than the academic courses.

To begin saving money for the study of law, Snedden took a job as schoolmaster of a one-room school in the abandoned log cabin of a homesteader. By 1892, he had been appointed principal of an eight-grade school and had won his Master's degree from St. Vincent's.

Snedden renewed his reading of Herbert Spencer while boarding in the home of a young, intellectually curious physician. He acknowledged in later years that Spencer's philosophy, more than any other, laid the groundwork for his thinking. Spencer had put a hard pragmatic test to education. Educational priorities, he said, should be determined by analyzing "the leading kinds of activities which constitute human life."

> those activities which directly minister to self-preservation; those activities which have as their end the rearing and discipline of offspring; those activities which are involved in the maintenance of proper social

---

[4]Drost, *op. cit.* The biographical details and intellectual history of Snedden are based on the biography by Drost.

and political relations; and those miscellaneous activities which make
up the leisure part of life devoted to the gratification of the tastes and
feelings.[5]

Years later, this list reappeared in the NEA's famous "Cardinal Principles" statement (1918) as: health, command of fundamental processes,
worthy home membership, vocation, citizenship, worthy use of leisure,
and ethical character. Spencer's insistence that education meet the
criteria of social efficiency and life adjustment made sense to the young
Western schoolmaster. He would find later, as he moved East, that
urban educators struggling with the question of what to do with city
children, would share his admiration for such ideas.

In 1895 Snedden enrolled as an undergraudate in education at
Stanford University. The school was only four years old then; but it
already had a reputation, under the leadership of David Starr Jordan,
for having a bright, aggressive young faculty. At Stanford, Snedden
encountered still other aspects of the "new education" in addition to
manual training—the child-study enthusiasm of Earl Barnes and the
Herbartian "center of interest" orientation. Snedden found greatest
inspiration, however, from his work with Edward A. Ross, the brilliant
and controversial young social economist. With his doctrine of social
control, Ross was emerging as one of the American pioneers in the new
field of sociology.

Between 1896 and 1898, Ross wrote a series of articles for the
American Journal of Sociology on the topic of "Social Control." They
formed the nucleus of his influential book under that title published in
1901.[6] In the Preface, Ross announced that his purpose was "to inquire
how far this order we see all about us is due to influences that reach men
and women from without, that is social influences." He described the
need for social control as rooted in the requirement to avoid chaos and
disorder; the *means* were analyzed as all sorts of instruments—religious, governmental and political organizations, folklore, traditions and
"even works of art." He found that "the moulding of the individual's
feelings and desires to suit the needs of the group" was "the most
difficult work of society."[7] Ross held that the efficiency of the social
system could be tested by its power to shape the individual.

Ross said religion was declining as a major influence for social con-

[5]Herbert Spencer, *Education: Intellectual, Moral, and Physical* (New York: Appleton, 1860), pp. 13–14. (The "Cardinal Principles" were formulated in 1918 by the NEA's
Committee on Reorganizing Secondary Education headed by Clarence Kingsley, who
was appointed High School Agent for Massachusetts by Snedden.)
[6]Edward Alsworth Ross, *Social Control* (New York: Macmillan, 1901; 1912 reprint).
[7]Edward Alsworth Ross, "Social Control," *American Journal of Sociology*, Vol. I
(March 1896), p. 518.

trol and foresaw *"an almost worldwide drift from religion toward education* as the method of indirect social restraint."[8] He predicted the new education would be "realistic, and its starting point will be the facts of personal and social life." In the spirit of Spencer, Ross recommended that schools must, above all, meet the test of utility.

Ross was subtle enough to discriminate between desirable and undesirable social control. The need for a new kind of social control based on *insight* into consequences of social acts became necessary as well-ordered *gemeinschaft* types of communities broke down. Education was the proper instrument to promote such insights, Ross, however, saw a need to be careful that the new kind of national social control would not intrude unduly on the individuality of persons.[9] Snedden, as we shall see, failed to grasp the discriminations which Ross made and interpreted "social control" as a doctrine which coincided with his emerging concept of "social efficiency."

After graduating from Stanford in 1897, Snedden became high school principal in Paso Robles. During his three years there Paso Robles adopted the new idea of a nine-year grammar school and Snedden became directly acquainted with the problems of the twelve-to-sixteen age group. He became a member of the County Board of Education and was encouraged to advance in the profession by influential members of the community. Teachers College, Columbia, was the place to go; and Snedden turned his attention to further study in sociology in preparation for graduate work in New York. He became excited by Lester Frank Ward's *Dynamic Sociology* and Franklin Giddings' *Principles of Sociology.*

From Ward, Snedden got the idea that education is "a system of extending to all members of society such of the extant knowledge of the world as may be deemed most important."[10] He rejected Ward's optimistic interpretations of evolution, with its hope that knowledge would reduce human inequality. Snedden found Giddings more persuasive on this latter point. Giddings interpreted Spencer's social evolution as holding that

> society, like the material world ... undergoes integration and differentiation. It passes from homogeneity and indefinitiveness of non-organization to the heterogeneity and definiteness of organization. The process of selection is based upon the differences growing out of the unequal conditions of both heredity and nurture to which man is born.

[8]Ross, *Social Control,* p. 176.
[9]*Ibid.,* pp. 418–419.
[10]Lester F. Ward, *Dynamic Sociology* (New York: Appleton, 1897), II, pp. 486–487, quoted in Drost, *op. cit.,* p. 40. This section on Snedden's experiences while at Paso Robles is based on Drost's Chapter II.

Inequality—physical, mental, and moral—is an inevitable characteristic of the social population.

Giddings concluded that "a population is therefore always differentiated into classes . . . created partly by the combinations of inheritance and partly also by the educational influence of association."[11]

While Snedden profited from his study of theory, he also took pride in being a realist. As a teacher and administrator, he saw clearly the general failure of schools with the majority of nonacademically oriented children. He was much impressed when he read an article in Albert Shaw's *Review of Reviews* in 1900 which described the program at Hampton Institute, Virginia. Shaw argued that "by all odds the finest, soundest, and most effective educational methods in the United States are to be found in certain schools for Negroes and Indians, and in others for young criminals in reformatory prisons." At Hampton Institute, for instance, said Shaw, the purpose is "the right kind of instruction" for the children of colored people, who having emerged from slavery "needed to be taught and trained in good conduct, the rudiments of book knowledge, and the plain tasks that go with farming, the ordinary handicrafts, and the duties of home and family." Shaw said that Hampton "never for one minute loses sight of the general conditions under which these children have been born and the range of social and industrial possibilities that the future has in store for them." The Institute focused on the practical question of "how plain boys and girls and men and women under conditions now existing in this country can make their lives useful and successful."[12] Washing, sewing, gardening, and a variety of vocational skills, plus moral exhortation, provided the bulk of the school program.

In Hampton Institute and the reform schools, Snedden found the school prototypes for the educational philosophy of social efficiency. Even before going east to Teachers College, Columbia University, he had clarified the educational problems he would make his own.

In the spring of his final year in California, Snedden was invited by Stanford to address its newly formed chapter of Phi Beta Kappa. He entitled his address, "Education for the Rank and File."[13] The speech summarized the thinking Snedden had done to that point. He drew on Spencer in picturing society, like nature itself, as governed by natural laws. With Ross, he noted that institutions find "their justification in their ultimate influence on general society" and held that the school "affected social evolution as [does] no other [institution.]"

---

[11]Franklin Giddings, *Principles of Sociology* (New York: Macmillan, 1896), p. 9.
[12]*Stanford Alumnus*, I (June 1900), pp. 185–198, quoted in Drost, *op. cit.*, pp. 42–45.
[13]*Ibid.*

Snedden argued that the ultimate aim of education was "the greatest degree of efficiency." We could afford to permit the universities to continue to provide adequate education for the professionals and the leadership class, he said. But we could not tolerate the failure of schools to provide for "those who do duty in the ranks . . . who will follow, not lead." Efficiency for "the rank and file" meant "not only training for culture's sake, but that utilitarian training which looks to individual efficiency in the world of work." Training in the trades and business, Snedden said, was a legitimate obligation of public education. The "old education" was judged to be "prescriptive and logical" and relied on the sacred "tripos" of Greek, Latin, and mathematics. This curriculum, more than poverty or the lure of employment, was what drove children from school. The "new education," he predicted, would be an elective program that included both a variety of child interests and a regimen designed to fit the child to his place in society. It would lead the child "toward the realities of present life"; and when the child was properly "fitted," he would possess "such an intelligent understanding of authority as [to] make the exercise of arbitrary authority unnecessary."

Snedden's advisor for his master's thesis was Samuel T. Dutton, who had become famous as the founder of the community school idea in Brookline, Massachusetts. Dutton's version of the "new education" regarded the school as the "fountain of inspiration" for improving the life of the entire community. The school should not hesitate to offer new community services if it was best equipped to do so—or it should coordinate its efforts with the home, church, library, art museum, and newspaper. Dutton endorsed dental and medical inspection for children, school baths, free nutritional lunches, corrective physical therapy, and the like.[14] He refused to join the popular attack on Latin but welcomed more time for new subjects—more science, art, music, and vocational subjects. He represented the kind of progressivism which emphasized the school as an instrument for social service and community improvement. He rejected the business efficiency stress espoused by followers of Frederick Taylor because, he said, the school is "not a factory and the schoolmaster not a foreman."[15] Snedden was presumably influenced by Dutton; for he avoided the Taylor brand of business efficiency. His later version of factorylike vocational schools was not aimed directly at economy for the taxpayer, but at producing high levels of differentiated vocational efficiency.

In his experience with Dutton, Snedden encountered the social

[14]See Samuel T. Dutton and David Snedden, *The Administration of Public Education in the United States* (New York: Macmillan, 1908), Chapter XXXI, "The Widening Sphere of Public Education."
[15]Drost, *op. cit.*, p. 50.

service branch of progressive thought. He had a knack, however, for selecting and interpreting ideas so as to reinforce his own mainline philosophy of social efficiency, and a capacity for blurring positions that really differed. In this case, Dutton's major emphasis was on using education to meliorate human ills and to raise the quality of community life by stimulating wider participation and involvement. Snedden's alterations of the social service orientation were subtle but profoundly important. He welcomed Dutton's ideas for an expanded social role for the schools but interpreted this as an opportunity for educators, armed with insights of the new social sciences, to play the role of a qualified elite in managing uplift for community life. He did not seem to sense that this was radically opposed to the vision of those who wanted to teach people the skills and attitudes of self-direction, social criticism, and democratic participation.

The truth is that contradictions like these permeated the whole fabric of the progressive movement, and reform rhetoric was loose enough to veil the differences. Thus Dutton could invite Snedden to be co-author of *The Administration of Public Education in the United States* (1908), which became one of the most influential texts of the period on school administration. The differences between social service and social efficiency were not consciously acknowledged.

After receiving his Master's degree, Snedden joined the staff at Stanford, where he taught Ross's old course "Education and Society." After a busy four years he decided to reenroll at Columbia for the doctor's degree at the urging of his Department Chairman, Ellwood Cubberley.

At Teachers College, Snedden encountered again the several value orientations of progressive thought. He took, for instance, three courses with John Dewey: one semester on "Social Life and Curriculum" and a full year of "Psychological Ethics." He also took work with professors trying to establish education as a science of behavioral control. He found this orientation more congenial than the philosophy of those who saw democracy as "a way of life." Snedden began to identify himself as a pioneer who would demonstrate how educational policy and practice could be based on the science of sociology. While he never exposed himself to the rigors of actual scientific research on sociological problems, he did take work in statistics with Franklin Giddings and two courses with E. L. Thorndike, "The Application of Psychological and Statistical Methods to Education" and an advanced course in "Genetic Psychology."[16]

The exact nature of Thorndike's influence on Snedden is not clear,

[16]Drost, *op. cit.*, p. 71.

but some major themes in Thorndike's work fitted hand in glove with the theory of social efficiency. Thorndike devoted his life to establishing foundations for the scientific study of education. His landmark dissertation on *Animal Intelligence* (1898) provided the base for years of enormously productive research in which he developed his connectionist (S-R) theory with "laws" of learning which, he believed, held significance for pedagogical science. He placed more emphasis on the role of heredity than did most of the other pioneers of the connectionist-behaviorist tradition; but he shared with them the conviction that training programs based on the laws of learning could be designed to shape behavior in accord with projected ends. This fitted Snedden's conviction that the good, progressive society could be achieved by placing directive control in the hands of scientifically qualified social engineers. A prime article of Snedden's faith was the conviction that a science of education could be built on the bases of the emerging social sciences. While a practicing investigator like Thorndike was humble before the enormous complexity of trying to create a "science of education," Snedden slipped easily into the assumption that sociology and psychology had given clear scientific warranty for the educational programs he espoused. Armed with this "authority," he could view his opponents with a condescension they did not always appreciate.

A number of Thorndike's basic doctrines were readily assimilated into the philosophy of social efficiency. While Thorndike held that his theory of learning as the establishment of conditioned responses provided a means for improving man's condition by conditioning behaviors that would be most useful, he also stressed that personality and behavior are the products of heredity. The goal of trying to provide equal education for all children on the high school level, therefore, appeared to him of little value. He recommended that the highly gifted become the target for special concern, and that on the mass level education be varied enough to prepare all young men and women for their probable future destinies. Each man "as nature has given him capacity" should assume his proper role in a good society. Individuals with superior intelligence and moral powers should occupy leadership positions. All others must be taught the attitude of "reasoned dependence," which is the ability to recognize their own limitations and the quality of leadership in others. They must, then, willingly place their fate in the hands of their scientific trustees. But, Thorndike reassured his readers, "nothing . . . need be lost for American independence, initiative and originality by greater obediance to the right masters, imitation of the right models, and learning the right facts in school."[17]

[17]Edward L. Thorndike, "Disciplinary Values of Studies; A Census of Opinions," *Education*, Vol. 35 (1914–15), p. 412. For the definitive study of Thorndike see Geraldine

The educational breakthroughs which Thorndike helped to effect influenced every educational innovation of the time. His work on measurement, on intelligence and mental testing, on genius and retardation, his recommendations for new classifications and groupings of students, for scientific curriculum development related to life needs, for new texts geared to the psychological needs of children, and his insistence on putting educational programs to the test of quantitative results were all related to various phases of progressive education. They could be interpreted in ways to fit the values of humanitarian reform or of social efficiency and control. Snedden welcomed the opportunity to use Thorndike's work as scientific blessing for his educational policies.

Snedden chose to do his dissertation with a recent appointee to the Teachers College staff, Edward T. Devine, who had been general secretary of the Charity Organization of New York. The topic of the dissertation was "Administration and Educational Work of American Juvenile Reform Schools." His research gave Snedden an opportunity to analyze the kind of school that perfectly exemplified the theory of social control. Snedden pictured reform schools as offering an advanced, superior form of education containing "the entire round of educational effort," including phases ordinarily carried on by home, church, and shop. As the home and church in urban communities relinquished their traditional controls, Snedden envisioned a time when the public schools would have to take over the total education of children. The reform school would provide the perfect model to follow.

Snedden assumed that schools ought to be efficient instruments for social control, shaping individuals in terms of their capacities and in accordance with desired social ends. Thus Snedden viewed education as a kind of "treatment."[18] Reform schools had special advantages because they could influence behavior for the entire twenty-four hours of every day.[19] Snedden argued that a well-engineered plan for total social control would place emphasis on the importance of physical education, moral education, and vocational training in addition to "school or literary" education. His dissertation devoted forty-eight pages to vocational education, thirty-six to moral education, and six to literary study.

Snedden broadened physical education to include instruction in cleanliness, habits of regular work and rest, and the counteraction of

Joncich, *The Sane Positivist: A Biography of Edward L. Thorndike*, (Middletown, Conn.: Wesleyan U. Press, 1968).
   [18]Drost, *op. cit.*, pp. 72–77.
   [19]The Russians have been lured by a similar vision of complete environmental control in their periodic plans to utilize boarding schools as a major part of Communist education.

vice. Moral education in a reform school setting intrigued him because of the possibility of developing a consistent pattern of control without interference from family or church. Generous time was provided for industrial education because the "class" of boys in these schools possessed special talent for mechanical and imitative work. Shop would teach them to be industrious. "Literary education" was confined to essentials in reading, writing, spelling, and arithmetic with "some opportunity for self-expression" in music, printing, and letter writing. Snedden maintained that the value of the literary subjects lay in their disagreeable nature. Their mastery would contribute to self-discipline. Literature should be taught, he said, for moral development; and librarians should be hired who could provide materials with the right exemplary content.

Reform schools were particularly effective in the classification of students. Children were sorted into groups on the basis of their intellectual aptitude and according to moral character as well, so that "the less hardened" could be protected from those who might contaminate them.

We may profitably use Walter Drost's summary of what Snedden learned from his dissertation.

[Snedden] believed the reform schools had already discovered that some children could become skilled workmen and others would forever remain in the ranks of the unskilled. They had discovered, too, that "the most potent means both of discipline and of education is work which is vocational in character," and by this reasoning he prognosticated "we shall go to the reform schools for their experience."

Classification was the second area of reform school experience Snedden believed public school people might appropriate to their advantage. According to him, the reform school had gone much more fundamentally into the program of grouping children for educational purposes. For Snedden "the group" was the unit of consideration and the individual who broke the "unity of the group," be he a "moral, mental, or physical misfit," claimed too much of the teacher's energy with little benefit to himself. He was especially concerned with that class of children whose parents were laborers and unable to exercise "adequate control over them." Snedden charged these were the children who frequently were truant and often suspended from the public schools, and for them classification promised a means toward "the most appropriate treatment." He concluded, "Society has a right to demand from parent and school an accounting for every child committed to their charge."[20]

[20]Drost, *op. cit.*, p. 77.

B. SNEDDEN AS PUBLIC SCHOOL OFFICIAL AND EDUCATIONAL THEORIST

By the time Snedden took over his duties as one of the chief school officers in the United States (1909), his philosophy of education for social efficiency was well developed. In the remainder of his career he would add only details or minor amendments. The doctrine of social efficiency contained an image of man, a vision of the good society, and a set of related recommendations for school practice.

Snedden confidently viewed the growth of the corporate-urban-industrial phenomenon as the best possible means for man's progress. A realist in his own eyes, he scorned those who questioned the new order as "simple-lifers" or "romantic impracticalists" who yearned for times that were gone forever. His endorsement of the status quo still comes through strongly in one of his last books, *Toward Better Educations* (1931).[21] The Great Depression was under way and social and educational criticism was widespread. Snedden quoted a wide variety of critics and refuted them one by one. To those who bemoaned the mechanization and depersonalization of modern economic methods, Snedden replied by comparing the higher standard of living for the majority to what it had once been.

> If we consider the satisfactions—that is, the securities, the nurtures, the longevities, the leisures . . . of the ninety percent of individuals best served . . . by ocean steamers, automobile factories, oil wells, tornado insurance, fireproof-housebuilding, yellow-fever control, sheep culture, deep sea-fishing, beet sugar production and urban-water supply—does it not become apparent that increasing *complication* of the functioning of social agencies has been at least paralleled by corresponding *simplification* of roles for individuals during the threescore and ten years of participation of each.[22]

One can almost see Snedden reviewing in his mind's eye these blessings as compared with the harsh deprivations of the California cabin in which he was reared.

Snedden acknowledged that gains had not been made without some sacrifice, but argued that social bookkeeping revealed that men preferred their current problems to the old ones. Modern men might be subjected to fragmented, routine job tasks; but production specialization and differentiation enabled them to live longer, more comfortably, and with the leisure to enjoy the arts. Moreover, the application of

[21]David Snedden, *Toward Better Educations* (New York: Bureau of Publications, Teachers College, Columbia University, 1931). See for example pp. 329–332.
[22]*Ibid.*, p. 364.

mass production methods to school life could make possible new social advances.

> No other course was open if public education was to be democratized. . . . Long before American manufacturers, miners, wheat growers . . . had clarified their applications of military methods to economic production the school administrators of our cities had been driven to apply such methods in their wars upon potential illiteracy and other ignorances of the children.
>
> Quantity production methods applied in education speedily give us school grades, uniform textbooks, promotional examinations, systems of handwriting, college admission standards, nine-month school years, certification of teachers, strictly scheduled programs, mechanical discipline and hundreds of other mechanisms most of which are unavoidably necessary if our ideals of universal education are to be realized.[23]

Snedden's faith that the new America was the most satisfying social system in human history developed early and never faltered. The task of education and other institutions was to keep this social order functioning as efficiently as possible: "to make the child a better *socius*," a more fit member of a complex society.[24]

Fortunately, argued Snedden, human beings fell into ability levels which paralled the hierarchical work requirements of modern society. With the aid of new social science instruments, people could be identified and channeled in to training that would benefit society and fulfill the individual.[25] Snedden concluded that schools needed to create differentiated "educations" beyond the elementary grades, appropriate to the capacities and "probable destinies" of the different children.

> Three kinds of differences are recognizable among children with reference to the extent and kind of education . . . they should receive. These are based on (a) native capacity, including strong interests and tastes; (b) economic conditions of the family and its capacity to support the child during the period of its higher education; and (c) probable educational destination.[26]

Educators were to be practical in calculating the future destinies of children by recognizing that aptitude was determined not only by inherited ability but by economic and social factors. Children of working-class parents were not likely to go to college, nor to enter profes-

---

[23] *Ibid.*, pp. 330–331.

[24] David Snedden, "History Study as an Instrument in the Social Education of Children," *J. Pedagogy*, Vol. 19 (June 1907), pp. 259–268.

[25] Snedden predated here Michael Young's vision of social life in the twenty-first century as described in *The Rise of the Meritocracy*.

[26] David Snedden, "Differences Among Varying Groups of Children Should Be Recognized," NEA *Addresses and Proceedings*, June 29–July 3, 1908, p. 753.

sional and directive groups in society. Scientific testing combined with vocational guidance would make it possible to identify people sharing common aptitudes, interests, and similar vocational futures. The new junior high schools would perform the initial task of sorting and allocating students to differentiated courses. Prevocational offerings in commercial subjects, industrial arts, agricultural arts, or household arts would be offered to those "who most inclined to them or have most need for them."[27] Thus students would have a chance to try programs geared to their probable interests. They would stay in school because their appetites would be whetted for more specialized study at the next level.

Snedden's rationale was agreeable to educational leaders in Massachusetts. Frederick P. Fish, President of AT&T and chairman of the State Board of Education, read a paper to the National Council of Education in 1910 that was a carbon copy of the ideas the new Commissioner of Education espoused.[28] Fish called for the schools to revise their values by providing training to meet "the practical needs of life" for "the rank and file." He advocated early determination of the student's place in life, since it would then be a simple matter to provide an appropriate, specific skill training program. Fish predicted the creation of a system of vocational schools, parallel to the regular type, that would appeal to the potential dropout and hold him in school for another two years. He was sympathetic to the progressive commitment to individualized instruction but argued that the enormity of the problem in a mass system required the use of one of Snedden's favorite plans, the identification of the individual with a group of other people to whom similar destinations had been ascribed. Everyone would be more comfortable if a proposal for class-oriented education could be brought in under an uplift label like "individualizing instruction." The progressives found it easy to believe that "naming it would make it so" —and that heritage would not die with them.

The Snedden-Fish regime was prepared to act as well as to talk. Snedden appointed his Teachers College colleague, Charles Prosser, as Deputy Commissioner for Vocational Education, to develop a comprehensive system of vocational schools for the major industrial centers. William Orr, Dupty Commissioner for general education, was asked to strengthen "the schools of the less densely settled areas"; Snedden reserved to himself the reform of the state normal schools. He assumed that normal school students were persons of "distinct social limitations"

<hr>

[27] *Ibid.*, p. 756.
[28] Frederick P. Fish, "The Vocational and Industrial School," NEA *Proceedings*, 1910, pp. 367–368.

with "only average capacity for . . . abstract thinking." The proper plan was to educate them to a mastery of the elementary curriculum rather than to encourage them in academic study. Following his bent for separate "educations," Snedden introduced specialized normal schools for teachers of agriculture, household arts, manual training, etc.[29]

Between 1910 and 1912 Snedden and Prosser clarified their ideas about vocational training. Snedden rejected manual training that claimed to provide general education values. What he wanted now was "real vocational education," by which he meant training programs designed to lead graduates to gainful employment in specific occupational fields. The time to begin such programs was when students entered high school at about age fourteen or fifteen. An elaborate system of such vocational schools for the "rank and file," or the "privates of industry," should exist parallel to traditional schools. The clear necessity for separate vocational schools, said Snedden, became apparent when one forced oneself to give forthright definitions of "vocational" and "liberal" to replace the typically fuzzy definitions of general educators. Vocational education in "its simplest and most significant sense . . . is some form of education designed to equip a young person for a recognized calling." Its content is to be discovered by "studying the requirements of recognized callings, such as medicine, teaching, bookkeeping, carpentering, printing, tailoring, cooking, and the like" and deriving from each the specific skills, ideals, and technical knowledge necessary to persons in the vocation. Such a definition made it clear that general educators simply were not equipped to design and administer these programs. "There is no satisfactory evidence that vocational education has been achieved to any satisfactory and economic degree in schools where such education is blended with the traditional processes of liberal education."[30]

When the U.S. Commissioner of Education, Philander P. Claxton, admitted to feeling a "shudder of abhorrence" at the "brutal efficiency" implied by this new and more effective education,[31] Snedden patiently and repeatedly explained that he, too, was for both vocational and cultural education. The proper definitions of cultural and vocational educations had to be derived, however, from an analysis of the social functions of each provided by insights from educational sociology, a new discipline of which Snedden was the foremost practitioner.

[29]Drost, *op. cit.*, pp. 103–108.
[30]David Snedden, "Fundamental Distinctions Between Liberal and Vocational Education," NEA *Proceedings*, 1914, pp. 154–155.
[31]Drost, *op. cit.*, p. 158, citing Claxton Papers, Special Collections, University of Tennessee.

> Man stands to the world about him, in a two-fold relationship. He is a
> producer of utilities on the one hand, and on the other, for his own
> growth and development, he must utilize utilities. That education
> which trains him to be a producer is vocational education. That educa-
> tion which trains him to be a good utilizer, in the social sense of that
> term, is liberal education.[32]

Vocational education was designed to make an efficient producer and
liberal education was intended to train the efficient consumer or utilizer. Trained to be more intelligent consumers of goods and services,
music, or art, men would also contribute to raising the quality of production.

The equation of liberal education with "consumer or utilizer education" reflected Snedden's long-time admiration for Herbert Spencer,
and his tendency to make broad ideological extrapolations from social
sciences to education. Snedden never strayed far from the question of
"what knowledge is of most use?" By use, he meant service to the
"social economy."

The meaning of Snedden's rationale for vocational education was
quite clear: it should consist of special courses designed to teach the
skills and techniques of specific callings. For the direction of its goals,
vocational education should "go consistently to the world of economic
activity. . . . It should be governed by or possess an advisory committee
containing men who are intimately identified with the occupation for
which it trains, both as employers and employees."[33] The methods of
vocational education, determined by its goal of producing definite skills
and powers, would stress painstaking application to detail.

The proper content of liberal studies, said Snedden the sociologist,
should be determined in a similar manner.

> Men as consumers, or utilizers, do not specialize. . . . But given
> sufficient leisure and economic resources, each one of us seeks to utilize
> literature, art, music, history, science, newspapers, the drama, and the
> various forms of service rendered by those who minister to us in pro-
> viding medical knowledge, means of travel, foodstuffs, clothing, shel-
> ter, and protection. In each of these directions, capacities for right
> utilization can be refined, elevated, and socialized.[34]

The proper criterion for the value of liberal studies was "higher utilization." Liberally trained men would be able "to make valuable choices
among the various utilities offered for man's utilization." In addition,
they might acquire certain useful intellectual skills, such as a foreign

[32]David Snedden, op. cit., p. 157.
[33]Ibid., pp. 159–160.
[34]Ibid., p. 157.

language, or techniques of the scientific method. Liberal education, concerned with developing "appreciations, refined tastes, and intellectual interests," had to be quite different from vocational education and therefore should be conducted in schools separate from those devoted to vocational training. Some liberal study, however, could go on in vocational schools; and some "prevocational" study could be included in general education. Schools of liberal learning might well offer courses in the so-called practical arts: manual training, household arts, commercial and agricultural education. Such studies would be conducted "in the spirit of the amateur" to promote "appreciation of the economic activities of life" and with a possible value for "vocational finding." They could properly be called prevocational but could never claim to be "real vocational education."

When viewing the total system of schools to be provided, Snedden spoke of "integrated education," which would contain elements needed by all students: physical education (Spencer's health for survival), vocational education, and moral and cultural education (sometimes referred to as "civism.") This rationale, harkening back to his dissertation, assigned to liberal education a special responsibility for moral and civic training. It became an instrument for social control and promoted efficiency for "complete living."

Snedden spoke to the New England History Teachers Association in 1914 to make available the new meaning of liberal study. He told them that "the spirit" of contemporary social economy required secondary education to be made purposeful and efficient for the new, larger high school enrollments. He characterized the chronological approach to history as "cold storage" education and said that for "the rank and file" at least, history had to be taught to satisfy "specific aims drawn from functional social needs." The great value of history, he said, was in training for citizenship. "Having once conceived of the citizen as we should like to have him, we can work back and by analysis find the numberless specific forms of training by which we can produce this type." Attitudes of mind had to be cultivated if the future citizen was to be equipped with "ideals of right social action."[35]

Some years later, Snedden wrote on the responsibilities of social studies teachers for teaching social values. He stated bluntly, "successful teaching of social values necessarily means that the teacher shall be an advocate, a pleader, perhaps a partisan."[36] On the question of which social values the teacher should advocate, Snedden said the teacher

[35]David Snedden, "Teaching History in Secondary Schools," *History Teachers Magazine,* Vol. 5 (November 1914), pp. 277–282, cited in Drost, *op. cit.,* p. 128.

[36]David Snedden, "Liberty of Teaching in the Social Sciences," *School and Society,* Vol. 13 (Feb. 12, 1921), pp. 185–186, 190.

should remember that he was a public servant. As such, he was under "heavy obligation" to present "the collective opinions and valuation of the controlling majority," or withdraw from their service. If the teacher held minority opinions, he should, as a teacher, conform to the position of the majority.

A critic charged that Snedden had described precisely what teaching *is not*, that he wanted to make teachers into nothing more than paid propagandists. Snedden dodged the attack by urging that every teacher be a "propagandist of the best moral and civic values" of the day.[38]

Snedden was, on occasion, stung by criticisms of his ideas by progressive philosophers of education like John Dewey, Boyd Bode, and H. Gordon Hullfish. Dewey charged that Snedden's narrow trade training was "social predestination,"[39] and Bode attacked Sneddenism as a plan to perpetuate class differences and promote passive acquiescence to the status quo.[40]

Snedden used a variety of arguments to meet his critics. He argued that "real vocational education" opened opportunities for economic betterment to the neglected rank and file and therefore was an antidote to undemocratic features of the regular system. When Bode spoke of the need for social democracy to complement political democracy, Snedden replied that by "social" democracy, Bode meant "industrial (production) democracy, marital democracy, cultural democracy, religious democracy, racial democracy," and so forth. Along all these fronts, movements were urging forward, Snedden said, but the enduring question remained, "how much can social efficiency stand of these several democracies?"[41] If the American people would be called upon to decide between social efficiency and democracy Snedden had little doubt about the choice they would make.

In the twenties, Snedden elaborated upon his rationale by describing the good society as analogous to a winning "team group." A team was made stronger by specialization of functions. Similarly, differentiated training programs would equip segments of the population for special roles. Above-average persons could attain a level of statesmanship for leading and coordinating. But a society, like an athletic team or a submarine crew, had to rely also on followers who were trained for

[38]"Discussion and Correspondence," *School and Society*, Vol. 13 (May 5, 1921), pp. 295–296.
[39]See, for example, John Dewey, "Industrial Education—A Wrong Kind," *New Republic* Vol. 2 (Feb. 20, 1915), pp. 71–73. (We shall compare Dewey and Snedden in the next chapter.)
[40]Boyd Bode, "Why Educational Objectives?" *School and Society*, May 10, 1924, pp. 531–539.
[41]Snedden, *Toward Better Educations*, p. 338.

their roles. The two kinds of men, fulfilling their proper functions, could produce the efficient society for the benefit of all.[42]

C. CHARLES PROSSER AND SOCIAL EFFICIENCY PHILOSOPHY IN THE SMITH–HUGHES ACT

The influence of the social efficiency philosophy was clearly evident in the educational features of the Smith-Hughes Act, the first piece of federal legislation providing financial support for precollegiate schools. The effective author of the Act was Charles A. Prosser, student and colleague of David Snedden, who spent his career working out the implications of social efficiency doctrines for vocational education.[43]

Prosser came from a family of steel workers in New Albany, Indiana. As a student and young professional, he was noted for his "get-up-and-go," a quality which later enabled him to win success when he moved to New York and the East. In 1898, while teaching physics, chemistry, and literature in the New Albany High School, Prosser succeeded in completing two years of legal training in one at the University of Louisville Law School. He won the honors of both classes and all the prizes for which he competed. The following year he was appointed Superintendent of New Albany Schools. While serving in that post (1900–1908), he became President of the Indiana State Teachers Association, "the youngest man ever elected to the position." He left Indiana to begin doctoral study at Teachers College, Columbia University. There he became a student under David Snedden and developed his first interest in vocational education. His dissertation was *A Study of the Boston Mechanic Arts High School.* He obviously impressed his mentor, for Snedden invited him in 1910 to become Deputy Commissioner for Vocational Education in Massachusetts. Prosser's meteoric rise was capped two years later (1912), when he was selected to become the full-time Executive Secretary of the prestigious National Society for the Promotion of Industrial Education. In this capacity, he became involved in the whirl of events which led to enactment of the Smith-Hughes law.

The Smith-Hughes Act was passed after years of preparation and political maneuvering. The final draft won the approval of groups as divergent as the National Association of Manufacturers and the Cham-

---

[42]David Snedden, "Education for a World of Teamplayers and Team Workers," *School and Society,* Vol. 20 (Nov. 1, 1924), pp. 554–556.

[43]Much of the material on Prosser has been derived from the research of Professor John Gadell of Wright State University who is completing a doctoral dissertation on Charles Prosser at Washington University in St. Louis.

ber of Commerce, the American Federation of Labor, the major farm organizations, settlement house leaders, and the National Education Association. The coming together of such ordinarily feuding factions is a rare event. It is even more remarkable to find them agreeing about a controversial matter like the introduction of federal power into the operation of public schools. Many men contributed to this agreement; but there is general agreement that the one individual most responsible for it was Charles Allen Prosser.

By the time Prosser received his appointment from NSPIE, the Society had decided to promote its cause by securing action through federal and State legislatures. Prosser immediately became active in helping to draft a bill by Senator Page of Vermont which, in fact, became the legislative source for both the Smith-Lever and Smith-Hughes Acts. (The Smith-Lever agricultural extension bill was passed first in 1914, as a concession to farm interests, in return for a promise from farmers to support vocational education later.) In January of 1914, Congress approved a joint resolution authorizing President Wilson to appoint a Commission to study national aid for vocational education. The Commission was conveniently composed of a group of Congressmen and citizens who had been ardent advocates of industrial education. Among them was Dr. Prosser. The Commission's two-volume final report[44] contained a section on "proposed legislation" which, with minor changes, became the text of the Smith-Hughes Act. Dr. Prosser's son, William, recalls seeing his father write the "proposed legislation" at their dining room table.[45]

Prosser was instrumental in working out the final wording of Smith-Hughes to satisfy the doubts of groups like the NEA and the AFL. After Congress approved the bill (1917), Prosser was named Executive Director of the newly created Federal Board for Vocational Education. His vigorous leadership was manifest as every state in the union accepted the provisions of the Act within a year. As the first chief administrator of the Act, Prosser saw that the bare bones of the law were filled in with operating procedures consistent with the principles he had built into the legislation.

We turn briefly, then, to examples of Prosser's theories of vocational education as they were reflected in Smith-Hughes.

Grant Venn, in *Man, Education, and Work*, pointed out that the Smith-Hughes Act established the pattern for nearly fifty years of federal aid in the field of vocational education. "In fact, its major provisions

---

[44]U.S., Report of the Commission on National Aid to Vocational Education, 2 vols. (Washington, D.C.: Government Printing Office, 1914).
[45]Interview with William L. Prosser, St. Louis, Missouri, September 1967.

remained untouched by amendment until 1963."[46] The great strength of the Act was that it was designed directly to meet a compelling need of the new America—the need to provide American industry with the complicated work skills required in a technological society. The genius of Charles Prosser lay in his capacity to focus energies unwaveringly on creating functional programs to accomplish this task.

Yet there were doubts in some quarters about the educational orientation of the Act from the beginning. Its strengths in securing quick short-term gains were also the source of its fundamental flaws.

A Commission appointed by President Franklin D. Roosevelt to review the effectiveness of the Act expressed misgivings in a report issued in 1938.[47] The Chairman, John D. Russell of the University of Chicago, stressed the point that the Act was marked by a specificity of prescription for programs and administration which was a feature of no other federal legislation for education, such as the Morrill or Smith-Lever Acts. This specificity, said Russell, tended to limit imaginative experimentation with curricula, and led to interference with institutions of higher education by prescribing details of teacher education. Narrow concentration on skill training resulted in almost total neglect of the cultivation of broad social and economic insights in students. The law seemed to foster a restricted quality of mind, as reflected in the type of leadership found in the federal office of vocational education. The Chairman thought he detected an inbred, parochial quality in the office and a tendency toward isolation from the mainstream of American education.

A look at some of the principles cherished by Dr. Prosser may help to explain both the strengths and weaknesses of the Act.

One of its cardinal tenets was the definition of vocational education so that it would accommodate only specific job training programs. Prosser was fond of quoting a friend, Charles R. Allen: "The purpose of vocational education is to help a person secure a job, train him so he can hold it after he gets it, and assist him in advancing to a better job."[48] Vocational education was, in brief, "training for useful employment"—period.

Prosser insisted that all of vocational content must be specific and that its source was to be found "in the experience of those who have mastered the occupation." The content must come from the minds of

[46]Grant Venn, *Man, Education, and Work* (Washington, D.C.: American Council on Education), 1964, p. 112.

[47]John D. Russell and associates, *Vocational Education:* Staff Study No. 8 (Washington, D.C.: Government Printing Office, 1938), pp. 25–40, 210–220 *et passim.*

[48]Charles A. Prosser and Thomas H. Quigley, *Vocational Education in a Democracy,* rev. ed. (Chicago: American Technical Society, 1950), pp. 454–455.

competent workers, and it will have "little or nothing in common with corresponding content in any other occupation. In setting up its program, therefore, the [all] day vocational schools must provide as many specific courses or groups of courses as there are occupations for which it proposes to train."[49] Prosser was convinced that to produce trained workers ready for useful employment, vocational programs had to be managed not by general educators but by those qualified and committed to advance "real vocational education." He pushed hard for "the dual system": for vocational education administered separately from general education.

Throughout his long career Prosser repeated endlessly the arguments for his position. Traditional scholastic education, he maintained, aimed to prepare the citizen for the worthy use of his leisure time. Traditional schoolmen, committed to the task of fostering "leisure culture," operated from the psychological tradition of faculty psychology and formal discipline. This they thought, would lead to general mental training and "cultural appreciations." There were several clear reasons why new programs of vocational training could not be entrusted to such men. "Culturists" were cut off from the practical world of work, and their outmoded theory of learning made them incapable of managing genuine skill training programs. "Vocational education," Prosser argued, "only functions in proportion as it will enable an individual actually to do a job. . . . Vocational education must establish habits: habits of correct thinking and of correct doing. Hence its fundamental theory must be that of habit psychology."[50] The new scientific psychology pioneered by Edward Thorndike, said Prosser, assumed that the mind is a habit-forming machine. There was an obvious fit between this psychological theory and vocational education, when the latter was conceived as "essentially a matter of establishing certain habits through repetitive training both in thinking and doing."[51] In contrast to the theory of general mind training of the discredited faculty psychology, Thorndike's theory taught that "all habits of doing and thinking are developed in specific situations." Prosser deduced correlatively that the content of vocational training should be determined by "the actual functioning content" of a given occupation. "If you want to train a youth to be an efficient plumber, you must select the actual experiences in the practice of the plumbing trade that he should have and see that he gets these in a real instead of in a pseudo way."[52] Furthermore, general studies like mathematics or science should ideally be broken

[49] *Ibid.*, pp. 286–287.
[50] *Ibid.*, pp. 215–220 *et passim.*
[51] *Ibid.*, p. 216.
[52] *Ibid.*, p. 228.

into short units which would bear "directly on specific needs of workers in the performance of specific tasks or operations." They should, when possible, be taught by the craftsman-teacher skilled in the task, rather than by general mathematics or science teachers.

A prototype of the plan favored by Prosser was established in the short unit courses which he developed while Director of the Dunwoody Institute in Minneapolis. "In garment making, one unit might deal with kimonos, one with underwear, and another with house dresses."[53] Training should be done either on the job, as in cooperative work programs, or in settings which duplicated as closely as possible the environment of the workshop itself. At the Dunwoody Institute, units were programmed in great detail to lead students step by step through the skill development cycle. Students punched in on time clocks and instructors behaved like shop foremen rather than public school teachers. A no-nonsense attitude prevailed. If students were not punctual, orderly, and efficient, they were asked to leave.

If this brief description of Dunwoody conveys a feeling of Prosser's orientation, some of the features he favored in Smith-Hughes can readily be understood. Approved programs had to meet the criterion of "fitting for useful employment" persons over fourteen but under college age who were preparing for work on farms, in trades, in industrial pursuits, and the like. Federal funds were given only for support of vocational training classes. General education costs were to be born by the States and local school districts. At least 50 percent of subsidized instruction had to be devoted to "practical work on a useful or productive basis." Funds for the training of teachers were restricted to those who "have had adequate vocational experience or contact in the line of work for which they are preparing."[54]

Since his rationale excluded general educators from the management of vocational training, Prosser fought as long as possible for a separately administered type of vocational education. In the final politicking prior to 1917, he had to make some concessions; but in the main, he created a framework which permitted vocational programs to stand apart. The Smith-Hughes Act did establish a Federal Board for Vocational Education, separate from the U.S. Office of Education and responsible only to Congress. The seven-member Board consisted of the Secretaries of Labor, Commerce, and Agriculture and three citizens representing labor, agriculture, and manufacturing and commerce. The Commissioner of Education was added partly to allay the anxieties of the NEA. Philander Claxton, Commissioner of Education, helped to

---

[53] *Ibid.*, p. 291.
[54] *Smith-Hughes Act of 1917*, in U.S., *Statutes at Large*, Vol. 39, Part I, pp. 929–936.

secure a separate board for vocational education by maintaining that the U.S. Office of Education staff was not properly constituted to administer the provisions of the Act.[55]

Prosser was immediately appointed Executive Director of the Federal Board and served in that office in its first two crucial years. He established the initial tone of administration. States were given the option of setting up separate boards, or of administering vocational education under the aegis of their general Boards of Education. In actuality, both the language of Smith-Hughes and the administrative style of Dr. Prosser assured that vocational education would function largely as a separate aspect of education within the States.

Vocational education became firmly established and expanded in the years ahead. Smith-Hughes turned out to be an effective instrument for adding practical training programs to the American school system. By the time John F. Kennedy became President and the Russians launched their first Sputniks, some shortcomings of Smith-Hughes, however, had become apparent. The feeling of urgency grew as discontented urban minorities faced job obsolescence as a result of their inferior education and training. Review procedures were established, and the first fundamental revision of vocational education legislation was readied for President Johnson's signature in 1963.[56] Detailed analyses of evolving economic conditions and recommendations for procedural changes in vocational training appeared in profusion. We shall mention a few of these shifts in orientation which could eventually lead to major philosophical and power changes in American education.

The critics of the 1960's identified two central failures of vocational education: (1) its lack of sensitivity to changes in the labor market, and (2) its lack of sensitivity to the needs of various segments of the population. Critics charged that Smith-Hughes programs had been confined to a very narrow part of the spectrum of work activities, and had failed to make imaginative adaptations to the demands of a fast-changing economy. By concentrating on the job requirements of industry and by restricting its efforts to secondary school age students, Smith-Hughes

---

[55]Melvin Barlow, *History of Industrial Education in the United States* (Peoria: Charles A. Bennett, 1967), pp. 114–115.

[56]See, for example, U.S. Department of Health, Education, and Welfare, "Education for a Changing World of Work," Report of Consultants on Vocational Education, 1963. For a comprehensive overview of shifts in policies and evaluation of their effects, see United States Senate, *Notes and Working Papers Concerning the Administration of Programs Authorized Under Vocational Education Act of 1963*, prepared for Subcommittee on Education of the Committee on Labor and Public Welfare (Washington, D.C.: Government Printing Office, March 1968). Hereafter referred to as *Working Papers*, 1968.

also failed to give priority to the vocational needs of all groups in the community.

The 1963 Act announced as its aim the development of vocational education for persons of all ages in all communities. This was to be accomplished with a unified concept of vocational education, rather than by sharply separated programs for vocational, agriculture, home economics, trade and industries, or distributive education. Special attention was to be paid to the needs of disadvantaged persons who had dropped out of school, lacked basic education skills, or needed retraining.

Several of the basic "operational principles" of the revision of the sixties illustrate dramatically the departure from Prosser's preferences.

> Vocational education cannot be meaningfully limited to the skills necessary for a particular occupation. It is more appropriately defined as all of those aspects of educational experience which help a person to discover his talents, to relate them to the world of work, to choose an occupation, and to refine his talents and use them successfully in employment. . . .
>
> The objectives of vocational education should be the development of the individual, not the needs of the labor market. . . .
>
> It is no longer possible to compartmentalize education into general, academic, and vocational components. Education is a crucial element in preparation for a successful working career at any level. . . . Culture and vocation are inseparable and unseverable aspects of humanity. . . .
>
> The practice of structuring teacher education along the traditional occupational category lines perpetuates fragmentation of vocational education, severs it further from general education and hinders adaptation to labor market conditions.[57]

The 1968 evaluators also suggested that pedagogical techniques inherent to vocational education, such as opportunities for multisensory experiences and the relation of classroom study to out-of-school experience, might also enliven general education. They suggested that studies which relate learning to the world of work could be important at all levels, from the elementary school on. Smith-Hughes legislation had denied funds for prevocational activities (excluding such creative new programs in industrial arts as American Industry projects at the junior high school level).[58]

Clearly, departures from Prosser's philosophy of education were in

[57] *Working Papers*, 1968, pp. 47–50, 37–39 *et passim*.
[58] See last chapter for descriptions of educational experiments which combine liberal and technological studies, but which fail to qualify for federal funding.

order. Long before, in the years preceding enactment of Smith-Hughes, John Dewey had set himself in sharp opposition to the social efficiency orientation of David Snedden and Charles Prosser. Dewey argued that the question of how to interrelate technical and liberal studies in American schooling was ultimately related to the question of what quality of life would obtain in American technological civilization. We turn next to Dewey's assessment of the educational problem.

8/ *"Vocational Aspects of Education"* in Dewey's Thought

> At the present time the conflict of philosophic theories focuses in discussion of the proper place and function of vocational factors in education. . . . Significant differences in philosophical conceptions find their *chief issue* in connection with this point. . . . John Dewey, *Democracy and Education*, p. 358. (Italics added.)

A. THE PHILOSOPHICAL RATIONALE OF DEWEY'S INTEREST IN THE VOCATIONAL-LIBERAL STUDIES ISSUE

John Dewey joined the Department of Philosophy at Columbia University in 1904 just as the wave of vocationalism was beginning to roll. *Democracy and Education* was published in 1916, the year in which President Wilson and the Congress made their final moves for the enactment of the Smith-Hughes law. Dewey once observed that for many years *Democracy and Education* was the one book in which his philosophy was most fully expounded—and noted wryly that critics of his philosophy refused to read it.[1] Even for those who have read it carefully, it may come as something of a surprise to discover how the book can be reinterpreted if read from the point of view of Dewey's statement that differences in philosophic reflection find their *chief issue* in the discussion of the proper place and function of "vocational factors in education."

Dewey was, of course, among the critics of traditional school practices. As he saw it, the industrial education movement contained possibilities for educational reform that might make all schooling more relevant to twentieth-century realities and might help this country realize its democratic promises. He was a critic, however, of the narrow utilitarianism of most vocational educators. He refused to be for or against "vocational education" in the vague sense in which it was often

[1] George P. Adams and William P. Montague (eds.), *Contemporary American Philosophy* (New York: Macmillan, 1930), pp. 22–23.

used. The problem, as Dewey saw it, was to determine the conditions under which "vocational aspects" might be helpful or harmful.

Unfortunately, for those who hunger for simple answers, Dewey's analysis of the problem was extremely complex. His general philosophy had a contextual quality that was based on the conviction that

> the more numerous and varied the forms of association into which anything enters, the better basis we have for describing and understanding it. . . . [The] adequacy of any philosophic account of things is found in the extent to which that account is based upon taking things in the widest and most complex scale of association open to observation.[2]

Dewey's educational thought cannot be understood apart from his assessment of the social situation and the philosophical issues of the time. Efforts to provide simplified interpretations for hard-working educators have resulted in reducing his ideas to feckless clichés. Dewey himself pointed to the contextual quality of his thinking about education in his Preface to *Democracy and Education:*

> [The] philosophy stated in this book connects the growth of democracy with the development of the experimental method in the sciences, evolutionary ideas in the biological sciences, and the industrial reorganization, and is concerned to point out the changes in subject matter and methods of education indicated by these developments.[3]

Dewey was convinced that any education which failed to provide the skills and attitudes for living in an era of science and technology was inadequate. The charge that he held a fatuous faith in science as the answer to all problems is, however, not warranted. Dewey was aware that science-technology had the power to debase life as well as the power to enrich it. In the late 1920's he wrote:

> Science . . . has played its part in generating enslavement of men, women and children in factories in which they are animated machines to tend inanimate machines. It has maintained sordid slums, flurried and discontented careers, grinding poverty and luxurious wealth, brutal exploitation of nature and man in times of peace and high explosives and noxious gases in times of war. Man, a child in understanding of himself, has placed in his hands physical tools of incalculable power. He plays with them like a child, and whether they work harm or good is largely a matter of accident.[4]

[2]John Dewey, *Philosophy and Civilization* (New York: Balch, 1931), p. 78.
[3]John Dewey, *Democracy and Education* (New York: Macmillan, 1916), p. v.
[4]John Dewey, *The Public and Its Problems* (New York: Holt, 1927), pp. 175–176.

With a haunting sense of the more ominous dangers still to come, Dewey added,

> Humanity is not, as was once thought, the end for which all things were formed; it is but a slight and feeble thing, perhaps an episodic one, in the vast stretch of the universe. But for man, man is the center of interest and the measure of importance.[5]

He was not, however, of a temperament to embrace existential despair. It man's own mind had created grave threats, it was also the source of his power to turn things around. "the more an organism learns . . . the more it has to learn in order to keep itself going; otherwise death and catastrophe."[6]

It was man's learning which had brought him face to face with a new order of problems related to technology. Retreatism was an illusion. Men had to formulate for themselves new possibilities for learning in order to find fulfillment and ward off disasters in a technological era. Dewey saw the promise of educational reform in his own special interpretations of vocationalism in education. These ideas in turn were intrinsic to his wider educational theory and his general philosophy.

B. THE BATTLE AGAINST DUALISMS

One way to grapple with the contextual quality of Dewey's work is to examine themes which cut across various facets of his thought. One such theme is his lifelong battle against dualisms. He thought contemporary life was shot through with crippling dualisms: America's religious heritage had set man apart from nature and put a Puritan conscience into conflict with man's sensual needs; psychology had divorced mind from body and separated the feeling of expressive self from the intellect; art was divorced from daily life and relegated to museums; school learning was disconnected from experiences outside the school door; work was as sharply distinguished from leisure as virtue was from sin. Mechanized work processes resulted in the isolation of laboring masses from meaningful contact with the few who controlled the great corporations. Even as a young man, Dewey experienced these schisms in American culture in a deeply personal way. They were, he said, "divisions by way of isolation of self from the world, of soul from body, of nature from God." He felt them as "a painful oppression—or, rather they were an inward laceration."[7]

---

[5] *Ibid.*, p. 176.

[6] See John Dewey, "The Philosopher Replies: Experience, Knowledge and Value" in Paul A. Schilpp, editor, *The Philosophy of John Dewey* (New York: Tudor, 1951), p. 523.

[7] John Dewey, "From Absolution to Experimentalism," George P. Adams and William P. Montague (eds.), *Contemporary American Philosophy* (New York: Macmillan, 1930), Vol. 2, p. 19.

Dewey located the beginnings of dualistic thinking in the world-view and social structure of the prescientific era. He felt that intellectuals like himself should assume the task of establishing a new humanism based on the realities of science, technology, and industry. Philosophers could provide insight about inheritances from the past which still hobbled men, and they could identify new antihuman forces in the present. Dewey's evolutionary orientation led him to analyze things genetically, with an effort to identify origins and lines of development.

The Platonic tradition, he said, presented us with a picture of man as a dual creature containing contrasting elements of mind and body.[8] The mind was portrayed as the immaterial thinking entity, capable in its highest form of contemplating eternal, abstract truths, or ideas. The mind was thought to be corrupted by its intimate contact with imperfect matter. Its refinement came through exercise with verbal and mathematical abstractions which progressively freed superior intellects from distortions engendered by matter and emotions.

An orientation like this suited an agriculturally based social order, where a tiny minority monopolized wealth and power and served as the directive class. The Platonic-Aristotelian tradition provided a convenient rationalization for the defense of the status of the privileged class. It assumed that men had been created with natures which classed them off from each other. A few were marked by superior intellects. When properly trained, these men had access to higher truths, which qualified them to lead. The mass of men, lacking true intellect, deserved no better than to serve dumbly and to do the heavy work. The medieval social order gave men an equal chance for salvation in the next world but kept them unequal in this one.

Western educational tradition provided its counterpart to the dual social structure. Universities prepared members of the elite for directive roles by training their intellects in the great literary and scholastic traditions, and by teaching them social graces in the company of their peers. For centuries, the masses of men received no formal education and lived their lives in ignorance. Later, when commerce and industry began to flourish, elementary education for the children of common people prepared them to be useful and obedient workers for new masters with money-based power.

Dewey made frequent references to this tradition as he tried to sketch social alternatives for a scientific–democratic age. More recently, as we have become disappointed and disillusioned with the fruits of technology, it has become popular to take a romantic view of life in the earlier centuries. The happy peasant is seen anchored securely in a

---

[8]See for example John Dewey, *Reconstruction in Philosophy* (New York: New American Library 1950), Chap. 1, "Changing Conceptions of Philosophy."

network of benevolent relations with God, nature, and the feudal order. Dewey's contemporary, Henry James, captured modern disaffections with his contrast between the Dynamo and the Virgin. Dewey and his progressive colleagues, however, saw little evidence to support this nostalgic view as they observed the conditions of the immigrant masses who were fleeing Europe.

Dewey felt that modern circumstances provided a chance for the American people to surmount old dualisms. If their tradition of democratic ideals were combined with the intellectual liberation of science, they might create a civilization which would give more people a chance to experience fullness as human beings. Unfortunately, American culture was thus far guilty of missing its opportunity. Dewey noted that it had not only perpetuated ancient dualisms but had created new ones. This was true of the nation's intellectual development where Americans rejected the facts of evolution; it was true of their social life, where an obsession with money led them to sell out the democratic dream for cheap materialism; it was true in education, where pressures were emerging to replace sterile rote-learning with pseudo-reforms of utilitarian trade training.

Dewey assigned philosophers and intellectuals the task of providing insight into the way things were and of projecting alternatives, and he followed his own advice. He prepared to stake out the outlines of a new kind of schooling which would capitalize on the educative possibilities inherent in the revolutionary processes of technology. Steeped in the perspective of the new social sciences, Dewey made it quite clear, however, that to concentrate only on school reform was to be guilty of tinkering about. The basic educator was the total pattern of culture. Any authentic conception of reform for the age of science had to be thought through across the board. He shared with Veblen and Beard a conviction about the centrality of economic influences on society. His writings on vocationalism in education were a component of his assessment of the meaning of the new corporate-industrial arrangements for American life. His ideas about educational reform can be understood only when laid alongside his economic critique.

C. THE ECONOMIC CRITIQUE

The main features of Dewey's ideas about the American economy and its effects had crystallized even before the vocational education movement of the early twentieth century got underway. Lewis Feuer, in a perceptive article on Dewey's work in the eighties and nineties, points out that Dewey "shared the kind of historical materialism which was the common property of the 'back to the people movement' " of the early progressive era.[9] He operated from the assumption that the modes of producing life's necessities had a pervasive effect on all other phases of life. Thus Dewey wrote in an anthropological essay that studies of hunting cultures demonstrated that mental patterns developed in the occupation of hunting were carried over into the whole gamut of cultural customs, feelings, and products. Approaches to courtship, war, art, and religion were psychologically linked to the characteristics and demands of the hunting vocation. The transition to an agricultural society brought with it new technical skills, social divisions of labor, and more complex mental habits.[10] Dewey saw that in our own time, all "occupations" and aspects of economic life were being radically changed by the impact of science and technology. He assumed that profound changes for all institutions and for man's "mind and personality" were inevitable. He felt that no task was more important than to analyze and assess the meaning of this set of events. It is not surprising to find that he gave a pivotal role to the study of "occupations" in his laboratory school and asked that history be taught in a way that would stress the "more fundamental and controlling influences of economic factors."[11]

There are parallels with Marxist thought in Dewey's insistence on the paramount importance of economic factors. But in Dewey's rationale, there was not the same ideological emphasis on the all-decisive role of class struggle. His tendency was to use the new anthropological perspective to discern the determinative factors of cultural change; to use a genetic analysis for perceiving historical lines of development; and to believe that educative activities of critical segments of society, including the press, could influence public opinion to make institutional changes through democratic processes. Dewey was a radical meliorist.

He became a critic of capitalist-industrial arrangements early in his career. While still at the University of Michigan in the 1890's, Dewey had been ready to collaborate with a radical reformer, Franklin Ford, in founding a newspaper committed to support of the idea that the economy ought to be directed by "the organization of intelligence" rather than the blind drive for profit. Michigan newspapers poured ridicule on the project. Dewey felt compelled to explain that he "planned no revolution" but wanted "to show that philosophy has some use." His paper would be designed for those who "are scientifically

---

[9]Lewis S. Feuer, "John Dewey and the Back to the People Movement in American Thought," *Journal of the History of Ideas*, Vol. 20 (October-December 1959), p. 664.

[10]John Dewey, "Interpretation of the Savage Mind," *Psychological Review*, Vol. 9 (May 1902), pp. 219–222.

[11]John Dewey, *School and Society* (Chicago: U. of Chicago Press, 1899), p. 29. For a discussion of the role Dewey's theory of occupations played in his Laboratory School, see Arthur G. Wirth, *John Dewey As Educator* (New York: Wiley, 1966), Chap. 9.

interested in the study of social questions."[12] The venture foundered before the first issue could be brought to press.

When Dewey went to Chicago in 1894, he met Jane Addams and progressive reformers of the Hull House circle who were committed to making democracy workable for the immigrants. In this company, Dewey became an admirer of Henry George and adopted the proposition "that economic needs and struggles have been the determining force in the evolution of all institutions."[13]

When Thorstein Veblen's *Theory of the Leisure Class* appeared in 1899, Dewey put it to use by locating the origins of "dualisms" in the leisure class. Philosophical dualisms, Dewey wrote, were a survival from a past "which was dualistic practically and politically, drawing fixed lines between classes, and dualistic intellectually." American culture, he said, "is still tainted with an inheritance from the period of the aristocratic seclusion of a leisure class—leisure meaning relief from participation in the work of a workaday world."[14] A new social democracy, he argued, would mean "an abandonment of this dualism." He wanted twentieth-century philosophy to join in the work of freeing America's "partial democracy" from the strictures of the leisure class and the cultural heritage accompanying it.

Dewey's interest in the analysis and critique of the American economic-industrial system was a central concern throughout his career. In order to express his convictions about the practical bearing of philosophy, he wrote regularly in popular journals. When *The New Republic* appeared in 1914, Dewey became a regular contributor along with Walter Lippman, Randolph Bourne, and other progressives. Some of his most searching articles on the vocational education movement appeared in this magazine. His major writings on social philosophy appeared in the twenties and thirties: *The Public and Its Problems* (1927), *Individualism Old and New* (1929), *Liberalism and Social Action* (1935), and *Freedom and Culture* (1939). For our purposes, it is appropriate to concentrate on *Individualism Old and New*, which was based largely on articles Dewey had written for *The New Republic*.

divided against itself." Anthropologically speaking, the United States of

1. Individualism Old and New

In *Individualism Old and New*, Dewey began by referring to the recently completed study of *Middletown* by Robert and Helen Lynd (1929). The study showed, said Dewey, that America was a "house

[12]Feuer, *op. cit.*, pp. 552–553.

[13]John Dewey, "James Bonar's 'Philosophy and Political Economy,'" *Political Science Quarterly*, Vol. 9 (1894), p. 743.

[14]John Dewey, "Are the Schools Doing What the People Want Them To Do?" *The Educational Review*, Vol. 21 (1901), pp. 470–471; Feuer, *op. cit.*, p. 567.

the 1920's had to be described as a money culture. It was committed to a "struggle for existence" which assumed that the unfettered pursuit of money was the means to all good: the fit should prosper in order that the rest could benefit from largesse filtering down from the top. Ironically, laissez-faire philosophy was based on economic determinism, while the spiritual heritage to which Americans also clung denied determinism. Laissez-faire doctrine preached that the "laws" of the market place were the chief social determinants; while espoused religious teachings frowned on materialistic creeds and encouraged people to use their free wills to plan social change instead of behaving like helpless pawns moved by impersonal forces. The fundamental cleavage, said Dewey, was a moral one. The nation gave priority to materialistic drives, while

> the spiritual factor of our condition, equal opportunity and free association and intercommunication is obscured and crowded out. Instead of the development of individualities which (the American founders) prophetically set forth, there is a perversion of the whole ideal of individualism to conform to the practices of a pecuniary culture. It has become the source and justification of inequalities and oppressions. Hence our compromises and the conflicts in which aims and standards are confused beyond recognition.[15]

Americans paid a heavy price for the unbalanced pursuit of monetary gain. Life had become marked by mechanization and the worship of technique as an end instead of means; by standardization and the concomitant homogeneity of thought and opinion instead of flexible, critical thinking; and by quantification, with consequent impersonality and "superficiality" of soul. When left unchecked, the new industrial system introduced both dramatic and subtle changes into the pattern of culture: the decline of family farms, the replacement of old-type artisans by assembly line machine tenders, the commercialization of college athletics, the sensationalism of the press, the manipulative thrust of advertising and public relations, and the tensions and compulsive drives of businessmen.[16]

[15]John Dewey, *Individualism Old and New* (New York: Capricorn, 1962; original pub. 1929),, p. 18.
[16]While writing these words, I read a column by James Reston on President Nixon's problems in making new Cabinet and administrative appointments. An aide to the President said that they were disturbed to discover how many times they would locate a prominent man, only to find that some physical or psychological weakness disqualified him for the job.
  "I had never realized," one Cabinet member remarked the other day, "what a toll the fierce competition of American business and professional life has taken on many of our most talented and successful men. Many of them have simply been worn out in the struggle. Many more have all kinds of family problems they cannot leave. In a great many cases, they have taken to drink to such an extent that the risk is too great. So we have had to go much slower than we expected." (Saint Louis *Post Dispatch*, June 26, 1969.)

Dewey felt that the right analysis of the human costs of a short-sighted, profit-driven economy might yield clues to reforms needed to restore balance to society. Here he took up again his theme of dualism. The new economic system was quilty of creating new dualisms that were possibly more harmful than the old. The ever-larger corporate bureaucracies concentrated power and decision making in the hands of a directive few (on matters of gravest importance for the whole of society), while more and more Americans were reduced to the role of helpless pawns. Men "not bound together in associations . . . are monstrosities," said Dewey.[17] If the schools in such a society do nothing more than fashion people to meet the needs of the system, if education fails to give people the insights to challenge the distortions of the system, then men are more enfeebled. More individuals will feel lost and disoriented, with recourse to nothing other than irrational outbursts. When millions are reduced to the inner despair of Dostoevesky's "underground man," the human waste becomes enormous. The survival of the democratic dream is finally at stake.

Dewey was specific in his indictment but did not believe that a ready-made answer was available: "No one person is going to evolve a constructive solution for the problem of humanizing industrial civilization, of making it and its technology a servant of human life."[18]

The major questions to which he addressed himself in *Individualism Old and New* were: How would individuals recover themselves as persons in the unprecedented social situation? What qualities should a new economic situation and a new education embrace which might restore the health of the American democratic soul, and reintegrate divided selves?

Dewey did have convictions about general courses of action to which his analyses pointed; his pragmatism was not paralyzed by existential *angst*. He began by ruling out defenses of the status quo and the faint-heartedness of science-hating humanists who yearned for the supposed harmonies of the pretechnological era, the advocates of "Forward to the Middle Ages." If a more humane culture could be created, it had to be built on the realities of science and technological industry.

His estimate of the possibilities markedly distinguished him from gloom-ridden prophets who saw the very nature of science and the new technique as a monster beyond control. Dewey envisioned prospects for a new humanism in the enterprise of science itself, although he was not greatly optimistic that men would make the choices required to establish it. His basic generalization was that "industry itself should become a primary educative and cultural force for those engaged in it"

[17]Dewey, *Individualism Old and New*, pp. 81–82.
[18]*Ibid.*, p. 141.

—and that it could not do that as long as it single-mindedly pursued profits without regard for human values.[19]

Dewey's argument centered on two points. (1) the scientific way of thinking was based on a set of attitudes and skills which opened new possibilities for growth in awareness. Modern industry was grounded in and permeated by the rationale of science. Men who worked in fragmented work processes might be completely unaware of the style of the scientific mode which energized the enterprise. Yet the possibility for tapping educative potential in industrial processes was there, remaining to be explored. (2) Corporate industrial organizations, so successful in effecting spectacular increases in production, were enterprises of collaborating human beings. They were witness to the power of conjoint human efforts. As they became more complex, they required greater degrees of intelligence and integration of procedures from workers. The trouble was that thinking about the corporate enterprise was dominated by a few men at the top who, under the pressure to make more money, introduced Taylorized production techniques that reduced people to impersonal cost items. The majority of workers were treated as "hired hands" rather than as whole persons, shut off from the processes of communication and participation.

Dewey did not say that a move to humanize industrial and commercial processes would be easy—or even likely. His point was that *if* one analyzed the contemporary situation from the standpoint of giving priority to human values, *then* one could begin to compare alternatives for reaching saner goals without rejecting the new techniques.

Dewey was perfectly aware that the power generated by science could be misused, but over and over again he fought the idea that science and scientific attitudes were the culprits responsible for our ills and discontents. He argued, as Jacob Bronowski did later in *Science and Human Values,* that scientific thinking was a refined example of man's creative mind at work. The community of scientists—the way scientists relate to each other in order to *do* science as truth-seeking could, in fact, operate as a model upon which to reconstruct other institutions in the technological era. Scientists are compelled to create communities which make it possible for men to build their lives around the pursuit of truth. To do this requires a combination of freedom and discipline. Each individual must be free to reflect on experience and to seek new ways of viewing things or reordering experiences. But in a community of truth seekers, the individual must be willing to submit his personal visions to public scrutiny in an atmosphere of free communication. Respect for individuality, participation, communication, criticism, dis-

[19] *Ibid.*, pp. 132–135.

sent are essential marks of men who form communities for creative work in science or the arts. In short, as Bronowski put it, "the society of scientists must be a democracy."[20] Dewey argued that the social conditions which are necessary to do science or art are the same conditions which must be created elsewhere if men are to be free to explore and extend experience.

> The general adoption of the scientific attitude in human affairs would mean nothing less than a revolutionary change in morals, religion, politics, and industry. The fact that we have limited its use so largely to technical matters is not a reproach to science, but to the human beings who used it for private ends and who strive to defeat its social application for fear of destructive effects upon their power and profit. *A vision of a day in which the natural sciences and the technologies which flow from them are used as servants of a humane life, constitutes the imagination that is relevant to our own time.* A humanism that flees from science as an enemy denies the means by which a liberal humanism might become a reality.[21]

Paul Goodman in "Can Technology Be Humane?"[22] describes the deep distrust of science which young Americans have developed since Dewey wrote. The reason is clear enough. Science has too often been coopted to serve the crasser needs of corporate industrialism or a rampant militarism. Goodman in effect calls for the application of Dewey's kind of humanistic test to the enterprise of science itself so that scientists and technologists would see themselves as responsible for the work they do and competent to judge the uses. That is a task of enormous importance and complexity for both capitalist and noncapitalist societies. Unlike some critics who now define science as diabolical and antilife, Goodman accepts the legitimacy of Dewey's identification of the ethical quality of the attitudes and disciplines required to advance understanding through scientific inquiry. The new order of urgency is to work out the problems of the ethical accountability of science.

In *The Public and Its Problems*, Dewey stated that the problem was to transform the Great Society—which produces enormously but which ruptures human relations and renders individuals anonymous—into the Great Community, built by persons with humane insights into the realities of the age of science who participate actively in the reconstruction of institutions.[23] Dewey's analysis led him to conclude that what was needed was a "cooperatively shared control of industry." He assumed

[20]Jacob Bronowski, *Science and Human Values* (New York: Harper, 1956), p. 80.
[21]Dewey, *Individualism Old and New*, pp. 155–156.
[22]Paul Goodman, "Can Technology Be Humane?," *New York Review*, Nov. 20, 1969, pp. 27–34.
[23]John Dewey, *The Public and Its Problems*, pp. 126–128, 147, 155–158.

that the trend was toward control of the economy by larger and fewer economic units. Only the myth remained of a market controlled by a myriad of small entrepreneurs.

> Economic determinism is now a fact, not a theory. But there is a choice between a blind, chaotic, and unplanned determinism, issuing from business conducted for pecuniary profit, and the determination of a socially planned and ordered development.[24]

Dewey never lost confidence in the idea suggested to him by journalist Franklin Ford in the early 1890's, of a new economy directed by "the organization of intelligence" rather than the unchecked drive for money. He could see only three general alternatives: (1) the chaotic determinism of the present, resulting in waste of natural resources, despoiling of the environment, and crippling of human lives; (2) state domination—"the road which Soviet Russia is traveling with so much attendant destruction and coercion;" or (3) a new kind of society planned "in accord with the spirit of American life . . . undertaken by voluntary agreement." Dewey foresaw the possibility of coordinating and directive councils in which leaders of industry and finance would meet with representatives of labor and public officials to plan the regulation of industrial activity.[25] He also predicted the appearance of kinds of governmental regulation and involvement which became a partial reality under the New Deal.

The task facing the twentieth century, said Dewey, is to build a humane society that will demand that science be "humanistic—not just physical and technical." American society could make a unique contribution to world civilization by combining its talents for technological achievement with its democratic traditions. If we could create a system of cooperative control of industry instead of coutrol by a few, Dewey predicted, there would be an enormous liberation of the American mind. People would experience the exhilaration that comes with participation and sharing in responsibility.[26]

> A new culture expressing the possibilities immanent in a machine and material civilization will release whatever is distinctive and potentially creative in individuals, and individuals thus freed will be the constant makers of a continuously new society.[27]

2. Education in the Industrial Society

Dewey maintained that the quality of schooling which might ensue in the new era was related to the decision the nation would make about

[24] *Ibid.*, pp. 118–120.
[25] *Ibid.*, p. 118.
[26] *Ibid.*, pp. 132–133.
[27] *Ibid.*, p. 143.

organizing economic life. He noted the American devotion to the universal common school but questioned the ends our system served. He acknowledged that the common school opened opportunities to many and that it aided in cultural unification. But, Dewey argued, if the system "merely turns out efficient industrial fodder and citizenship fodder in a state controlled by pecuniary industry, as other schools in other nations have turned efficient cannon fodder, it is not helping to solve the problem of building up a distinctive American culture; it is only aggravating the problem."[28] Schools used primarily to help people get ahead, to fill job needs, and to parrot textbook clichés nourished a kind of infantilism.

Dewey stressed the point that a genuine renewal of individuality could not be accomplished by school reform alone, but had to be accompanied by economic-social reconstruction as well.

> I can think of nothing more childishly futile, for example, than the attempt to bring "art" and aesthetic enjoyment externally to the multitudes who work in the ugliest surroundings and who leave their ugly factories only to go through depressing streets to eat, sleep, and carry on their domestic operations in grimy, sordid homes.

He felt hopeful about the growing interest of the young in the arts but felt that it could turn into a mere escape mechanism,

> unless it develops into an alert interest in the conditions which determine the esthetic environment of the vast multitudes who now live, work and plan in surroundings that perforce degrade their tastes and that unconsciously educate them into desire for any kind of enjoyment as long as it is cheap and "exciting."[29]

Economic and social reconstruction was required of American society. The question remained whether a "new education" could help prepare the way for a humane technological society. Dewey turned a critical eye to the industrial education movement and saw it as containing possibilities for educational reform and possibilities for exaggerating evils already far advanced.

[28] *Ibid.*, p. 127.
[29] *Ibid.*, pp. 130–131.

9/ The "Vocational" as a Means for Liberalizing Education

The unique fact about our own civilization is that if it is to achieve and manifest a characteristic culture, it must develop, not on top of an industrial and political substructure, but out of our material civilization itself. It will come by turning a machine age into a significantly new habit of mind and sentiment, or it will not come at all. . . . It is a qualitative question. Can a material, industrial civilization be converted into a distinctive agency for liberating the minds and refining the emotions of all who take part in it? . . . A "humanism" that separates man from nature will envisage a radically different solution of the industrial and economic perplexities of the age than a humanism entertained by those who find no uncrossable gulf or fixed gap. The former will inevitably look backward for direction; it will strive for a cultivated elite supported on the backs of toiling masses. The latter will have to face the question of whether work itself can become an instrument of culture and of how the masses can share freely in a life enriched in imagination and esthetic enjoyment. This task is set not because of sentimental "humanitarianism," but as the necessary conclusion of the intellectual conviction that while man belongs in nature and mind is connected with matter, humanity and its collective intelligence are the means by which nature is guided to new possibilities.[1]

If we are to understand Dewey's stand on the vocational-liberal studies issue, we have to see the interrelationships of key points in this passage. (1) The only hope for civilizing the technological society is to cultivate "new *habits* of mind and sentiment." (2) These cannot be formed by approaches which reject the machine culture—but somehow the industrial society itself, including man's work in it, must be converted into an agent for human liberation. (3) Both man's mind and machine age culture must be seen as emergents within nature. The habits of intelligence which may become the instruments for salutary

---

[1]John Dewey, *Individualism Old and New* (New York: Capricorn, 1962), (original publication 1929), pp. 124–126.

change must be identified and consciously cultivated, both in schooling and through the workings of all institutions. (4) A "dualistic humanism" which separates mind from matter and turns to intellectualist elitism must be rejected as futile. (5) The changes effected by technology have such a radical effect on human life that the new habits of intelligence required to cope with change must be cultivated throughout the entire population. An enlightened elite would be doomed to failure because it could not move a mass that lacked refined skills and attitudes; therefore, a democratization of the new "habits of mind and sentiments" throughout the population will be required for survival.

We shall comment on aspects of Dewey's philosophy which led him to such conclusions, and note the position he took on the role of the "vocational" in the reform of general education.

One of the most effective efforts to get at the heart of Dewey's concept of man is found in John E. Smith's *The Spirit of American Philosophy.*[2] Smith's account is valuable because it helps explain why Dewey was the philosopher of democracy—of the "back to the people movement;" why he held elitism to be untenable; why he stressed the need for a new liberalizing quality in education for the entire population.

Dewey often contrasted his position on the nature of man with that of other philosophers—the British empiricists who defined man in psychological terms, or the idealists who stressed mind and reason. Dewey, by contrast, conceived of man in naturalistic, biological terms. Smith points out that no one can grasp Dewey's thought who does not take this fact seriously.

> It does not mean that Dewey thought of man solely in physiological terms; his position is far more subtle. It does not mean that man is not to be understood primarily as a theoretical knower who merely represents the world through the "ideas" in the mind. For Dewey we do not start within the mind and we do not start with elements of certainty —simple ideas of sense or clear and distinct ideas of reason. We start instead with man as a complex organism set within an environment of change, flux, precariousness, and instability. The biological orientation means setting out from the organism-environment polarity and then showing how all of the distinctions of complex and mature sense experience emerge from that primordial situation.[3]

Like Freud, Dewey started from the assumption that planet Earth had not been tailor-made to meet man's need. It contained elements

[2]John E. Smith, *The Spirit of American Philosophy* (New York: Oxford U. Press, 1963), Chap. 4, "John Dewey."
[3]*Ibid.*, pp. 126–127.

which give man a chance to live, but it was also full of the contingent, unpredictable and perilous. Dewey interpreted man's characteristic responses to such a environment—his propitiation of the gods, magic, ritual practices, art, and, most recently, scientific intelligence—as efforts at control. Being on earth, essentially, is to have a chance to live. The task is to keep life going and to explore its possibilities. The basic trait of existence—its uncertain, doubtful, and hazardous character— gives the clue to man's distinctive nature. Man is the being who has developed awareness of this generic trait of his situation. He can perceive and confront the precarious and doubtful *as such*, and, by seeing obstacles as problems, he can respond to the challenges with his resources. Man's capacity to gain control over his environment has emerged slowly, and is based on his capacity to attain insight into what threatens or supports his survival and growth. Man *has* to grow in insight and skill, for nature changes of itself—and it changes through the effects of man's actions on it.

Dewey held that the capacity for reflective thought was an evolutionary biosocial emergent. It had grown out of man's interaction with nature and his fellow men, and was related to other aspects of his human nature—impulses and habits. This evolutionary view of the origin of man's capacity to think provided an alternative explanation to dualist traditions which had made thinking an attribute of an immaterial entity, "mind." In this older sense, "mind" was essentially an unexplainable "something"—outside and apart from nature. It was an intrinsic part of the dualist image of man which Dewey so deplored. Some passages from *Reconstruction in Philosophy* may give a feeling of Dewey's counterview of "minded behavior" as an emergent from man's dynamic interactions with his world.

> Wherever there is life, there is behavior, activity. In order that life may persist this activity has to be both continuous and adapted to the environment. This adaptive adjustment . . . is not a mere matter of moulding of the organism by the environment. . . . There is no such thing in a living creature as mere conformity to conditions. . . . In the interests of the maintenance of life there is transformation of some elements in the surrounding medium. The higher the form of life, the more important is the active reconstruction of the medium.[4]
>
> From this point of view, experience becomes an affair primarily of doing. The organism does not stand about, Micawberlike, waiting for something to turn up. . . . The living creature undergoes, suffers, the consequences of its own behavior. This close connection between doing and suffering or undergoing forms what we call experience.[5]

[4]John Dewey, *Reconstruction in Philosophy* (New York: New American Library, 1950, p. 82).
[5]*Ibid.*, pp. 82–83.

Reflective thinking emerges out of experience. It is the process of discerning the connections and meanings in situations and of projecting ideas as hypotheses, testing them by acting on them, and observing the consequences. It is through this process that men build knowledge of their world.

The biosocial image of man enabled Dewey to show the relation of thought to other aspects of man's nature. Human development, he held, starts with impulse and passes into habits which become embodied in customs. Intelligence or "minded behavior" emerges as men become aware of the *meaning* of their impulses and habits. Unlike that of the lower organisms, man's life is fortunately not rigidly determined by instincts and impulses. Impulses can be modified, controlled, and directed. But what about habits—the learned responses men develop as a response to conditions they encounter? Habits tend to persist and may be inflexible. Can they, too, be transformed by intelligence so tht man may gain control over himself?

A distinctive feature of Dewey's philosophy was the importance he assigned to habit. In many respects, he felt, our habits determine who we are in a more fundamental way than do conscious choices. In Peirce's vivid phrase, habits as ideas "become fixed in our muscles." But habit and reflective thought are not mutually exclusive. Reflective thought or intelligence may be brought into play when habits become rigid and fail to meet new requirements. Habits are amenable to change as men gain insight into the need for change.

As John Smith put it,

> The singling out of habit as the essential feature of man is of the most importance to Dewey's entire outlook. For if man is primarily a creature of habit and habits are accessible to human intelligence, many of the most pervasive ills of human history can be attacked, and they should be, in principle at least, subject to elimination.[6]

Dewey's concern with the idea of universal education grew out of this orientation. We typically associate universal schooling with the ideal of widening and equalizing opportunity, but

> there was a more subtle reason behind the idea of universal education in Dewey's thinking; it means the education of an *entire* people, the education of a nation and, through them, the education of an age. *It means the redirection of impulse and the modification of habit all across the culture at large.* This is something very different from the education, in an established tradition, of a few whose task it will then be to guide and direct the others. It is rather the enterprise of redirecting the entire culture at a most elemental level. Social transformation

[6]Smith, *op. cit.*, p. 132.

—the changing of basic social, economic, and political conditions—has a better chance of success if the total population is involved.[7]

Cultural transformation would also have a better chance of success if a working model of the desired new attitudes and skills were available. As we noted in the last chapter, Dewey felt that the values and processes of science itself provided such a model. He had hopes that something of the essential spirit of science could be taught to the population at large because, from his biological perspective, he saw science simply as a refined form of inquiry that had emerged from the evolutionary process. The habits of problem solving, of treating ideas as hypotheses, of making judgments in terms of the observation of consequences, of tolerating discrepant ideas, had grown out of human experience and could be cultivated and taught. Science, then, was the best and most vivid example of the marriage of theory and action. By using experimental science as a model, Dewey stressed the philosophical point that action, practice, and behavior cannot be alien to thought but are necessary to it. This demonstrated, he felt, that the ancient tendency to disparage practice as compared to contemplative thought was mistaken.

In education Dewey opposed practices which treated learning as a passive process of absorbing information. He stressed the importance of learners being physically and mentally active as inquirers. The popular image of Dewey's position is contained in the slogan "learning by doing," and there is warrant for it. But Dewey was equally concerned with *meaning*, and his famous definition of education combines the features of action and meaning-seeking. "[Education] is that reconstructing or reorganizing of experience which adds to the meaning of experience, and which increases ability to direct the course of subsequent experience.[8]

The test of whether an experience is educative, is not whether mere activity is involved, but *whether it leads us to see new meanings about the world or ourselves.* To gain a new meaning, said Dewey, is to acquire "increased perception of the connections and continuities of the activities in which we are engaged," and to gain added power of control. "The chief business of life at every point is to make living contribute to an enrichment of its own perceptible meaning."[9]

Dewey was aware that science and its applications could bring "new modes of unloveliness and suffering."[10] It was equally important, therefore, that men grow in their capacity to examine the conse-

---

[7] *Ibid.*, pp. 132–133. (Italics added.)
[8] John Dewey, *Democracy and Education* (New York: Macmillan, 1916), pp. 89–90.
[9] Dewey, *Reconstruction in Philosophy*, pp. 145–147.
[10] Dewey, *Individualism Old and New*, p. 153.

quences of thought in action. Here the role of democracy entered Dewey's rationale. The democratic ideal held that only those actions were justified which opened opportunities for all human beings to grow in experience. In an oft-quoted statement, Dewey put it this way:

> All social institutions have a meaning, a purpose. That purpose is to set free and to develop the capacities of human individuals without respect to race, sex, class or economic status. . . . [The] test of their value is the extent to which they educate every individual into the full stature of his possibility. Democracy has many meanings, but if it has a moral meaning, it is found in resolving that *the supreme test of all political institutions and industrial arrangements* shall be the contribution they make to the all-round growth of every member of society. [11]

Dewey applied that test to the uses of technology in the industrial system and to American schooling and found both of them wanting. If there was a chance for reform, Dewey felt it could be accomplished only through a combination of the humane aspects of science with the ideals of democracy. He was clear that the necessary restructuring of habits and attitudes would be nourished ideally by a total cultural reorientation, with all institutions contributing. But beginnings had to be made somewhere; and Dewey and other progressives held school reform to be of strategic importance because the habits and minds of the young were still pliable and unformed.

Dewey encountered the pressures for vocational education as the twentieth century opened. He evaluated the movement in terms of his philosophical frame of reference.

A. "THE OCCUPATIONS" AS THE MODEL FOR EDUCATIONAL REFORM

Both practically and philosophically the *key to the present educational sitiatuion* lies in a gradual reconstruction of school materials and methods so as *to utilize various forms of occupations typifying social callings, and to bring out their intellectual and moral content.* . . . This educational reorganization *cannot be accomplished* by merely trying to give a *technical preparation for industries and professions as they now operate*, much less by merely reproducing industrial conditions in the school. *The problem is not that of making the schools an adjunct to manufacture and commerce, but of utilizing the factors of industry to make school life more active, more full of immediate meaning, more connected with out-of-school experience. The problem is not easy of solution.* There is a standing danger that education will perpetuate the older traditions for a select few, and effect its adjustment to the new

[11]Dewey, *Reconstruction in Philosophy*, p. 147. (Italics added.)

economic conditions more or less on the basis of acquiescence in the untransformed, unrationalized, and unsocialized phases of our defective industrial regime. Put in concrete terms, there is *danger that vocational education will be interpreted in theory and practice as trade education; as a means of securing technical efficiency in specialized future pursuits.*

Education would then become an instrument of perpetuating unchanged the existing industrial order of society, instead of operating as a means of its transformation. . . . The [needed] change is essentially a change in the quality of mental disposition—an educative change. This does not mean that we can change character and mind by direct instruction and exhortation, apart from a change in industrial and political conditions. Such a conception contradicts our basic idea that character and mind are attitudes of participative response in social affairs. But it does mean that we may produce in schools a projection in type of of the society we should like to realize, and by forming minds in accord with it gradually modify the larger and more recalcitrant features of adult society.[12]

This passage from "Vocational Aspects of Education" in *Democracy and Education*[13] bears careful reading. It points toward some of Dewey's major prescriptions for the reform of public education. The key recommendation is to use "occupations", interpreted as the new mode of getting work done in a technological society in a way *"to bring out their intellectual and moral content."* We are promised that this innovation will make school life more active and more relevant to out-of-school experience; and, that schools so organized can influence mental dispositions in ways to help transform "our defective industrial regime." The chapter title indicates that the author is not writing directly on "vocational education" but on "vocational aspects of education."

1. The Definitional Problem

If Dewey insisted that the introduction of the study of "occupations" into American schools was to be a major feature of educational reform, it seems strange that progressive educators who followed Dewey did not give the concept more attention. The idea was not ignored in some of the "project method" proposals, but it is hard to think of educators other than Dewey who made "occupations" a leading term in their vocabularies.

Dewey's tortured style of writing in discussing the terms "occupations," "vocation," and "calling," provides a partial explanation as to

---

[12]Dewey, *Democracy and Education*, pp. 369–370. (Italics added.)
[13]*Ibid.*, Chap. XXIII.

why educators shied away from concepts which for Dewey had so much meaning. The terminological problem is illustrated in his chapter "Vocational Aspects of Education" in *Democracy and Education.*

On the one hand, Dewey spoke of "occupations" in referring to forms of work available to men in the industrial era. In this case he described how work in industry and commerce was being transformed by scientific and technological factors. On the positive side, there was a reduction in the physical drudgery required of men.

> Industry has ceased to be essentially an empirical, rule of thumb procedure, handed down by custom. Its technique is now technological: that is to say based upon machinery resulting from discoveries in mathematics, physics, chemistry, bacteriology, etc. . . . Industrial occupations have infinitely greater intellectual content and infinitely larger cultural possibilities than they used to possess. The demand for such education as will acquaint workers with the scientific and social bases and bearings of their pursuits becomes imperative, since those who are without it inevitably sink to the role of appendages to the machines they operate.

His last phrase indicates Dewey was not blind to the fact that men pushed out of craft occupations could be reduced to mindless machine tenders.

> While the intellectual *possibilities* of industry have multiplied, industrial conditions tend to make industry, for the great masses, less of an educative resource than it was in the days of hand production for local markets. The burden of realizing the intellectual possibilities inhering in work is thus thrown back on the school.[14]

In practice, however, said Dewey, the schools were not seizing upon opportunities to draw on the intellectual possibilities involved in the revolution in modes of work. The trend instead was to introduce the "vocational" component into education in the form of narrow trade training designed to teach specific salable skills. Such a conception of "vocational" should be rejected, he argued, because "mere training" did not meet the criterion of an "educative experience;" that is, premature training for job skills neglected the liberalizing dimension of exploring things in terms of their broader meanings and of raising questions about human values. Public school trade training, because of its sharp focus on job skills, tended to create members of a permanent, subordinate working class. If denied insight into the profound consequences for human experience of the revolution in techniques workers would not be prepared to help transform an unsatisfying industrialism into something more civilized.

[14]*Ibid.*, p. 367.

In that same chapter, however, Dewey also used the terms "occupation" or "vocation" in ways which had nothing to do with earning a living. We must avoid, he said, using vocation or occupation to apply only to activities where tangible commodities are produced, or to imply that each person has only one vocation. In its broader definition an occupation "is a continuous activity having a purpose."[15] In this sense, it is something which *occupies* an individual personally; it is something in which he is interested and to which he is committed. Each individual, in this sense, has a variety of "occupations," "callings," or "vocations." He may earn his living as a garment worker or an engineer. But he also may be a member of a family, may be active in community affairs and in political organizations, or may be passionately committed to playing the oboe. We tend, Dewey said, to name a person's vocation according to his employment. "But we should not allow ourselves to be so subject to works as to ignore and virtually deny his other callings when it comes to the vocational phases of education."[16]

Dewey employed a kind of accordion usage of the term "occupation." In a constricted sense, Dewey used it to refer to specific jobs and concomitant training programs; more broadly, he used it to point to fundamental changes in the nature of work effected by science and technology. Beyond paid employment, he used "occupation" to apply to activities where one's deepest personal purposes or interests were involved; and at its fullest extension he said "the dominant vocation of all human beings at all times is living—intellectual and moral growth."[17] It is no wonder that there was puzzlement about the meaning of Dewey's statement that the key to educational reform lay in the use of "various forms of occupations" and their intellectual and moral content.

There *is* a genuine problem in the style of Dewey's writings; nevertheless, it is possible to clarify his intentions. We shall refer to the use he made of "occupations" in his own Laboratory School at the University of Chicago.

B. THE "OCCUPATIONS" IN DEWEY'S LABORATORY SCHOOL

The inclination to learn from life itself and to make the condition of life such that all will learn in the process of living is the finest product of schooling.[18]

[15]Dewey, *Democracy and Education*, p. 361.
[16]*Ibid.*, p. 359.
[17]*Ibid.*, p. 362.
[18]*Ibid.*, p. 60.

Dewey came to the University of Chicago in 1894 with an appointment as Chairman of the combined Departments of Philosophy, Psychology, and Pedagogy. He began very soon to plan the founding of a Laboratory School, formally launched with a dozen or so children in 1896. As the school grew, Dewey remained its Director until he left Chicago in 1904.[19] The school gained its widest fame through his references to it in *School and Society* (1899). His major educational treatise, *Democracy and Education*, is based on the theory and practice represented in his Laboratory School.

Before looking directly at his ideas about the occupations, it may help to review the kinds of criticisms Dewey and his colleagues were making of schooling. In a famous chapter, "Waste in Education" in *School and Society*, Dewey pinpointed some of the shortcomings of traditional education.[20] He used the term "waste" not to describe the schools' financial inefficiency, but to charge that they failed to make any significant differences in the lives of the students. Factors in the out-of-school lives of children were not drawn upon in class, and school-room recitations had little relevance for students when they fled at the end of the day. Periods were filled with "teacher talk," which no one ever used except in classrooms. The result, said Dewey, was that schools were isolated from life. Their own internal operations accented the "isolation." The separate subjects remained unrelated to each other, and there was a lack of correlation between the elementary, middle, and higher parts of the system. In addition, outdated psychologies of learning prevailed that assumed students brought empty minds to school to be filled. This author's father, for example, quit school in 1906 at age thirteen when the teacher assigned for memorization a long list of American explorers with the dates of their births and deaths. The result of such learning theory was that classrooms were places of passive, rote learning where the dominant method was the ancient practice of reciting teacher-assigned material. Dewey said, "There is much of utter triviality of subject matter in elementary and secondary education." No wonder, then, that the majority of children were leaving school well before the end of the elementary grades. Dewey was angry about the human waste.

In Dewey's school, the occupations represented the most dramatic departure from standard school programs. They consisted of activities such as gardening, cooking, printing, textile work, simple carpentry and metal work, and dramatics. Projects were generated out of activities

---

[19]See Katherine C. Mayhew and Anna C. Edwards, *The Dewey School* (New York: Appleton, 1936) and Arthur G. Wirth, *John Dewey as Educator* (New York: Wiley, 1966).

[20]John Dewey, *School and Society*, rev. ed. (Chicago: U. of Chicago Press, 1923), Chap. 3.

like these to which academic study was related.

Dewey said that progressive educators had been making use of such activities, but that their reasons for doing so were painfully inadequate. They generally defended manual training, for example, on the grounds that it engaged the spontaneous interest of children, kept them active and alert instead of passive, and taught useful skills for home life. These reasons, while not insignificant, missed the main point about "the occupations": their social significance. The main functions of the occupations, said Dewey, should be, first, to give children examples of the types of processes men utilize to create the primal necessities of communities; second, to reveal how changes in techniques have enabled men to advance from primitive to civilized stages; and finally, to provide opportunities for children to practice community living rather than mere competitive striving.[21]

In one of his many elaborations about the value of the occupations, Dewey noted in *Democracy and Education* that

> education through occupations consequently combines within itself more of the factors conducive to learning than any other method. It calls instincts and habits into play; it is a foe to passive receptivity. It has an end in view; results are to be accomplished. Hence it appeals to thought; it demands that an idea be steadily maintained, so that activity cannot be either routine or capricious. Since the movement of activity must be progressive, leading from one stage to another, observation and ingenuity are required at each stage to overcome obstacles and to discover and readapt means of execution.[22]

The occupations, he said, can transform the whole spirit of a school. They create opportunities for children to feel a sense of personal involvement, to engage in manipulative and expressive as well as mental activities, and to grow in social insight. Instead of being a transmitter of auditory input, the school could become an ally of the arts, and a center for the study of science and history.

Dewey was convinced also that use of the occupations could help overcome another troublesome "dualism"—the separation of academic studies from each other. Perhaps the best way to give a comprehensive view of Dewey's ideas on the educative value of the occupations is to quote some passages at length from *Democracy and Education* in which he summarized his position.

> Aside from the fact that active occupations represent things to do, not studies, their educational significance consists in the fact that they may typify social situations. Men's fundamental common concerns

---

[21] *Ibid.*, p. 14.
[22] Dewey, *Democracy and Education*, p. 361.

center about food, shelter, clothing, household furnishings, and the appliances connected with production, exchange, and consumption. Representing both the necessities of life and the adornments with which the necessities have been clothed, they tap instincts at a deep level; they are saturated with facts and principles having a social quality.

To charge that the various activities of gardening, weaving, construction in wood, manipulation of metals, cooking, etc., which carry over these fundamental human concerns into school resources, have a merely bread and butter value is to miss their point. If the mass of mankind has usually found in its industrial occupations nothing but evils which had to be endured for the sake of maintaining existence, the fault is not in the occupations, but in the conditions under which they are carried on. *The continually increasing importance of economic factors in contemporary life makes it the more needed that education should reveal their scientific content and their social value.* For in schools, occupations are not carried on for pecuniary gain but for their own content. Freed from extraneous associations and from the pressure of wage-earning, they supply modes of experience which are intrinsically valuable; they are truly liberalizing in quality.

Gardening, for example, need not be taught either for the sake of preparing future gardeners, or as an agreeable way of passing time. It affords an avenue of approach to knowledge of the place that farming and horticulture have had in the history of the race and which they occupy in present social organization. Carried on in an environment educationally controlled, they are means for making a study of the facts of growth, the chemistry of soil, the role of light, air, and moisture, injurious and helpful animal life, etc. There is nothing in the elementary study of botany which cannot be introduced in a vital way in connection with caring for the growth of seed. Instead of the subject matter belonging to a peculiar study called botany, it will then belong to life, and will find, moreover, its natural correlations with the facts of soul, animal life, and human relations. As students grow mature, they will perceive problems of interest which may be pursued for the sake of discovery, independent of the original direct interest in gardening—problems connected with the germination and nutrition of plants, the reproduction of fruits, etc., thus making a transition to deliberate intellectual investigations.

The illustration is intended to apply, of course, to other school occupations—woodworking, cooking, and on through the list. It is pertinent to note that in the history of the race the sciences grew gradually out from useful social occupations. Physics developed slowly out of the use of tools and machines; the important branch of physics known as mechanics testifies in its name to its original associations. The lever, wheel, inclined plane, etc., were among the first great intellectual discoveries of mankind, and they are none the less intellectual because they occurred in the course of seeking for means of accomplishing practical ends. The great advance of electrical science in the last generation was closely associated, as effect and as cause, with application of electric agencies to means of communication, transportation, lighting of cities and houses, and more economical production of goods. These are *social* ends, moreover, and if they are too closely associated with notions of private profit, it is not because of anything in them, but because they have been deflected to private uses:—a fact which puts upon the school the responsibility of restoring their connection, in the mind of the coming generation, with public scientific and social interests. In like ways, chemistry grew out of processes of dying, bleaching, metal working, etc., and in recent times has found innumerable uses in industry.

Mathematics is now a highly abstract science; geometry, however, means literally earth-measuring: the practical use of number in counting to keep track of things and in measuring is even more important today than in the times when it was invented for these purposes. Such considerations . . . indicate the possibilities—greater today than ever before—of using active occupations as opportunities for scientific study. The opportunities are just as great on the social side, whether we look at the life of collective humanity in its past or in its future. The most direct road for elementary students into civics and economics is found in consideration of the place and office of industrial occupations in social life. Even for older students, the social sciences would be less abstract and formal if they were dealt with less as sciences (less as formulated bodies of knowledge) and more in their direct subject-matter as that is found in the daily life of the social groups in which the student shares.

Connection of occupations with the method of science is at least as close as with its subject matter. The ages when scientific progress was slow were ages when learned men had contempt for the material and processes of everyday life, especially for those concerned with manual pursuits. Consequently, they strove to develop knowledge out of general principles—almost out of their heads—by logical reasonings. It seems as absurd that learning should come from action on and with physical things, like dropping acid on a stone to see what would happen, as that it should come from sticking an awl with waxed thread through a piece of leather. But the rise of experimental methods proved that, given control of conditions, the latter operation is more typical of the right way of knowledge than isolated reasonings. Experiment developed in the seventeenth and succeeding centuries and became the authorized way of knowing when men's interests were centered in the question of control of nature for human uses. The active occupations in which appliances are brought to bear upon physical things with the intention of effecting useful changes is the most vital introduction to the experimental method.[23]

[23]Dewey, *Democracy and Education*, pp. 234–237. (Italics added.)

1. The Role of Occupations in Providing Continuities Between Levels of the Educational System

The disjunctions between the different levels of the school system was another instance of the "separations" which pained Dewey. He felt that the concept of the occupations might provide themes to establish better transitions and integrations between the levels. In the Laboratory School, children were introduced to school with initial experiences in the occupations. Dewey and his colleagues felt that this provided an opportunity to capitalize on the educative possibilities of children's play. Creative play through the occupations helped establish continuities with home life and it introduced children to inquiry-oriented ways of learning. Play gave the child an early chance to experience learning as something that involved all facets of himself; his interests and goals, manipulative and expressive impulses, his ideas and their relation to actions.

In the elementary grades, projects centering on occupations became more elaborate and required longer time spans to complete. Techniques had to be cultivated, and study and research were required to carry projects through to completion. Play passed over into productive work. Word and number studies were needed to handle more ambitious undertakings; thus the need for the basic skills received a functional warranty. At the upper elementary levels, occupation-centered activities were related more systematically to studies in history, the sciences, or mathematics.

Dewey hoped that by the time students entered secondary school, they would have developed a personal sense that knowledge grows out of interaction with the world, and is a natural product of man's effort to cope with his situation in a physical and social environment. They would then be ready to begin a more systematic study of organized branches of knowledge.

> It is the time for formulating in generalizations the chief principles which are fundamental to various lines of study and for amassing the detailed stores of information which embody and illustrate the general principles. If the elementary period has been adequately lived through, so that the child has secured positive experience in all these directions, has had intellectual hunger kept alive and quickened, and has acquired working use of the main lines of investigation, there is no doubt that a very large amount of technical generalization and of special detail can be acquired in a comparatively short time.[24]

[24]John Dewey, "The University Elementary School: History and Character," *University Record*, Vol. 2, No. 8, (May 1897), p. 75.

Dewey's long-time desire to add a high school extension was not realized until the last year of his stay in Chicago. He had not had time to give serious attention to the problems at this level. His secondary plan was based on the incorporation of the Chicago Manual Training School with an academic study component. Experiences in the shops were to be available to all students, including the affluent, so that they might have firsthand knowledge of the techniques which underlay American industry, including concepts and scientific modes in their technical applications.

In higher education, Dewey viewed with mixed feelings the intrusion of a phalanx of new practical courses—journalism, commerce, agriculture, pharmacy, engineering, teaching, forestry, library science, and domestic arts. It was clear that these newcomers had appeared in response to the needs for higher technical proficiency. Yet Dewey sided in part with those humanists who deplored the pressures on universities to operate as service stations for special groups. He saw the danger that practical programs would take their shape solely according to the wishes of their sponsors and would serve simply to help students to "get on" in the system. If the new studies were not guided by liberal values, he said, they could become "narrow and hard, tending not merely to the utilitarian in its restricted sense, but even toward the brutal and inhuman."[25]

There was a counterdanger, however, in traditional concepts of liberal education which lacked relevance to the realities of a scientific-industrial age. If liberal studies were retained as esoteric remnants of an earlier life, they could become "genteel" and lose their vitality. The vocational element, on the other hand, if properly conceived might become the significant factor both personally and socially in the liberalization of a young person's life.

Dewey referred to remarks by President Arthur E. Morgan of Antioch College who had seen the educative potential in imaginative work-study programs.

> In so far as the liberal arts college stands for a perpetuation of the traditional conflict between vocation and culture, it seems doomed to play a constantly decreasing role in education. In a day when most of the occupations of men involved little more than manual skill and the repeated application of a few rule-of-thumb formulae, the concept of vocational as illiberal may have had some basis. With the modern applications of all the sciences and arts to vocations, and the successful scientific search for principles within the operations and purposes of

[25]John Dewey, *The Way Out of Educational Confusion* (Cambridge: Harvard U. Press, 1931), pp. 26–27.

the vocations themselves, it is no longer true. It is rapidly becoming a fact that the study within one's vocational preparations is an important means of freeing and liberalizing the mind. This being true, the inevitable trend in education is toward the thinning of the traditional educational wall between vocational and cultural. The liberal arts college will survive and render service in proportion as it recognizes this fact and brings its course of study, and administrative set-up into conformity with it.[26]

These remarks, Dewey said, applied with equal force to the high school.

He held that nothing was more important than to effect a genuine liberalization of study: but he rejected the tendency to accept automatically as "liberal" those subjects which campus scholars had traditionally labeled as Liberal Arts. When properly taught, these studies might be tremendlusly exciting in opening new perspectives. But they also could be sterile, trivial, and irrelevant. Just so with technical studies, which could be either narrow and limiting, or a means of stimulating intellectual inquiry and moral reflection. Nothing was guaranteed by the label; it all depended on the quality of the experience. There is a criterion, Dewey said, for deciding whether a given study is liberalizing:

> Any study is cultural in the degree in which it is apprehended in its widest possible range of meanings. Perception of meanings depends upon perception of connections of context. To see a scientific factor or law in its human as well as in its physical and technical context is to enlarge its significance and give it increased cultural value. Its direct economic application, if by economic is meant something having money worth, is incidental and secondary, but a part of its actual connections. The important thing is that the fact be grasped in its social connections—its function in life.[27]

Dewey's point was that the vocational component had tremendous potential for the liberalizing of experience. This recalls the particular meanings he assigned the terms "vocation," "occupation," "calling." One must recall his flexible usage of the terms.

Vocation in the sense of one's work could give an individual a sense of identity and meaningful relatedness to society:

> An occupation is the only thing which balances the distinctive capacity of an individual with his social service. To find out what one is fitted to do and to secure and opportunity to do it is the key to happiness. Nothing is more tragic than failure to discover one's true business in life, or to find that one has drifted or been forced by

[26] *Ibid.*, pp. 27–28.
[27] *Ibid.*, p. 336.

circumstances into an uncongenial calling. A right occupation means simply that the aptitudes of a person are in adequate play, working with the minimum of friction and the maximum of satisfaction.[28]

Thus Dewey supported the importance of school guidance efforts and educational programs designed to help students find themselves "vocationally." However, he opposed early and fixed determinations of vocational objectives, since these might hinder a subsequent change of directions, or merely reflect the needs of the local job market.

Dewey refused to limit the meaning of vocation, however, to its usual connection with one's job. People could have important "callings" or "vocations" beyond employment: for example, one's calling as a parent, or as a dedicated worker in community causes, or as an explorer of the arts. In such cases Dewey spoke of "vocations" as one's *central concerns*.

His rather complex point was that one's vocation, both in the sense of one's work and of one's central concerns, plays a critical role in self-fulfillment and continuing education.

> A calling is also of necessity an organizing principle for information and ideas; for knowledge and intellectual growth. It provides an axis which runs through an immense diversity of detail, it causes different experiences, facts, items of information to fall into order one with another. The lawyer, the physician, the laboratory investigator in some branch of chemistry, the parent, the citizen interested in his own locality, has a constant working stimulus to note and relate whatever has to do with his concern. He unconsciously from the motivation of his occupation, reaches out for all relevant information, and holds to it.[29]

In this sense the schools had an important function in helping people find their vocations, though in a genuinely humane community, all the other institutions would have this function too.[30]

---

[28] *Ibid.*, p. 360.

[29] *Ibid.*, p. 362.

[30] In a somewhat related fashion, Thomas F. Green argues that a central problem of our time is to help people find a work (or a calling) to accomplish. Green argues that because automation reduces many jobs to monotonous routines, we should stop identifying work with jobs. We should start viewing a person's work as including activities which enable him to be creative in, for example, community work or the arts outside his job role. See Thomas F. Green, *Work, Leisure, and American Schools* (New York: Random House, 1968).

Frederick Herzberg, on the other hand, asks us to explore the possibilities of reorganizing job life so that more people may experience a sense of meaningful vocation within thier employment roles. See Frederick Herzberg, *Work and the Nature of Man* (New York: World Publishing, 1966).

Dewey's rationale would suggest that both avenues should be pursued.

C. THE EDUCATIONAL MODEL IN PRACTICE: "SCHOOLS OF TOMORROW"

Dewey welcomed a variety of alternatives to traditional education and spotted and encouraged them throughout his career. At the same time he used his own frame of reference to evaluate and criticize them. As we have seen, his model was quite complex. Unwary observers who seize upon single aspects of Dewey's thought usually wind up doing violence to his central goals. This happened to the vocational educator, David Snedden, for example—who sought to make Dewey his ally on the basis of an incomplete reading.

What Dewey did favor may be clarified by examples of school programs he endorsed. While preparing for the writing of *Democracy and Education* in 1916, Dewey engaged in a parallel project with his daughter, Evelyn. Their purpose was to describe actual school practices which were consistent with their educational theory. Evelyn Dewey did most of the school visiting and then collaborated with her father in writing *Schools of Tomorrow*.[31]

A variety of experiments in both private and public schools in various parts of the country were reported. Mrs. Henrietta Johnson's "Organic Education" in Fairhope, Alabama; Caroline Pratt's Play School in New York City; and J. L. Meriam's Elementary School at the University of Missouri, were described as efforts which tapped children's interests and tried to make educative use of play and work activities. In public education, the Deweys said, "schools all over the country are finding that the most direct way of vitalizing their work is through closer relations with local interests and occupations."[32]

They endorsed the work of Mr. Valentine, principal of an all-Negro school in Indianapolis, which they described in a chapter called "The School as a Social Settlement." They said that Valentine was trying to turn his plant into "a true school; that is, a place where the children of the neighborhood shall become healthy, happy, and competent both economically and socially, and where the connection of instruction with the life of the community shall be directly recognized both by children and parents.[33]

The Deweys were particularly impressed with aspects of the Indianapolis program which were designed to improve family and neighborhood life through community involvement. The cooking program emphasized knowledge of nutrition and the skills of food purchasing

---

[31]John and Evelyn Dewey, *Schools of Tomorrow* (New York: Dutton, 1915).
[32]*Ibid.*, p. 205
[33]*Ibid.*, p. 207.

and preparation. Valentine had taken the initiative in establishing shops and sewing rooms which were open all day and at hours when adults could make use of the facilities with children. Local tailors, cobblers, carpenters, and plumbers were brought in to teach children how to use a variety of tools and repair personal and school equipment. They helped the boys convert an old house into club rooms and to rehabilitate a gymnasium for use by the whole community. Some children developed interests out of these experiences which they later followed into careers. Projects were planned jointly with participation of children, teachers, and parents. It was an example of the kind of communication and democratic procedure which could transform a neighborhood from a bit of geography into a self-directing community. It was the Community School idea in action—one of the creative innovations of the progressive era, and one which will surely be revived and extended again.[34]

In a section called "Education Through Industry," the Deweys reported on other urban experiments designed to help children become "intelligent in all the activities of their life, including the important one of making a living." Gary, Chicago, and Cincinnati were selected as examples.

The Deweys made an important qualification about industrial training. Most programs of industrial education, they said, had been tailored to meet the labor requirements of the two or three largest industries in the area. "The problem of general public-school education is not to train workers for a trade, but to make use of the whole environment of the child in order to supply motive and meaning to the [school] work."[35]

They felt that one of the best examples of using industry for *educative* purposes was the work of Henry Wirt in the steel-town of Gary. Wirt had made financial savings from his "platoon plan" of administration and used the money to introduce a variety of science laboratories and shops for carpentry, metal work, printing, forging, and home economics. Children worked under skilled craftsmen to make school repairs and to construct equipment or facilities needed in the schools. The school's power plant was used as a lab in which to demonstrate principles of heat and lighting to children working as helpers. The Deweys particularly liked the activities which brought children of all ages into actual working relationships. "The little children go into the shops as helpers and watchers much as they go into the science laboratories, and

---

[34]Years later, at the close of his career, Dewey gave his support to community school programs that were being imaginatively employed to rehabilitate the blighted lives of miners and hill country people in West Virginia and Kentucky. See Elsie Ripley Clapp, *The Use of Resources in Education* (New York: Harper, 1952). Dewey's introduction was his last published writing on education.

[35]*Ibid.*, p. 252.

they pick up almost as much theory and understanding of processes as the older children possess."

All children, whether college-bound or not, took a variety of shop courses.

> [The pupils] are not taking the courses to become carpenters, or electricians, or dressmakers but to find out how the work of the world is done. . . . To keep on growing [the child] must have work which exercises his whole body, which presents new problems, keeps teaching him new things, and thus develops his powers of reasoning and judgment. Any manual labor ceases to be educative the moment it becomes thoroughly familiar and automatic.[36]

When industrial education was kept genuinely educative, they argued that

> it is just as valuable for the man who works with his brain to know how to do some of the things that the factory worker is doing, as it is for the latter to know how the patterns for the machine he is making were drawn, and the principles that govern the power supply in the factory. In Gary the work is vocational in all these senses.[37]

Experiences in industrial education were thus felt to quicken interest in academic studies. Chemistry included the chemistry of cooking; botany and zoology made use of plants and animals from the school grounds; arithmetic included material relevant to shop problems; English teachers related their work to the skills of paragraphing, spelling, and punctuation needed in the printing shop; drawing included dress designing, house decoration, and pattern drawing for metal working.

The Deweys felt that the Gary program was effective in introducing the children of immigrant peasants to the realities and modes of thinking needed in industrial society. If pupils left school early, they were encouraged to return whenever they felt ready.[38]

The Deweys noted with favor, also, industrial education and related

---

[36] *Ibid.*, pp. 256–257.
[37] *Ibid.*, pp. 264–265.
[38] The Gary plan became something of a rage for a number of years. We lack a careful study to learn what happened to it. Like so many educational innovations, it seems to have become diluted and distorted when disseminated beyond the point of origin. Business efficiency enthusiasts seized on its "platoon system" aspects as a device for saving money. Wirt was brought to New York in 1914 as a midwest knight of school reform. The faddists forced a too-rapid spread of the idea and the Gary Plan foundered in the rough waves of New York politics. See Sol Cohen, *Progressives and Urban School Reform* (New York: Bureau of Publications, Teachers College, Columbia University, 1964), pp. 86–93.

Dewey commented on the situation: "All of the better informed of the friends of the now defunct Gary system in New York have been aware for some time that its success was fundamentally compromised if not doomed by the autocratic way in which it was formulated and imposed from above." John Dewey, "Public Education on Trial," *New Republic*, Dec. 29, 1917, p. 246.

202 — Philosophical Issues: Education and the Industrial State

reforms introduced into Chicago by Superintendent Ella Flagg Young, Dewey's former colleague in the Laboratory School. Among her other activities, Miss Young had waged a fierce battle against business groups who pushed for a separately administered system of trade training schools.[39] The Deweys commented in particular on the program in the new Lane Technical High School, where imaginative integrations were being effected between shop and academic work.

> A problem being set to a group of students, such as the making of a gasoline engine or a vacuum cleaner, the different elements in its solution are worked out in the different classrooms. For the vacuum cleaner, for instance, the pupils must have reached a certain point in physics and electrical work before they are capable of trying to make the machine, since each pupil becomes in a sense the inventor, working out everything except the idea of the machine. When they are familiar with the principles which govern the cleaner they make rough sketches, which are discussed in the machine shop and altered until the sketch holds the promise of a practical result. In mechanical drawing, accurate drawings are made for the whole thing and for each part, from which patterns are made in the pattern shop. The pupils make their own molds and castings and when they have all the parts they construct the vacuum cleaner in the machine and electrical shops. . . . The pupil does everything connected with its production himself, from working out the theory in the laboratory or classroom to screwing the last bolt. The connection of theory and practice not only makes the former concrete and understandable, but it prevents the manual work from being routine and narrow. When a pupil has completed a problem of this sort he has increased knowledge and power. He has tested the facts he learned and knows what they stand for in terms of the use the world makes of them; and he has made a useful thing in a way which develops his own sense of independent intelligent power.[40]

In Cincinnati, the Deweys found the cooperative work-study plan of "great suggestive value." They contrasted it with the typical continuation school, where dropouts of age fourteen or fifteen were put on jobs and then returned to the classroom a few hours each week for supplementary instruction. Continuation schools helped the young person who needed immediate employment; but, the Deweys added, "they do not give him that grasp of present problems and conditions which would enable him intelligently to choose the work for which he is best

[39]See also John T. McManis, *Ella Flagg Young and a Half Century of the Chicago Public Schools* (Chicago: McClurg, 1916).
[40]John and Evelyn Dewey, *op. cit.* pp. 277–278. (The reader will note that this is a classical example of the instrumentalist theory of knowing and learning in practice.)

suited.[41] The cooperative plan, on the other hand, was commended because it took advantage of the educational value of the important industries in the community. Two groups of students alternated: one was in school for a week while the other worked in factories or stores. The factory shops thus became school shops. The Deweys described the intention of Cincinnati educators to extend this plan into the program of the City College, so that engineering and architectural students might have experience in the machine shops and drafting rooms of the city, and domestic science students work as cooks or bookkeepers in the city's hospitals. Careful records were kept of students' progress in work situations as well as in school. Vocational guidance programs were related to these experiences.

Again the Deweys hammered home their point:

> The work is not approached from the trade point of view; that is, the schools do not aim to turn out workers who have finished a two years' apprenticeship in a trade and are to that extent qualified as skilled workmen for that particular thing. The aim is to give the pupil some knowledge of the actual conditions in trade and industry so that he will have standards from which to make a final intelligent choice.[42]

Programs like these incorporated various aspects of Dewey's rationale: the combination of theory with practice; the use of inquiry-oriented approaches which would give students a chance to act on their world and get feedback; the relation of study to out-of-school life; the integration of work project activities with academic conceptualization; the practice of democratic planning and participation. The programs neglected, however, to deal with value issues. As Dewey saw it, the habit of raising value questions about the consequences of industrial development was a matter of hard-headed practicality. The entire population, both workers and managers, had to get into the habit of evaluating the effects of industrialization. Technology was too powerful a force to be set loose without careful social monitoring.

Dewey remained alert to projects where education was a partner to community and socioeconomic reform. He looked overseas as well as at home. In 1926 he referred to the rural school reforms of the Mexican revolution as an ecucational renaissance. For the first time schooling was being extended to the Indians to free them from a condition of near-slavery. He visited rural schools which, he said, demonstrated "more of the spirit of intimate union of school activities with those of the community" than he had found anywhere else in the

---

[41] *Ibid.*, p. 280.
[42] *Ibid.*, p. 284.

world.[43] The Indians were experiencing human dignity and freedom for the first time, as the revolutionary government followed a policy of fostering cooperatively managed "small industries" to take the place of giant feudalistic or foreign capitalist holdings. Native arts and cultural traditions were renewed as the Indians began to gain control over their lives. Schools were beginning to function as an integral part of community life, combining a simple academic curriculum with programs featuring the agricultural and manual industries. Hygiene, physical education, and the arts were incorporated into general studies. The educational catchword was *escuela de accion*. Dewey said that while enthusiasm often out-distanced performance, there was no doubt about a tremendous lifting of national morale.

> Night schools are held in each building, to which come young men and women who are at work during the day; their eagerness to learn is symbolized in the fact that they walk miles to reach the place of instruction, each one bringing a candle by whose glimmering light the studying is done. And the Indian teachers work practically all day and then again in the evening for a wage of four pesos a day.[44]

All of this, said Dewey, confirmed an old belief of his that "backward" countries freed from long-established institutional patterns "could start afresh with the most educationally advanced countries."

In 1928 Dewey was invited to Russia to observe the new communist education. He was determined to rule out preconceptions as much as possible in order to look at the situation through his own eyes. He reported his observations in a series of articles for *The New Republic*. He met and talked with dedicated leaders of the new order like Schatzsky, director of an educational colony, and Lenin's widow, Krupskaya. His reports contain a mixture of positive, occasionally laudatory remarks with a foreboding that Russian idealism might become the victim of Marxist dogmatism.

Dewey saw that the distinctive features of Russian communist educational theory was the linking of all education procedures with a single, comprehensive social purpose. School activities were dovetailed with out-of-school experiences where economic practice was, in theory at least, based upon the cooperative principle. In the early 1920's, Dewey said, the Russians had borrowed the progreessive education idea that

[43]John Dewey, "Mexico's Educational Renaissance," *Characters and Events*, I, (New York: Holt, 1929), p. 367. (Originally in *The New Republic*, Sept. 22, 1926.)

For further comments on the rural school reforms sponsored by Mexican reform leaders like Vasconcelos and Saenz, a student of Dewey's, see Louise Schoenhals, "Mexican Experiment in Rural and Primary Education: 1921–1930," *Hispanic American Historical Review*, Vol. 44, No. 1 (1964), pp. 22–43.

[44]*Ibid.*

"work is the chief stimulus and guide to self-educative activity on the part of pupils, since such productive work is both in accord with the natural and psychological process of learning; and also provides the most direct road to connecting the school with social life, because of the part played by occupations in the latter."[45] The polytechnical rationale had been followed up with an emphasis on Marxist ideology as the only legitimate tool of social criticism. Education and work were united under the ideal of "socially productive labor." Dewey saw that there was at least a theoretical advantage to this unity, especially when compared to progressive educational efforts in capitalist countries that conflicted with the competitive drives in economic life.

Dewey took a favorable view of official Russian policy which stated that "at the basis of the whole program is found the study of human work and its organization: the point of departure is the study of this work as found in its local manifestations." He saw children experiencing "socially productive labor" through school-directed activities—helping to improve local sanitation and hygienic conditions, assisting in the campaign against illiteracy, taking care of younger children in clubs and on excursions, and participating in activities designed to increase economic production.[46]

Dewey allowed himself to be challenged by the spirit, and the provocative, fresh ideas of enthusiastic Russian educators. He was not a Marxist, however. He felt that Marxism was flawed at its core by pseudo-scientific claims of having discovered "laws" of history based on economic materialism. This dogmatism, together with rationalizations which conceded uncontrolled power to Communist party leadership, betrayed Marxist aspirations for effecting human liberation.[47] Stalinist terror of the 1930's was just around the corner. Dewey led an investigating committee to Mexico which exposed the murder of Trotsky by Stalin's agents, and he was branded a bourgeois reactionary by the Party faithful.

Enough has been said to make clear that Dewey rejected the idea that some single curriculum or school method alone was consistent with his educational philosophy. He sketched a complex picture of the human situation in our time and tried to identify features of institutional life and school practice which might foster creative life in an age of

---

[45]John Dewey, "New Schools For A New Era," *Characters and Events*, Vol. I, p. 414; see also pp. 378–431. (Originally in a series of articles for *The New Republic* from Nov. 14, 1928 to Dec. 19, 1928.)

[46]*Ibid.*, p. 417.

[47]See, for example, John Dewey, *Freedom and Culture* (New York: Putnam, 1939). Note especially Chap. 4, "Totalitarian Economics and Democracy. See also John Dewey, "Education and Social Change," *Social Frontier*, Vol. 3 (May 1937), pp. 235–238.

technology. Science and industry had the potential to tyrannize and corrupt human affairs or to act as forces for release and betterment. In the controversy over industrial education, Dewey centered his attention on these two faces of science, and asked that choices be made in terms of a full awareness of them.

10/Dewey and the Vocational Education Debate

> The question of industrial education is fraught with consequences for the future of democracy. Its right development will do more to make public education truly democratic than any other one agency now under consideration. Its wrong treatment will as surely accentuate all undemocratic tendencies in our present situation, by fostering and strengthening class divisions in school and out.[1]

The reader is by now aware that profound differences distinguished Dewey's views from those of the social efficiency vocationalists. Dewey was writing on the subject of industrial education as the century opened; he stepped up his efforts as state and federal legislation was being readied prior to 1917. We have already noted that he pointed to his version of industrial education as a major feature of educational reform in *Democracy and Education.*

Dewey's strategy was to describe the possibilities for imaginative educational uses of industrialism and to contrast these with wrong tendencies in the vocational education movement. In a 1916 article, "American Education and Culture," Dewey said

> To transmute a society built on an industry which is not yet humanized into a society which wields its knowledge and its industrial power in behalf of a democratic culture requires the courage of an inspired imagination.
>
> I am one of those who think that the only test and justification of any form of political and economic society is its contribution to art and science—to what may be called culture. That America has not yet so justified itself is too obvious for lament. . . . To settle a continent is to put it into order, and this is a work which comes after, not before, great intelligence and great art. . . . It means nothing less than the discovery of a method of subduing and settling nature in the interests of a democracy, that is to say of masses who shall form a community of directed thought and emotion in spite of being masses. That this has not been effected goes without saying. It has never been attempted

[1]John Dewey, "Some Dangers in the Present Movement for Industrial Education," *Child Labor Bulletin*, Vol. I (February 1913), p. 70.

before. . . . That the achievement is immensely difficult means that it may fail.[2]

Dewey assumed that the twentieth century would be a testing period revealing how Americans would respond to the pressures of an emerging technologism. Some, he said, would retreat to asylums and hospitals; some would be caught in "the meshes of a mechanical industrialism;" and others would commit themselves to the long fight to "subdue the industrial machinery to human ends until the nation is endowed with soul."[3]

In 1906, the year of the founding of NSPIE and the appearance of the Douglas Commission Report, Dewey published an assessment of the new stirrings over vocational education. The time had arrived, he said, to face not the question of "What shall the school do for industry?" but of "What shall industry do with the school?"

Business, said Dewey, was the dominating force in American life, affecting everything and everyone, whether educators were aware of it or not. The ideals and methods that controlled business "take possession of the spirit and machinery of our educational system." Pressures were strong to put the schools in the service of business interests—to introduce industrial education to promote the cause of American economic supremacy (to which end an emulation of German education was urged); to create a stable group of workers who would produce efficiently while becoming passive and contented under the reward of higher wages.[4]

These trends were reinforced, Dewey said, by the habitual ways in which business and educational leaders thought about education. They still thought in terms of a European tradition which from the time of Aristotle, distinguished "education" for the directive and leisured classes from "training" for the menial, servile masses. At present, said Dewey, the vast majority of children leave school at the end of the fourth or fifth grade—a pattern which until recently served industry's need for a large supply of unskilled labor. The school dropouts were taught little more than reading, writing, and 'rithmetic—a schooling which made them into nothing more than economically useful tools.

---

[2]John Dewey, "American Education and Culture," *Characters and Events*, II, 1929, p. 500. (Originally in *The New Republic*, July 1, 1916.) One is reminded of a comment by John Smith in *The Spirit of American Philosophy:* "The candor, the concern for fact, and the unwillingness to abandon an ideal merely because it is difficult to realize are traits which we must associate at once with the mind of Dewey."

[3]*Ibid.*, p. 501.

[4]See also John Dewey, "The Need of an Industrial Education in an Industrial Democracy," *Manual Training and Vocational Education*, Vol. 17 (February 1916), pp. 409–414; and "A Policy of Industrial Education," *The New Republic*, Vol. 1 Dec. 19, 1914), pp. 11–12.

They entered jobs which were routine, repetitive, and demeaning; and after a short while they became unfit for further special training. They were, moreover, relatively helpless to protest their plight, since they had been denied the kind of education which would equip them with "initiative, thoughtfulness, and executive force." Many businessmen were quite content with this arrangement, said Dewey. They demanded that schools stick to the three R's and attacked "fads and frills" —knowing full well that their own children would receive enriched experiences which they deplored for the masses.[5] The new trend in favor of vocationalism, Dewey maintained, derived from the fact that more complex industrial processes required a better trained work force.

From time to time, Dewey pinpointed specific dangers as the focus of his criticism. In an article for the *Child Labor Bulletin* written in 1913, he pointed to abuses arising from the new enthusiasm for vocational guidance. The tendency, he said, is to use a high-sounding phrase like "vocational guidance" for what is nothing more than a plan to find jobs for children under sixteen. These plans become mischievous or worse when they actually encourage young people to leave school to fill job openings in local industries.

Vocational guidance enthusiasts, he said, should encourage children to stay in school to get an education they could build on later; they should work to modify school programs by providing opportunities for students to have study experiences connected to the out-of-school environment; and they should seek to establish supplementary centers where young people could get advice and further ecucational experience aftr they took jobs.[6] He called for an alliance between educators and settlement house workers to counteract pressures for narrow training orientations. They should advocate community schools which might serve as centers for each neighborhood's social, artistic, and educational life. Such schools, open day and night, should offer avenues for exploration of personal interests or "callings," or for vocational self-improvement; they should stimulate the thinking and the skills necessary for social action.

As late as 1928, Dewey reported to the NEA that a study of NAM documents on education revealed that organization's inclination to give many reasons why large numbers of children should drop out of school. They pointed to the increases in high school enrollments in terms of

[5]See John Dewey, "Learning to Earn," *Education Today* (New York: Putnam, 1940), pp. 126–132. Originally in *School and Society* Vol. 5 (March 24, 1917), pp. 331–335, based on an address to the NEA.
[6]Dewey, "Some Dangers In the Present Movement for Industrial Education," pp. 69–70.

escalating costs. They charged that many of the public schools and colleges promoted socialism or bolshevism. Some manufacturers concluded that the best way to protect workers was to get them early into the factories, where they could be protected from subversive ideas.[7]

Dewey also followed closely the vocational education bills that were being considered by the state legislatures. In 1915, for example, he described an Indiana law as "a wrong kind." He endorsed comprehensive features of the law which included provision for agricultural and domestic education as well as industrial training; and he felt provision was rightly made for evening school programs and "continuation" schools. The latter provision was spoiled, however, by limiting state aid to instruction which was connected with a man's regular employment. The consequence, said Dewey, was that workers were denied the chance to change their minds, or to seize other work opportunities. Furthermore, provisions for full-time vocational schools specified that vocational programs should be open only to those who were already in that field of work or who indicated their intention to enter employment related to the specific training programs. The law was written to deny aid to schools giving general industrial or prevocational courses designed to help students explore career alternatives or to lay a broad base for future vocational decisions. Dewey said that the Indiana law was an object lesson in the kind of absurdity which could result when legislators rushed hurriedly into specific educational details without consulting intelligent school men.[8] The defensible alternative, Dewey argued, was for the states to pass statutes with only the broadest provisions, so that state Boards of Education could exercise discretionary powers in their execution. Such laws would permit necessary experimentation and could prevent the hobbling of schools by inflexible legislative prescriptions in a period of rapid social change. If State Boards of Education were weak the task was to strengthen them, rather than to attempt to administer schools by legislative enactment.

A. THE FIGHT AGAINST "THE DUAL SYSTEM"

In the years immediately prior to enactment of the Smith-Hughes law, Dewey concentrated his criticism on efforts to pass state and federal legislation which would establish separate systems of vocational schools alongside the general common school.

[7]John Dewey, "The Manufacturers' Association and the Public Schools," *Journal of the National Education Association*, Vol. 17 (February 1928), pp. 61–62.

[8] John Dewey, "Industrial Education—A Wrong King," *The New Republic*, Vol. 2 (Feb. 20, 1915), pp. 71–73.

One of the most notable battles was the struggle against the Cooley Bill in Illinois. It was formally presented to the legislature in 1914 and 1915 and triggered a bitter controversy before finally being defeated. Dewey joined educators, labor and Settlement House leaders, and other progressives in a concerted resistance to this bill. Support for the measure came from powerful segments of the business and manufacturing community and from vocational education leaders of the Prosser-Snedden persuasion.

The Cooley Bill proposed a separate State Commission of Education to administer all forms of vocational education for youth over age fourteen. Dewey quoted Mr. Cooley, an ex-Superintendent of Chicago Schools and a spokesman for the Chicago Commercial Club, as saying that the proper task of vocational schools was to provide "the direct training in vocational life of the youth who *must* leave the ordinary school at fourteen," aדd that "vocational education must be shaped to dovetail with the industry in which the group of pupils happened to be."[9] With this definition of vocational education, it is not surprising, said Dewey, to find Mr. Cooley arguing that the enterprise requires "different methods of administration, different equipment" from those of the unified school system.

Dewey said that proponents of the bill denied that the plan was designed to serve the interests of employers and argued that separate vocational schools would be more effective in meeting the needs of youth forced to leave school at fourteen. The plan, it was claimed, would raise the general level of industrial efficiency and thus benefit the whole community. Further, the interests of labor would be protected because labor representatives would sit on local and state advisory boards. One could assume the best of intentions in supporters of the bill, said Dewey, but still conclude the measure should be resolutely opposed.

The real issue, he insisted, was whether the school system would be split so that "a sharp line of cleavage shall be drawn as respects administrative control, studies, methods and personal associations of pupils, between schools of the traditional literary type and schools of a trade-preparatory type."[10] Dewey predicted a series of evil consequences if the bill were passed. It would, he said, divide and duplicate administrative machinery and thus lead to frictions and wastes of funds.[11] Secondly, at a time when industrialism was already polarizing class

---

[9] John Dewey, "Splitting Up the School System," *The New Republic*, Vol. 2 (Apr. 17, 1915), p. 284.

[10] *Ibid.*

[11] Dewey, "Some Dangers in the Present Movement for Industrial Education," pp. 70–71.

divisions, the separation of pupils along these lines would accentuate this tendency.

One of the ironies of the Illinois situation, Dewey thought, was that the Cooley law would split the schools just when urban education had begun to come alive under the leadership of Ella Flagg Young.

> More than half of the pupils in the high schools of Chicago today are engaged in "vocational" work. There are industrial centers in twenty elementary schools; were there funds they would have been established in twenty-six more. There are four or five schools for workers in the apprenticeship trades and preparations for three more. Under unified control, the pupils are kept in constant personal association with youth not going into manual pursuits; the older type of school work is receiving constant stimulation and permeation. Technical subjects are taught by practical men and women whose horizon and methods are broadened by contact with wider educational interests, while the teachers in the more theoretical subjects are brought into living touch with problems and needs of modern life which in the isolated state they might readily ignore.
>
> In short, a complete education system preserving the best in the old and redeeming the heritage of lively association with studies, methods, and teachers representing newer social needs, is in active development.[12]

It would not be surprising if a closer look revealed that Dewey, in the heat of argument, had given a rosier picture of Chicago's schools than the facts warranted. His statement does reveal, however, the aspirations he had for public school work.

In one more shot at Mr. Cooley, Dewey commended him for his report on "Vocational Education in Europe"—but charged him with violating his own analysis of the advice of Kerschensteiner, the Munich educational reformer. Cooley himself, said Dewey, had reported Kerschensteiner's insistence that all technical and trade work be taught in its scientific and social context and that industrial education be offered more for the sake of the citizen than of the manufacturer.

Cooley, Snedden, and Prosser all favored the dual plan of school administration but saw themselves as part of progressive reform. They were taken aback by Dewey's slashing attack.

Cooley, in a tempered reply, denied that his bill would interfere with reform movements in the public schools; after all, it did not involve elementary education. The whole purpose was to do for the two-thirds who dropped out after age fourteen what the high schools and universities had long been doing for the professional and managerial classes: "to

---

[12] *Ibid.*

supply, on the basis of the elementary school instruction, an application of science and art to the various occupations of men and women."[13] These new schools, said Cooley, would encourage the development of character, civic responsibility, and joy in work—absolute essentials for the happiness and self-respect of the individual. The decision to propose dual administration was made upon primarily practical grounds: experience had shown, Cooley said, that the people who had already allowed public education to become ineffectual were not capable of providing the leadership required for a reformed system. He concluded that "while I dislike to differ with Dr. Dewey on any question, I must insist that the argument is against him in this case."

David Snedden, who had been a student and colleague of Dewey at Columbia University, was stung to a sharper reply. Snedden began a two-page letter to *The New Republic* as follows:

> Sir: Some of us school men, who have profound respect for the insight of Dr. Dewey where the underlying principles of social organization and of education are under discussion, are somewhat bewildered on reading the contributions which he has recently made to *The New Republic*. Those of use who have been seeking to promote the development of sound vocational education in schools have become accustomed to the opposition of our academic brethren, who, perhaps unconsciously, still reflect the very ancient and very enduring lack of sympathy, and even the antipathy, of educated men towards common callings, "menial pursuits" and "dirty trades." We have even reconciled ourselves to the endless misrepresentations of numerous reactionaries and of the beneficiaries of vested educational interests and traditions. But to find Dr. Dewey apparently giving aid and comfort to the opponents of a broader, richer, and more effective program of education, and apparently misapprehending the motives of many of those who advocate the extension of vocational education in schools designed for that purpose, is discouraging.[14]

Snedden went on to say that, in his opinion, the question of so-called unit or dual control was not fundamental at all. A decision concerning the administration of vocational education was "merely one of securing the greatest efficiency." In order to decide the issue it was important to have a clear definition of vocational education: "vocational education is, irreducibly and without unnecessary mystification, education for the pursuit of an occupation."[15]

[13] Edwin G. Cooley, "Professor Dewey's Criticism of the Chicago Commerical Club and Its Vocational Education Bill," *Vocational Education*, Vol. 3 (September 1913), pp. 24–29.

[14] David Snedden, *The New Republic*, Vol. 3 (May 15, 1915), p. 40.

[15] *Ibid.*, p. 41.

He said that, like all thoughtful educators, he was of course in favor of liberal education; but that the question was what kind of training was proper for youth about to embark on wage earning. These young people had a right to the same kind of specific training which universities gave to those headed for professions. A boy of fourteen, said Snedden, will already have had a general education. He "should be able to concentrate his efforts largely in learning the occupation selected. It is not desirable to blend so-called liberal and vocational education at this period, it being always within the possibilities of the youth to continue in the regular or general elementary or high school if he so selects."

Snedden said that it was incredible that men acquainted with economic conditions should think that state-supported vocational education would be beneficial chiefly to employers. It was, in fact, designed for the hitherto neglected majority. Vocational programs would tend to their needs, and the whole society would benefit. Snedden said that candor required admission of the fact that business men were suspicious of the "so-called academic mind." "They feel assured neither of the friendliness nor of the competency of our schoolmasters in developing sound industrial education. For that reason they often favor some form of partially separate control, at least at the outset of any new experiment." To get best results, said Snedden, it is better to admit that "school men, however well intentioned, are apt to be impractical and to fail to appreciate actual conditions."[16]

If Snedden thought his letter would mollify Dewey, he was doomed to disappointment. Dewey replied that Snedden had simply failed to meet the heart of his argument, and he attempted to repeat it in one sentence: "I argued that a separation of trade education and general education of youth has the inevitable tendency to make both kinds of training narrower, less significant and less effective than the schooling in which the traditional education is reorganized to utilize the industrial subject matter—active, scientific, and social of the present day environment."[17]

Snedden's insistence on a narrow definition of vocational education designed for a specific segment of students was at loggerheads with Dewey's highly complex model aimed at a reformed education for all. Dewey said so. He refused to accept an identification of "vocation" with certain trades that could be learned before eighteen or twenty; and he rejected any conception of vocational education which did not have as its "supreme regard the development of such intelligent initiative, in-

16 *Ibid.*, p. 42.
17 *Ibid.*

genuity and executive ability as shall make workers, as far as may be, the masters of their own industrial fate."[18]

Dewey said that his difference with Snedden was not so much narrowly educational as it was profoundly social and political.

> The kind of vocational education in which I am interested is not one which will "adapt" workers to the existing industrial regime; I am not sufficiently in love with the regime for that. It seems to me that the business of all who would not be educational time-servers is to resist every move in this direction, and to strive for a kind of vocational education which will first alter the existing industrial system, and ultimately transform it.[19]

He challenged Snedden to indicate whether he favored substituting the dual features of the Cooley bill for the kinds of efforts to integrate liberal and industrial studies that were going on in Chicago and Gary. For whatever reasons, Snedden did not reply. The goals of the two educators were disparate, and it was probably just as well to let the issue rest.

B. DEWEY AND THE SMITH-HUGHES BILL

Dewey's misgivings about the Smith-Hughes bill were related to his growing doubts about proposals of the state legislatures for vocational programs. We have noted NSPIE's aggressive drive to get state and federal action to which Congress responded by creating in 1914 a Commission on National Aid to Vocational Education. Dewey commented on these developments in an article entitled, "A Policy of Industrial Education."[20]

He began by observing that citizens generally approved the notion that education in the United States ought to be "kept out of politics." Educators had accepted this dictum and, as a result, had played feeble roles in struggles over questions of national policy. This was evident, said Dewey, in the current drive for vocational education, in which public school men remained on the sidelines while nonpublic school groups took the initiative. Moreover, not one of the new Congressional Commission's five lay members was a professional educator. (The five, it may be noted, were active *vocational* education leaders, headed by Dr. Prosser.)

Dewey urged a "go slow" policy and expressed grave doubts about the drive for immediate solutions to educational problems. Educators

---

[18] *Ibid.*
[19] *Ibid.*
[20] John Dewey, "A Policy of Industrial Education," *The New Republic*, Vol. 1 (Dec. 19, 1914), pp. 11–12.

had not had time to think through how "the vocational" could become an imaginative aspect of general educational reform. The case for federal aid for vocational education was based instead on an ill-digested set of reasons aimed at serving needs of various interest groups. These included the demands of employers for more skilled workers; the fear of dropping behind in international commercial competition; the need to find a substitute for declining apprentice training; *and* the need for a more "vital" kind of instruction. The temptation to copy Germany was strong, but doing so would be a fatal mistake. American businessmen might envy the German arrangement, said Dewey; but they should recognize that such a school system perpetuates class divisions and eventually leads to an increased class conflict.

There were important reasons, said Dewey, why we should reject federal policies for education that were designed primarily to improve industrial efficiency rather than general education. Even the practical arguments put forward for special trade training ignored significant features of industrial development. The main problem was not to provide workers for the skilled crafts. These trades already had effective unions, with organized training programs and the strong resolve to avoid an oversupply of workers. The revolutionary factor and the heart of the problem, said Dewey, was the introduction of automatic machines, which reduced labor to highly specialized operations.

This meant, Dewey continued, that the only defensible approach was to incorporate a new kind of industrial education as part of general education reform whose aim would be to cultivate "industrial intelligence" throughout the population. While Dewey picked up a popular term, he insisted on giving it his own definition: the "initiative and personal resources of intelligence" which would enable the American worker to infuse existing industrial arrangements with democratic values. While we did not yet know fully how to accomplish this, Dewey said, preliminary efforts had been made in school systems like those of Gary and Chicago. "The aim has not been to turn schools into preliminary factories supported at public expense, but to borrow from shops the resources and motives which make teaching more effective and wider in reach."[21]

In 1917 Dewey was still trying to promote an understanding of his scheme for universal ' industrial education designed to promote industrial intelligence." It would aim at

> preparing every individual to render service of a useful sort to the community, while at the same time it equips him to secure by his own initiative whatever place his natural capacities fit him for. . . . Instead

[21] *Ibid.*, p. 12.

of trying to split schools into two kinds, one of a trade type for children whom it is assumed are to be employees and one of a liberal type for the children of the well-to-do, it will aim at such a reorganization of existing schools as will give all pupils a genuine respect for useful work, an ability to render service, and a contempt for social parasites whether they are called tramps or leaders of "society." Instead of assuming that the problem is to add vocational training to an existing cultural elementary education, it will recognize frankly that the traditional elementary education is largely vocational, but that the vocations which it has in mind are too exclusively clerical, and too much of a kind which implies merely ability to take positions in which to carry out the plans of others. It will indeed make much of developing motor and manual skill, but not of a routine or automatic type. It will rather utilize active and manual pursuits as the means of developing constructive, inventive and creative power of mind. It will select the materials and the technique of the trades not for the sake of producing skilled workers for hire in definite trades, but for the sake of securing industrial intelligence—a knowledge of the conditions and processes of present manufacturing, transportation and commerce so that the individual may be able to make his own choices and his own adjustments, and be master, so far as in him lies, of his own economic fate. It will be recognized that, for this purpose, a broad acquaintance with science and skill in the laboratory control of materials and processes is more important than skill in trade operations. It will remember that the future employee is a consumer as well as a producer, that the whole tendency of society, so far as it is intelligent and wholesome, is to an increase of the hours of leisure, and that an education which does nothing to enable individuals to consume wisely and to utilize leisure wisely is a fraud on democracy. So far as method is concerned, such a conception of industrial education will prize freedom more than docility; initiative more than automatic skill; insight and understanding more than capacity to recite lessons or to execute tasks under the direction of others.[22]

Neither Congress nor the people were of a mind to heed such talk. By 1917, the urgent need to increase military production provided the special motivation required to spur federal action. Congress and the President gave Charles Prosser and his colleagues the measure for which they had worked so long and hard.

[22] Dewey, "Learning to Earn," pp. 131–132.

11/*The Value and Policy Issues*

Frank Tracy Carlton was right, of course, in his statement to the NEA in 1910 that "industrial organization quietly forces its peculiar impress upon each and all." Our story has shown that all sectors of American society experienced culture shock in their contact with technology. The interest groups with a stake in educational policy were torn by value dilemmas which were reflected in the two philosophies of education that came into being in response to the industrial education movement: the social efficiency philosophy of David Snedden and Charles Prosser and the experimentalism of John Dewey.

Both philosophies agreed that traditional schooling was failing in urban America. Compulsory school attendance laws confined children to classrooms for years of verbal recitations on dull, standardized textbooks. The school and its youthful population were "isolated from life." Children chafed under classroom conditions which denied them the chance to explore and actively discover the contours of the real world. They fled school in large numbers despite endless administrative efforts to induce them to stay.

Both philosophies agreed that vocationalism as affected by science and technology ought to play a prominent role in a reformed education. Their conception of the form that vocationalism should take, however, and their ideas of how it should be related to the larger society, differed sharply.

Pedagogically, Snedden and Prosser articulated the position that a straightforward set of specific skill training programs should be added as an overlay to academic studies. Such a curriculum would be the public school equivalent of professional training in the universities, and it would be concentrated at the point which preceded the student's entry into work. The content of training programs would be derived from a study of the needs of industry.

To Snedden and Prosser, it seemed apparent that the way for all Americans to serve their own best interests was to retool public schools to meet the needs of the nation's fabulously productive economic machine. The social efficiency philosophy assumed that the goals of increased productivity, material wealth, and social power represented the culmination of human well-being. In this view Snedden and Prosser were merely expressing one of the major articles of faith of the American people. As Samuel Hays observed in his comments on life in the United States in 1914,

> The American people subordinated religion, education, and politics to the process of creating wealth. Increasing production, employment, and income became the measure of community success, and personal riches the mark of individual achievement.[1]

It must be acknowledged, however, that vocational leaders like Charles Prosser spoke to a real and important problem. They had the imagination and energy to develop the rationale for manpower training programs to replace the outdated apprenticeship tradition. They brought into the open a set of complex and critically important questions: Which training programs should be offered? By whom? For whom? At what levels and for what age groups? Such questions are essential to the functioning of the technological society; they must be faced constantly and answered anew as this era unfolds.

The weakness of the early proponents of vocational education was the narrowness of their vision. They wanted to downgrade considerations other than the development of efficient training programs. They defined themselves so that they literally were trainers rather than educators. This led them to miss the significance of the underlying revolution in science and technology that was transforming life, and prevented them from seeing the potential use of technological and vocational studies to bring reform and relevance to general education.

The passion for practicality of the early vocationalists ultimately flawed even their conceptions of vocational training. Prosser's style of designing detailed training programs to meet specific industrial needs was reflected in the features of the Smith-Hughes law and the mode of administering it. Such specificity handicapped vocational education from attaining the flexibility required to meet the demands of fast-moving technical and social change. Vocational education became marked by a quality of separatism as its leaders remained suspicious of collaboration with general educators. Parochial attitudes resulted, and vocational experiences tended to be limited to young people headed for immediate employment in industry. Federal legislation was drawn so that narrowly defined vocational training could be funded; experiments

---

[1] Samuel P. Hays, *The Response to Industrialism* (Chicago: U. of Chicago Press, 1957), p. 12.

aimed at effecting interesting integrations between liberal and vocational studies were excluded.

John Dewey, the foremost educational philosopher of the time, brought a different perspective to the debate. He had relatively little to say on the question of how to develop effective manpower training programs, a matter which dominated the attention of the vocationalists.

He was motivated by another concern—that the quality of human experience was being changed by the advent of science, technology, corporate-industrialism, and urbanism, and that these developments contained potentials for debasing and dehumanizing life and for undermining the ideals of the democratic dream. He was convinced that only the most far-reaching economic, social, and educational reform could turn these trends toward human good. Dewey took on the task of delineating what he thought was the nature of the modern challenge: what the dangers were and what was needed in the way of institutional reconstruction. He took the position that major philosophical questions were at issue "in discussion of the proper place and function of vocational factors in education." Dewey saw, for example, the strong temptation of Americans to copy the German technocratic system, which chose unquestioningly to put schooling at the service of material gain and national power. He joined those who chose to resist such moves. He also rejected the position of those intellectuals who viewed science and technology as intrinsically alien to humane values.

A distinctive feature of Dewey's philosophy was his conviction that cultural renewal could be engendered from within the very system of science and technology which threatened men. Since he thought that necessary institutional change depended on man's developing new insights and attitudes, he assigned a pivotal role to education. His ambitious plan was to employ an interpretation of science, together with a reconstituted view of vocation, as the means for a general reform of education.

Dewey differed from those who insisted that science and technology lead inevitably to dehumanization and estrangement, because he saw scientific thought as part of an evolving human experience. Scientific thinking was a form of learning which had grown out of the history of man's interaction with the world. It was a form of learning which had enabled men to reconstruct and extend their understanding of nature and of themselves. Dewey also assumed that the attitudes and habits intrinsic to scientific inquiry could be generalized and made available to men everywhere: the habits of thinking hypothetically, of testing conjectures against experience, of freely exchanging results and conclusions, of creating communities tolerant of maverick ideas and life styles as prerequisites to further insights and growths. In short, Dewey found congruence between the values of the scientific community and those cherished by the democratic tradition. This position might seem hopelessly dated and naive to many as they witness the deep disillusionment with and violent rejection of science and technology by influential intellectuals and the young of radical persuasion.

The fact that Dewey's interpretation of the positive possibilities of science can still be convincing to humanistic educators is illustrated by comments on Dewey by George Dennison, a pioneer in the modern Free School movement.

> Dewey stressed again and again . . . that it was not the external procedures of empirical science that needed to be adopted, but the dynamics between science and experience. Science organizes experience in a unique, and uniquely imitable, way. It cannot afford rigidity, or merely rhetorical reverence, yet it builds upon the past. It is instrumental, wholly alive to the present, yet it is open to the future and is no enemy of change. Free thought is its essence, yet it is disciplined by its devotion to emergent meaning. It places the highest value upon ideas, cannot function without them, defines them scrupulously, yet never enshrines them into final truths. It is always collaborative. Egotism, vanity, the power lusts of the individual will—all these are chastened by the authority of truth and the demonstrable structure of the natural world. These were the attributes Dewey cited in proposing empirical science as a model for the social effort we call education.[2]

And Paul Goodman in 1969 called for a social reformation in which our institutions would "return to the pure faith"—to the authentic values of science—prudence as to consequences, ecological concern, and decentralized modes of work and community living. He reminded his readers that it was on such values that "John Dewey devised a system of education to rear pragmatic and experimental citizens to be at home in the new technological world rather than estranged from it."[3]

In order to make the theoretical model operational, Dewey drew upon the concept of vocation. He saw possibilities for changing the dynamics of school practice through imaginative use of "the vocational aspects of education." The idea of establishing connections between the concepts of science and of vocation still *seems* strange. But Dewey's effort is understandable if we recall once again his commitment to an evolutionary view of human experience. In this view, men were related

---

[2] George Dennison, *The Lives of Children* (New York: Random House, 1969), p. 248.
[3] Paul Goodman, "Can Technology be Humane," *New York Review*, Nov. 20, 1969. pp. 27–34.

to the rest of nature through their work—through their basic patterns of producing what was required for survival and growth. As Dewey saw it, each change in the mode of production or work form led to transformations in the total patterns of culture. It was through vocations that men engaged in their basic interaction with nature and with each other. Thought, feeling, and action were combined through vocations, and patterns of human relations and communication were established. Theory was wedded to practice in the mechanical and social techniques developed to get the work of the world done and in the pursuit of personal interests passionately held. The new education which Dewey projected was to be permeated with humane conceptions of science, art and vocation.

In actuality, public education repudiated both the educational approach recommended by John Dewey and the policies of social efficiency urged by Snedden and Prosser. The nation produced as a compromise the comprehensive secondary school which promised both to preserve the egalitarian values of the common school tradition and to satisfy the skill requirements of industrialism. The actual performance of the schools demonstrated the strength of the pressures of the technocratic system. The use of ability tracks and differentiated courses tended to reflect and preserve the social class ordering of society. Prosser's kind of vocationalism isolated vocational training from academic courses. Imaginative integrations of liberal with vocational studies which might have served to enliven each were not effected. Students in "voc. ed." tended to move in a world separate from classmates headed for the university.

Technology has flourished in America for more than half a century since the passage of Smith-Hughes. Yet as we approach the bicentennial anniversary of the republic, we appear to be on the verge of social breakdown. In spite of a largely successful quest for material gain, Americans have failed to demonstrate that they can create a humane social order. Technological waste poisons the environment. Sensibilities are violated by the visual ugliness of our communities and by the cheap deceits of the advertising industry. Racist hatreds erupt into social conflict. Bitter differences over involvement in foreign wars alienate youth from their elders. In the major cities, more than half of all secondary-age students still choose to leave before completing high school. Disaffection has spread to the young of the suburbs, who question the life style of their parents. In their confusion, the youth pathetically turn for relief to drugs or to strange cults of the irrational. Their hunger is for a civilization which is worthy of allegiance.

The compelling question of our time remains whether it will be possible to humanize life under technological conditions: whether democratic traditions of responsible participation can be revitalized, and whether individuals can attain a sense of personal meaning under conditions of the urban-industrial society.

Evidence of our willingness to reorder priorities will be revealed in ideas we generate for the education of our children. There is no better indication of the real values of a people than the kinds of schooling they create for their youth.

The temptation to proceed by seeking greater efficiency through a technocratic model, adding a variety of well-financed manpower training programs to traditional school studies, will remain strong. Such approaches enable us to stay within established routines and to fulfill the skill needs of industry and business. One of the critical tests of our intentions will be our answer to an important federal policy question: Will federal funding be limited to vocational training in the narrower sense, or will it be broadened and extended to include experiments and practice at all levels in which imaginative use is made of the "vocational aspects" of study in relation to general or liberal education?

The latter approach, in the Deweyan tradition, might indicate that we are ready to scrutinize the quality of our social life in terms of our espoused humane-democratic traditions. To believe that the answers to our educational problems can be found intact in Dewey's philosophy is absurd. His was a loose system with puzzling ambiguities. There is no single answer available to us now, and we would be better off if we gave up the search for one. We ought to take seriously the advice to "let a thousand flowers bloom." What can be said with confidence is that Dewey's thought was the most serious American philosophical effort to establish humanistic connections between education, science and technology, and the democratic ideal. It might be fruitful once again to reflect upon this part of our intellectual heritage.

12/The Technological and the Liberal in General Education: Examples from Contemporary School Practice

One of the major challenges as we enter the last quarter of the twentieth century will be to create life styles which will overcome the divorce of technology from humanistic conerns. A task for educators in all countries will be to create imaginative approaches which integrate science and technology with liberal study. This is not an easy point of view to explain. Two major traditions lead us to think of the technological and vocational as separate from liberal education: The technocratic tradition thinks in terms of training programs whose legitimate purpose is solely to serve the efficiency needs of industry, business, and government; classical humanist traditions define the technological as a dehumanizing evil to be kept away from general education as long as possible.

The materials which follow describe contemporary educational programs in which new tries are being made to integrate the technological and the liberal. They show that such approaches may be made at every level from the primary grades through the university. Included are "The Technology for Children Project" for elementary (K–6) children in the Trenton, New Jersey, area; the "American Industries Studies" programs developed for junior high schools at the Ohio State University and Stout State University, Menomonie, Wisconsin; and interdisciplinary senior high school projects sponsored by the Center for Technological Studies of San Francisco State College.

No one yet has brought them together in a unified way. The prospect remains for some urban area to take on that interesting challenge.

224

A. THE NEED FOR DESIGNING SCHOOL PROGRAMS WHICH INVOLVE INTERACTION OF CLASSROOM STUDY WITH THE "REAL WORLD"

We may not understand completely the new mood of the young but several aspects are clear. Large numbers of students from all social classes are expressing discontent with their schooling. Many of their feelings such as their distrust of authority, their feelings of the irrelevance of classroom talk, their scepticism about textbook learning derive from their bitter reaction to the Vietnam War and their anger about the ways adults have handled it. The roots of their disaffection are, of course, much more complex, Some obvious factors from the nature of life in the technological society contribute: (1) Young people have been exposed to the multifaceted stimulation of the media and many have traveled widely in the United States and abroad. In the face of such experiences, the classroom props of the bland textbook, "discussion," and unending test-giving become less and less convincing. (2) The demands for a more highly trained work force have caused us to embrace a goal of universal free education for at least two years beyond the high school. As a consequence we move toward a policy of holding our youth in classrooms until they are well into their twenties. As many students see it the lengthening of the school process does not result in providing them with experiences appropriate to their needs and abilities, but becomes simply "more of the same." In their eyes this means being given assignments that are trivial, being tested endlessly, and being certified in order to be made socially useful. They feel that they are denied the chance to play meaningful roles in the larger society and denied opportunity to have control over significant aspects of their lives. (3) The sheer size and style of the school operation makes many students feel that they are being processed as objects. The school routine itself begins to come through as oppressive. (4) The most disaffected have come to feel that basic life satisfactions cannot be found in institutions of the corporate society. They seek to create new life styles outside the system. Let us assume also that there is oversimplication in their complaints. Let us assume that their disaffection cannot be ignored. When at their best, the young are making a call for a schooling that will be related more meaningfully to the real world, that will help them experience themselves as whole persons, and that will help American society to take seriously its oft-repeated allegiance to humane values.

We must disabuse ourselves of the notion that there are simple answers. My own hunch is that we should encourage more plurality of efforts. We have to find our way by projecting imaginative ideas, by acting on them, and learning as we go. It is in that spirit that I describe some school programs which seem promising.

B. SCHOOL PROGRAMS

1. Technology for Children Program—Elementary Level, Trenton, New Jersey, Suburban and Inner-City Areas

A basic feature of this program is its assumption that the elementary classroom should be transformed into a "responsive environment"—a place where children have a chance to manipulate, construct and interact with a broad range of materials while learning. Its designers note that before coming to school, children explore their environment with all of their senses: auditory, tactile, visual, kinesthetic, olfactory, gustatory, etc. Compared to the varied set of interactions in the out-of-school environment the classroom may be experienced as restrictive, adult-centered, dull, limited largely to verbal activities.

The program's rationale assigns to the school the task not only of establishing continuity with the child's earlier activities, but of extending experiences through contacts with realities in the larger society. Science-technology is seen as a major transformer of the quality of modern life. A critical task of modern education is to help the young gain insights and qualities of mind to enable them to live in the technological era.

Technology is viewed as a product of man's thinking, and as an extension of his efforts to deal effectively with his material world. Its power can be used to debase life or for human good. The program rejects the notion that an adequate understanding of the rich complexity of the technological society can be attained primarily by descriptive chapters in books. The classroom is turned into a place where children can have direct experiences with materials, tools, techniques, and modes of thought represented in technology.

A deliberate effort has been made to avoid creation of prescribed structures for the use of the materials. Teachers are encouraged to be flexible and imaginative in discovering ways to utilize materials in connection with other studies in the elementary currciculum. Grants from the Ford Foundation have made it possible to provide $600 "classroom kits" of tools and equipment for teachers who volunteer to work in this way. Summer workships are provided to help teachers gain confidence in moving in the new direction, and supervisory consultants are made available during the year. In the workshops teachers gain experience with the kinds of materials and activities they will be exploying in the classroom. Random examples include making paper, printing, use of simple jigsaw, and other power-driven tools; experiments with electricity, refrigeration, exploration of the insides of clocks, cameras, telephones, crystal radio sets, and hydraulic brake systems.

I visited classes in which students were using some of these techniques in connection with units on map making and transportation in addition to employing them in science-oriented projects. The program encourages an atmosphere of freedom in which individuals or small groups may develop special-interest projects. Children seem to respond with enthusiasm to the opportunities presented. I remember vividly the look of satisfaction on the faces of several black boys in a ghetto school when they had succeeded in sawing through a board more or less according to plan.

The out-of-school environment becomes a well-spring of information. During a unit on refrigeration one class visited a local refrigerator factory and watched the assembly-line process from beginning to end. It could be seen as an extension of their own simplified explorations in class.

Human relations learnings are intrinsic to classrooms which require children to cooperate in handling recalcitrant materials or tools. In this kind of situation teachers may be experienced as guides and helpers in a warm, supportive atmosphere. The good teachers learn the difficult discipline of restraining their impulses to intervene except when absolutely necessary.

This approach is not without problems. The right resources have to be provided and teachers need special training and sensitive supervision to overcome their insecurities. It is important to note that this program has been tried only with teachers who volunteered to enter it. Like a lot of other good ideas in education it could be killed if expanded rapidly on a mass basis.

2. The American Industries Projects

American Industries Projects have been developed at the Ohio State University and Stout State University with special reference to the junior high school level. Essentially they involve a complete rethinking of industrial arts as general education. They stemmed from a realization that American students are ill-informed about the industrial system, and that traditional industrial arts program with emphasis on a few hand-skill techniques, such as wood and metal working, are inadequately designed to remedy the situation.

Because of the complexity and diversity of modern industry a decision was made to create a conceptual structure that would reveal activities basic to all industries. The conceptual framework was developed with the collaboration of specialists in areas such as industrial design, engineering, personnel management and psychology. The model calls attention to features and processes of industry like: the use of energy and materials, production design, modes of construction, merchandising, cost accounting, research, and the organization of personnel.

Students are given opportunities to "learn by doing." Students study the conceptual analysis of industry and follow through with an industrial project conducted by themselves. In the Nova schools of Dade County, Florida, I saw an eighth-grade group at work on a project in which students manufactured and sold desk nameplates and megaphones for use at school sports events. They developed the engineering design for manufacturing the products with working drawings and prototype models. One committee took responsibility for the financial records, another worked on operation control problems including the use and training of personnel. Students procured the materials, used tools and power-driven machinery in an assembly-line type of production, and conducted inspections on the quality of the product. They worked out advertising and sales techniques. Students invested their own money, sold in the school market, and took the losses or profits.

More students apply for admission to the courses than can be accommodated. A check with a number of suburban parents brought comments to the effect that they found their children spontaneously engaged in hours of talking and planning for the projects—"It gives them a chance to do something that they have control over."

At Nova these courses, as general education, are open to all students and serve a number of useful functions for guidance purposes. Teachers in related areas such as mathematics, science, social studies and English are exploring possibilities for integrating their subjects with the industrial projects.

3. Programs of the Center for Technological Education— San Francisco Bay Area

The Center for Technological Education of San Francisco State College gives guidance for some forty interdisciplinary senior high school programs in the greater San Francisco Bay area.

These programs, begun in the early sixties, grew from an awareness that large numbers of students of average ability (IQ's 90–115) were bored by traditional schooling and were doing poorly or dropping out. While such students were leaving school a growing need was developing for more and more persons with at least two years of education beying the high school. Efforts to understand the situation led to several conclusions: (1) Students did not see the significance of subjects studied without relation to each other, yet the contemporary world of work requires persons who can use language, mathematics, science, and human relations skills in an integrated way; (2) Students were not motivated by classroom approaches limited to verbal exercises; they wanted to be active manipulators and doers in projects that would relate school work to community life. A decision was made to design new curricula which would correlate several academic studies with experimental activities in lab-shop settings and in the community.

The Richmond Pre-Tech program is an example. In order to overcome the isolation of subjects a team of teachers was formed—in this case from English, physics, mathematics and the technological laboratory-shop. Instead of presenting teachers with a preestablished curriculum they were brought together in two summer workshops to develop their own tentative plans of work. Central concepts from science or technology were identified and plans were made to relate these in ways designed to improve communications and mathematical skills. A distinctive feature was an insistence that the team have time for daily planning meetings so that projects could be designed and modified in process. A unit on heat, for example, was tentatively scheduled for three weeks but actually ran for eleven weeks. In the unit, apparatus was constructed in the tech-lab to conduct experiments; the study of heat in physics was related in mathematics to first-degree equations; the English teacher helped students prepare written and oral reports.

Teaching teams are granted considerable autonomy and are encouraged to develop projects in depth with a stress on individual and group interests—rather than on cursory coverage of a long list of topics. It must be emphasized that the approach is one of general education rather than vocational education. The technological laboratory provides opportunities for students to *apply* theoretical knowledge. It is not craft-training centered. Special efforts are made to arrange for field trips to industrial laboratories, government experiment stations, or industrial plants. On some occasions students spend as much as a week on special work projects in one of these situations.

The Pre-Tech program happens to have an emphasis which points its students toward the middle-level technician training programs of the local community colleges. But many other kind of programs using a similar rationale can and do exist. There is, for example, an interdisciplinary program involving Social Studies, math and English at the San Lorenzo High School, and a program in Food Education and Service Technology in Oakland. In the Oakland program, science, math, and English are related to a home economics laboratory. An advisory committee with representatives from local businesses and unions has been established.

The San Francisco programs have concentrated on under-achieving students of average ability. The rationale, however, could easily be adapted as a motivating device for students with college-level potential.

Imaginative educators might see possibilities for bringing together suburban and inner city students on common projects.

Such programs are based on concepts of learning consistent with
the Deweyan tradition and with more recent psychological studies of
the developmental needs of the young. For example, Erik H. Erikson
in *Identity: Youth and Crisis* refers to critical stages in the development
of healthy personalities. For the very young child it is essential that he
acquire a sense of basic trust in people and the world. For the elementary age youngster the critical task is to develop a feeling of personal
competence. As the child comes to school, says Erikson,

> He is eager to make things, to share in constructing and planning.
> . . . Children . . . want to watch and imitate people representing
> occupations which they can grasp—firemen and policemen, garden-
> ers, plumbers and garbage men. . . . This is socially a most decisive
> stage. Since industry involves doing things besides and with others, a
> first sense of division of labor and of differential opportunity—that is,
> a sense of the technological ethos of a culture—develops at this time.
> Therefore, the configuration of culture and the manipulations basic to
> the prevailing technology must reach meaningfully into school life,
> supporting in each child a feeling of competence—that is, the free
> exercise of dexterity and intelligence in the completion of serious tasks
> unimpaired by an infantile sense of inferiority. This is the lasting basis
> for cooperative participation in productive adult life.[1]

Erikson reminds us of an ancient educational maxim—children
need to have visceral as well as verbal experiences—they need to have
opportunities to get hold of their world manipulatively. Erikson argues
that if children miss the chance to gain a sense of competence in these
ways it may have crippling effects on subsequent development.

All of the programs which I described engage children or youth in
problem-oriented projects. Classrooms are transformed into situations
where children are made to respond to the challenges of a stimulating
environment. Students must do things to get answers. They must work
cooperatively and communicate constantly with each other. As in the
integrated curriculum projects in California, students are forced to
work so that knowledge from mathematics, science, English, and
laboratory situations are interrelated. Students work on scaled-down
problems which illustrate the basic dynamics of complex social institutions. Field experiences become an intrinsic part of basic studies.

Erikson also points out that as technological needs put more time
between early school life and eventual work, it puts more of a strain on

---

[1] Erik H. Erikson, *Identity: Youth and Crisis* (New York: Norton, 1968), pp. 122–127
et passim.

the struggle for identity of adolescents. If youth lack clarity about vocational goals and feel they are not gaining competencies required to "make it" in the real world, they are forced to seek identity in the ideological trends of the time.

> In general it is the inability to settle on an occupational identity which most disturbs young people. To keep together they temporarily over-identify with the heroes of cliques and crowds to the point of an apparently complete loss of individuality.[2]

The programs I have described are *not* vocational education in a training sense, but they put students in contact with a wide range of occupations and adult workers. As such they convey to students a sense that teachers and schools are anxious to help them with their personal search for vocation. The programs provide a basis for realistic guidance, and for more specific vocational or professional training beyond the high school. In addition they provide opportunities for students to learn by interacting with a variety of adults engaged in work in the real world. Such approaches counter one of the depressing features of mass schooling—the isolation of students with age mates and a handful of teachers in classrooms.

4. Other Examples

In order to show that these examples of educational practice for integrating liberal and technical studies are not parochial American ideas, we choose to add a quotation from Sir Eric Ashby's *Technology and the Academics*.[3] Sir Eric argues that the study of technology at the University level could "become the cement between science and humanism."

> A case could be made, therefore, for including technology among the ingredients of a liberal education. But technology in universities could be made to play a far more important part than this: it could become the cement between science and humanism. Far from being an unassimilated activity in universities, it could become the agent for assimilating the traditional function of the university into the new age. For technology is inseparable from men and communities. In this respect technology differs from pure science. It is the essence of the scientific method that the human element must be eliminated. Science does not dispense with values but it does eliminate the variability of human response to values. It concerns itself only with phenomena

[2] *Ibid.*, p. 132.
[3] Sir Eric Ashby, *Technology and the Academics: An Essay on Universities and the Scientific Revolution* (London: Macmillan, 1958), pp. 81–85.

upon which all qualified observers agree. It describes, measures, and
classifies in such a way that variation due to human judgment is eliminated. Unlike science, technology concerns the applications of science
to the needs of man and society. Therefore technology is inseparable
from humanism. The technologist is up to his neck in human problems
whether he likes it or not. Take a simple example: the civil engineer
who builds a road into a new territory in tropical Africa. He may assert
that it is not his business to take into account the effect his road will
have on primitive villages up-country; but his road is in fact a major
experiment in social anthropology. He does not need to be a professional anthropologist, but he cannot afford to be utterly ignorant of the
implications of his work. He is a technologist, not a pure scientist: the
social consequences of his work are therefore an integral part of his
profession. Take another example from one of the most ancient tech-
nologies: medicine. Chemotherapy and preventive medicine and con-
traceptives between them have enormously altered the pattern of
family life. The next generation will inherit from us a surplus of elderly
people. This situation sets problems which have given rise already to
a new subject called gerontology. Now the problems of gerontology
are not merely scientific; they involve some of the perennial issues of
humanity—family affection, group loyalty, and social justice. The practitioner in social medicine is a technologist: he cannot repudiate these
involvements.

What, then, is missing in a scientific or technological education?
It is not a smattering of art or architecture which is missing, nor is it
an acquaintance with history or literature. Indeed it is not primarily
a lack of subject-matter at all: the fault lies in what Whitehead called
"a celibacy of the intellect which is divorced from the concrete con-
templation of the complete facts." It is a preoccupation with abstractions from reality, an escape from the whole of reality. Thirty years ago
in *Science and the Modern World*, Whitehead warned us that this
would become the great danger of professional education. Each
profession, he said, makes progress in its own groove of abstractions,
"but there is no groove of abstractions which is adequate for the com-
prehension of human life." And this is how he summed up the kind of
adaptation which a university needs to make in order to assimilate
science and technology:

> "There is something between the gross specialised values of
> the mere practical man, and the thin specialised values of the
> mere scholar. Both types have missed something; and if you add
> together the two sets of values, you do not obtain the missing
> elements. When you understand all about the sun and all about
> the atmosphere and all about the rotation of the earth, you may
> still miss the radiance of the sunset. There is no substitute for the
> direct perception of the concrete achievement of a thing in its
> actuality. . . . A factory, with its machinery, its community of

operatives, its social service to the general population, its dependence upon organising and designing genius, its potentialities as a source of wealth to the holders of its stock is an organism exhibiting a variety of vivid values. What we want to train is the habit of apprehending such an organism in its completeness."

The habit of apprehending a technology in its completeness: this is the essence of technological humanism, and this is what we should expect education in higher technology to achieve. I believe it could be achieved by making specialist studies (whatever they are: metallurgy or dentistry or Norse philology) the core around which are grouped liberal studies which are relevant to these specialist studies. But they must be relevant; the path to culture should be through a man's specialism, not by by-passing it. Suppose a student decides to take up the study of brewing; his way to acquire general culture is not by diluting his brewing courses with popular lectures on architecture, social history, and ethics, but by making brewing the core of his studies. The *sine qua non* for a man who desires to be cultured is a deep and enduring enthusiasm to do one thing excellently. So there must first of all be an assurance that the student genuinely wants to make beer. From this it is a natural step to the study of biology, microbiology, and chemistry: all subjects which can be studied not as techniques to be practised but as ideas to be understood. As his studies gain momentum the student could, by skilful teaching, be made interested in the economics of marketing beer, in public-houses, in their design, in architecture; or in the history of beer-drinking from the time of the early Egyptian inscriptions, and so in social history; or, in the unhappy moral effects of drinking too much beer, and so in religion and ethics. A student who can weave his technology into the fabric of society can claim to have a liberal education; a student who cannot weave his technology into the fabric of society cannot claim even to be a good technologist.

The European interest in rethinking the relations between technical and liberal studies is not limited to the kind of thinking represented in the statement by Sir Eric Ashby. In Sweden, for example, a broad reform of preuniversity education is under way which represents a break with the class-oriented, dual-school tradition. An official of the Ministry of Education and Cultural Affairs said in 1970, "We want to do away with the past situation, where the upper class generally went to schools that led to the university while the lower class entered vocational training schools."[4] The educational reforms are part of a broad social effort to democratize relations between the classes and the sexes. All children are to be brought together in new two-to-four year secondary schools which will offer everything from training for construction

---

[4] *New York Times*, Nov. 10, 1970, p. 16.

work to linquistics, history, and general academic subjects. The goal is to develop an understanding of the interrelatedness of occupations and to promote respect for manual, technical and professional work. In addition a conscious effort is being made to reexamine traditional social roles of the sexes. Swedish children are to be taught "equality of the sexes" in both the family and the labor market. The young will learn to assume that women may legitimately aspire to the same occupational goals as the men.

In our own country experiments like the Parkway Program (Philadelphia) attempt to offer alternatives to schoolroom-centered learning. The plan aims to use as a learning laboratory the ongoing institutions and organizations in the community, e.g., the Franklin Institute, General Electric Company, Insurance Company of North America, the Police Department, and City Hall. An assumption behind such an approach is that young people can be sent into the community for educative purposes—that opportunities to interact with people at work will provide liberalizing experiences which could not be achieved by classroom studies alone.

Before embracing too enthusiastically such ideas it might be well to recall the worries of some of the early progressives. They saw that such programs could easily be captured for narrow training purposes—employers would see the chance to give early job training to potential recruits and the young could be lured by the opportunity to make "useful contacts." The school operation becomes then a tool for facilitating adjustment to the status quo. If the society were in a condition of vibrant health one might entertain the notion that training for social entry might coincide with humane education. But our cities are sick, our psyches are in disarray—our values distorted. A sense of the human hurts of the technological system led the early progressives to ask, "Will 'the industies' be worthy of the children we send them?" The question was based on the realization that the basic educator is the total pattern of culture. The work of creative teachers cannot assure healthy human beings if the institutions surrounding the schools are sick.

It was John Dewey who worked out the philosophical argument that a people who wanted humane democratic institutions with technology could not afford an education that would merely "adapt workers to the existing industrial regime." People had to learn to insist that the technological-corporate system be made subordinate to human needs.

Dewey called for a kind of education that would help to "first alter the existing industrial system, and ultimately transform it." He specified a moral criterion for judging all social organizations: "the supreme test of all political institutions and industrial arrangements shall be the contribution they make to the all-around growth of every member of society." A society with democratic commitments would demand that science and technology be "humanistic—not just physical and techni-cal."[5]

In order for such a transformation to take place Dewey argued that modifications of habit were needed all across the culture. Skills of reflec-tive thinking and problem solving were to replace the blind following of custom, Dewey made much of that. But equally important was the habit of raising questions about the consequences of technological-cor-porate practice. Paul and Percival Goodman made the point in *Com-munitas* with a passion that expressed Dewey's depth of feeling on the matter better than did his own writings. They sought to clarify the criterion they would employ to evaluate community planning proposals —*beauty* in the form of a proportion of means and ends.

> We therefore, going back to Greek antiquity, propose a different line of interpretation altogether: form follows function, but let us sub-ject the function itself to a formal critique. Is the *function* good? *Bona fide?* Is it worthwhile? Is it worthy of a man to do that? What are the consequences? Is it compatible with other, basic, human functions? Is it a forthright or at least ingenious part of life? Does it make sense? Is it a beautiful function of a beautiful power? We have grown unused to asking such ethical questions of our machines, our streets, our cars, our towns. But nothing less will give us an esthetics for community plan-ning, the proportion of means and ends. For a community is not a construction, a bold Utopian model; its chief part is always people, busy or idle, en masse or a few at a time. And the problem of community planning is not like arranging people for a play or ballet, for there are no outside spectators, there are only actors; nor are they actors of a scenario but agents of their own needs—though it's a grand thing for us to be not altogether unconscious of forming a beautiful and elabo-rate city, by how we look and move. That's a proud feeling.
>
> What we want is style. Style, power, and grace. These come, burn-ing, from need and flowing feeling, and that fire brought to focus by viable character and habits."[6]

If we have grown "unused to asking such ethical questions" we must begin to ask them again. The best place to start is with the young. Fortunately for us they are primed for the task.

The school programs described at the beginning of this chapter seemed to be weakest in failing to involve students in raising questions about the consequences of industrialization and technology. Their op-erations and content, however, place student in positions where they

---

[5]See pp. 180–181 and p. 215 in this book.
[6]Goodman, Percival, and Paul Goodman, *Communitas*, New York: Vintage Books 1947, 1960, pp. 19–20.

could engage men of industry, labor and government in explorations of value issues of basic importance for our times.

It may be difficult to imagine that persons holding power in unions, corporations and government bureaus would permit themselves to be drawn into serious discussions with questioning students. It is less difficult to imagine the kinds of questions young people, concerned with the quality of life they will face in the twenty-first century, might ask. Black students might want to question leaders of the building trade unions about admission policies. Girls might want to find out what career opportunities will be open to them in private or public employment. Questions might be asked about the basic functioning of giants like General Electric or General Motors—are they merely private firms whose policies are controlled by forces of the free market, or do they function as quasi-monopolies free from public accountability? How are their governing boards selected? Why do Boards of Directors contain no members representing blocks of shareholders like labor unions, educational institutions, consumers, and the like? What are the environmental and esthetic effects of production policies? What are the moral effects of manipulative advertising campaigns?

On the other hand, the young might have to relinquish many simplistic assumptions if they had more firsthand chances to watch imperfect humans struggling with intractable realities. Sharing duty-hours with patrol car officers, for instance, might raise questions about indiscriminate use of the term "pig."

Not even the early progressives were so naive as to assume that the questionings of the young would usher in economic and social reorderings. The progressive faith however, was that the critical, question-raising qualities of mind which were to characterize reformed school efforts, were to be part of a broader social criticism—a free press, muckraking journals, and gadfly jabs by special-cause organizations like the American Civil Liberties Union, or Nader's Raiders. These would provide the dynamics for institutional change that would turn us away from dehumanizing drives of the technological system.

Succeeding traumas have shattered whatever hopes might have existed for automatic progress. More recently the basic faith that the American system can engender social transformation from within has come into doubt.

If the hard-headed radicals are right those with power in the corporate system can be budged only by violent revolutions operating outside the political process. Leftist doctrine asserts that leaders of the system will resort to fascist repression rather than give way to significant change.

Time is running out on the option of acquiescing to mindless, technocratic productivity. We are called on to find out if the American social-political system can transform itself and subordinate technological power to human—democratic ends. If it cannot we can expect more serious social disorders and growing confrontations.

If we make it, educational reform and social renewal will go on together. The emergence of wide varieties of educational experiments aimed at providing humanizing experiences within the realities of technology will be one kind of sign. The flourishing of bland, well-engineered school efforts to serve narrow technocratic efficiency needs will be a counterindication. The inner conflict over which kind of society Americans want to create with the power of science and technology continues—only the stakes are getting higher.

Bibliography

Adams, George P. and William P. Montague (eds.). *Contemporary American Philosophy*. New York: Macmillan, 1930.

Addams, Jane. *Twenty Years at Hull-House*. New York: Macmillan, 1910.

American Federation of Labor. *Proceedings*, 1902–17.

American Federation of Labor. Report of the Committee on Industrial Education. Senate Document No. 936, 62nd Cong., 2nd Sess., Vol. 4 (Washington, D.C.: Government Printing Office, 1912).

American Federationist. December 1909.

Ashby, Sir Eric. *Technology and the Academics: An Essay on Universities and the Scientific Revolution*. London: Macmillan, 1958.

Auchmuty, Richard T. "An American Apprentice System," *The Century*, New Series Vol. 15 (November 1888–April 1889), pp. 401–405.

Ayres, Leonard P. *Laggards in our Schools: A Study of Retardation and Elimination in City School Systems*. New York: Charities Publication Committee (Russell Sage Foundation Publication), 1909.

———. "Studies in Occupations," U.S. Bureau of Education *Bulletin*, No. 14 (Washington, D.C.: Government Printing Officce, 1914), pp. 27–30.

Bagley, William C. *The Educative Process*. New York: Macmillan, 1905.

Barlow, Melvin L. *History of Industrial Education in the United States*. Peoria, Ill.: Bennett, 1967.

Bawden, William T. "Leaders In Industrial Education—Charles Allen Prosser," *Industrial Arts and Vocational Education*, Vol. 41 (September—November 1952) and Vol. 42 (January 1953).

———. *Leaders in Industrial Education*. Milwaukee: Bruce, 1950.

Beatty, Albert James. *Corporation Schools*. Bloomington: Indiana U. Press, 1918.

Becker, Carl L. *Cornell University—Founders and the Founding*. Ithaca, N.Y.: Cornell U. Press, 1943.

Bemis, Edward W. "Relation of Labor Organizations to the American Boy and to Trade Instruction," *Annals of the American Academy of Political and Social Science*, Vol. 5 (September 1894), pp. 209–241.

Bennett, Charles Alpheus. *History of Manual and Industrial Education, 1870–1917.* Peoria, Ill.: Manual Arts Press, 1937.

Blauch, Lloyd E. "Federal Cooperation in Agricultural Extension Work, Vocational Education, and Vocational Rehabilitation." U.S. Office of Education *Bulletin,* 1933, No. 15. Washington, D.C.: Government Printing Office, 1935.

Bloomfield, Daniel (ed.). *Selected Articles on Employment Management.* New York: Wilson, 1920.

Bloomfield, Meyer. "The Aim and Work of Employment Managers Associations," National Society for the Promotion of Industrial Education *Bulletin,* 1916, Appendix, p. 44.

_____. "The New Profession of Handling Men," in Daniel Bloomfield (ed.), *Selected Articles on Employment Management.* New York: Wilson, 1920.

_____. *The Vocational Guidance of Youth.* Boston: Houghton Mifflin, 1911.

Bode, Boyd. "Why Educational Objectives?" *School and Society,* May 10, 1924.

Borow, Henry (ed.). *Man in a World at Work.* Boston: Houghton Mifflin, 1964.

Bossing, Nelson, and Roscoe Cramer. *The Junior High School.* Boston: Houghton Mifflin, 1965.

Bourne, Randolph. *Education and Living.* New York: Century, 1917.

Brewer, John M. *The Vocational-Guidance Movement, Its Problems and Possibilities.* New York: Macmillan, 1924.

Brisbane, Albert. *A Concise Exposition of the Doctrine of Association.* New York: Redfield, 1844.

Bronowski, Jacob. *Science and Human Values.* New York: Harper, 1956.

Bruner, Jerome. "Culture, Politics and Pedagogy," *Saturday Review, Inc.,* May 18, 1968.

Bundy, George. "Word of the Employment Department of the Ford Motor Company," National Society for the Promotion of Industrial Education *Bulletin,* 1916, Appendix, p. 63.

Bunker, Frank Forest. *The Junior High School Movement—Its Beginnings.* Washington, D.C.: Roberts, 1935.

_____. Reorganizing the Public School System, U.S. Bureau of Education *Bulletin,* No. 8, 1916.

Burks, Jesse. "Introductory Address," National Education Association Report on *The Place of Industries in Public Education,* 1910.

Callahan, Raymond E. *Education and the Cult of Efficiency,* Chicago: U. of Chicago Press, 1962.

Carlton, Frank Tracy. *Education and Industrial Evolution.* New York: Macmillan, 1908.

———. "The Industrial Factor in Social Progress," National Education Association Report on *The Place of Industries in Public Education*, 1910.

———. *The Industrial Situation: Its Effect Upon the Home, the School, the Wage Earner and the Employer*. New York: Revell, 1914.

Clapp, Elsie Ripley. *The Use of Resources in Education*. New York: Harper, 1952.

Clark, Burton R. *Educating the Expert Society*. San Francisco: Chandler, 1962.

Clark, Harold F., and Harold S. Sloan. *Classrooms in the Factories:* An Account of Educational Activities Conducted by American Industry. Rutherford, New Jersey: Institute of Research, Fairleigh Dickinson University, 1960.

Cochran, Thomas C., and William Miller. *The Age of Enterprise*. New York: Macmillan, 1942.

Cohen, Eli E., and Louise Kapp (eds.). *Manpower Policies for Youth*. New York: Columbia U. Press, 1966.

Cohen, Sol. "The Industrial Education Movement, 1906–17," *American Quarterly*, Vol. 20, No. 1 (Spring 1968).

———. *Progressives and Urban School Reform*. New York: Bureau of Publications, Teachers College, Columbia University, 1964.

Commons, John R., et al. *History of Labour in the United States*. New York: Macmillan, 1918, 1961.

Commonwealth of Massachusetts. *Report of the Commission on Industrial and Technical Education*. New York: Teachers College Educational Reprints, No. 1 (1906).

Cooley, Edwin G. "The Argument for Industrial Education from the Success of Germany," National Society for the Promotion of Industrial Education *Bulletin*, No. 15 (1911).

———. "Principles that Should Underly Legislation for Vocational Education," National Society for the Promotion of Industrial Education *Bulletin*, No. 16, 1912.

———. "Professor Dewey's Criticism of the Chicago Commercial Club and Its Vocational Bill," *Vocational Education*, Vol. 3 (September 1913), pp. 24–29.

Country Life Commission. *Report*. Senate Document 705, 60th Cong., 2nd Sess.

Counts, George S. *School and Society in Chicago*. New York: Harcourt, 1928.

Cremin, Lawrence A. *The Transformation of the School*. New York: Vintage Books, 1961.

Cubberley, Ellwood P. *Changing Conceptions of Education*. Boston: Houghton Mifflin, 1909.

242

Bibliography

Curoe, Philip R. V. *Educational Attitudes and Policies of Organized Labor in the United States.* New York: Teachers College 1926.

Curti, Merle. *American Paradox: The Conflict of Thought and Action.* New Brunswick, N.J.: Rutgers U. Press, 1956.

_____. *The Growth of American Thought.* New York: Harper, 1943.

Davenport, Eugene. "Industrial Education—a Phase of the Problem of Universal Education," National Education Association, *Addresses and Proceedings,* 1909.

Davis, Jesse Buttrick. *The Saga of a Schoolmaster.* Boston: Boston U. Press, 1956.

_____. *Vocational and Moral Guidance.* Boston: Ginn, 1914.

DeGarmo, Charles. "Relation of Industrial to General Education," *The School Review,* Vol. 17, No. 3 (March 1909), pp. 145–153.

Dennison, George. *The Lives of Children.* New York: Random House, 1969.

Dewey, John. "American Education and Culture," *Characters and Events,* Vol. II. New York: Holt, 1929.

_____. "Are the Schools Doing What the People Want Them To Do?" *Educational Review,* Vol. 21 (1901).

_____. *Democracy and Education.* New York: Macmillan, 1916.

_____. "Education and Social Change," *Social Frontier,* Vol. 3, (May 1937), pp. 235–238.

_____. *Freedom and Culture.* New York: Putnam, 1939.

_____. "From Absolution to Experimentalism," in George P. Adams and William P. Montague (eds.), *Contemporary American Philosophy.* New York: Macmillan, 1930.

_____. "Industrial Education—A Wrong Kind," *The New Republic,* Vol. 2 (Feb. 20, 1915), pp. 71–73.

_____. "Interpretation of the Savage Mind," *Psychological Reviw,* Vol. 9 (May 1902).

_____. "James Bonar's 'Philosophy and Political Economy,'" *Political Science Quarterly,* Vol. 9 (1894).

_____. "Learning to Earn," *Education Today.* New York: Putnam, 1940.

_____. "The Manufacturers' Association and the Public Schools," *Journal of the National Education Association,* Vol. 17 (February 1928).

_____. "Mexico's Educational Renaissance," *Characters and Events,* Vol. I. New York: Holt, 1929.

_____. "The Need of an Industrial Education in an Industrial Democracy," *Manual Training and Vocational Education,* (February 1916).

———. "New Schools for a New Era," *Characters and Events*, Vol. I. New York: Holt, 1929.

———. "The Philosopher Replies: Experience, Knowledge, and Value," in Paul A. Schilpp (ed.), *The Philosophy of John Dewey*. New York: Tudor, 1951.

———. *Philosophy and Civilization*. New York: Balch, 1931.

———. "A Policy of Industrial Education," *The New Republic*, Vol. 1 (Dec. 19, 1914).

———. *The Public and Its Problems*. New York: Holt, 1927.

———. "Public Education on Trial," *The New Republic*, Vol. 12 (December 1917), 245–247.

———. *Reconstruction in Philosophy*. New York: New American Library, 1950.

———. *School and Society*. Chicago: U. of Chicago Press, 1899.

———. "Some Dangers in the Present Movement for Industrial Education," *Child Labor Bulletin*, Vol. 1 (February 1913).

———. "Splitting up the School System," *The New Republic*, Vol. 2 (April 17, 1915).

———. "The University Elementary School: History and Character," *University Record*, Vol. 2, No. 8 (May 1897).

———. *The Way Out of Educational Confusion*. Cambridge: Harvard U. Press, 1931.

———, and Evelyn Dewey. *Schools of Tomorrow*. New York: Dutton, 1915.

Dodd, Alvin E. "Training for Industrial Life," *The Nation's Business*, Vol. 3 (November 1915), pp. 8–11.

Donnelly, Thomas E. "Some Problems of Apprenticeship Schools," National Society of Corporation Schools *Papers*, Vol. 1, 1913.

Donohue, John, S.J. *Work and Education*. Chicago: Loyola U. Press, 1959.

Dorfman, Joseph. *Thorstein Veblen and His America*. New York: Viking, 1934.

Douglas, Paul H. "American Apprenticeship and Industrial Education," *Studies in History, Economics and Public Law*, Vol. 95, No. 2. New York: Columbia U. Press and Longmans, 1921.

Downey, James E. "A Modern High School of Commerce," *The Nation's Business*, Vol. 4 (February 1916), pp. 20–21.

Draper, Andrew S. "Desirable Uniformity and Diversity in American Education." National Education Association, *Addresses and Proceedings*, 1908.

———. "The Adaptation of the Schools to Industry and Efficiency." National Education Association, *Addresses and Proceedings*, 1908.

Drost, Walter H. *David Snedden and Education for Social Efficiency.*
    Madison: U. of Wisconsin Press, 1967.
Du Bois, W. E. B. *The Philadelphia Negro.* Philadelphia: U. of Pennsyl-
    vanis Press, 1899.
Duffy, Frank. "Industrial Education and What Labor Unions Are Doing
    to Promote It," *American Federationist*, Vol. 19, No. 5 (May 1912),
    pp. 392–396.
Dutton, Samuel T., and David Snedden. *The Administration of Public
    Education in the United States.* New York: Macmillan, 1908.
Eliot, Charles W. "Industrial Education as an Essential Factor in Our
    National Prosperity," National Society for the Promotion of Indus-
    trial Education *Bulletin*, No. 5, 1908.
_____. "The Value During Education of the Life Career Motive," Na-
    tional Education Association *Proceedings,* 1910.
Ellul, Jacques. *The Technological Society.* Introduction by Robert Mer-
    ton. New York: Knopf, 1964.
Feldman, Marvin J. "Why Manpower Training Should be a Public
    School Mission," *American Vocational Journal*, Vol. 42, No. 8
    (November 1967).
Fellows, G. E. "The Value of General Culture in Technical Courses in
    the Land-Grant Colleges," Bulletin 212. Washington, D.C.: U.S.
    Experiment Stations Office, July 10, 1909, pp. 65–68.
Feuer, Lewis. "John Dewey and the Back to the People Movement in
    American Thought," *Journal of the History of Ideas*, Vol. 20 (Octo-
    ber–December 1959), pp. 545–568.
Fish, Frederick. "The Vocational and Industrial School," National Edu-
    cation Association *Proceedings,* 1910.
Fisher, Berenice M. *Industrial Education: American Ideals and Institu-
    tions.* Madison: U. of Wisconsin Press, 1967.
Gabriel, Ralph Henry. *The Course of American Democratic Thought.*
    2nd ed. New York: Ronald, 1956.
Gallington, Ralph O. "Industrial Arts for the Disadvantaged," *American
    Vocational Journal*, Vol. 42, No. 8 (November 1967).
Giddings, Franklin. *Principles of Sociology.* New York: Macmillan,
    1896.
Gillie, Angelo C. "Needed: A New Program of General Education for
    Ghetto Youth," *American Vocational Journal*, Vol. 42, No. 8
    (November 1967).
Gompers, Samuel. "Labor and Its Attitude Toward Trusts," *American
    Federationist*, Vol. 14 (November 1907).
_____. *Seventy Years of Life and Labor:* An Autobiography. Revised
    and edited by Philip Taft and John A. Sessions. New York: Dutton,
    1957.

Goodman, Paul. "Can Technology Be Humane?" *The New York Review of Books,* Nov. 20, 1969, pp. 27–34.

———. *Compulsory MIS-Education.* New York: Horizon Press, 1964.

———. *People or Personnel and Like a Conquered Province.* New York: Vintage Books, 1968.

Goodman, Percival and Paul. *Communitas.* New York: Randon House, 1947.

de Grazia, Sebastian. *Of Time, Work, and Leisure.* New York: Twentieth Century Fund, 1962.

Green, Marguerite. *The National Civic Federation and the American Labor Movement 1900–1925.* Washington, D.C.: Catholic University of America Press, 1956.

Green, Thomas F. *Work, Leisure, and American Schools.* New York: Random House, 1968.

Grob, Gerald N. *Workers and Utopia:* A Study of Ideological Conflict in the American Labor Movement 1865–1900. Evanston, Ill.: Northwestern U. Press, 1961.

Handlin, Oscar. *Children of the Uprooted.* New York: Braziller, 1966.

Haney, James Parton. "Manual Training as a Preventive of Truancy," *Education,* Vol. 27, No. 10 (June 1907), pp. 634–641.

Hanus, Paul H. "Industrial Education," *Atlantic Monthly,* January 1908, pp. 60–68.

———. "Vocational Guidance and Public Education," *The School Review,* Vol. 19, No. 1 (January 1911), pp. 51–56.

Harvey, Lorenzo D. "The Need, Scope, and Character of Industrial Education in the Public-school System," *Journal of Proceedings and Addresses* of the Forty-seventh Annual Meeting of the National Education Association, held at Denver, Colorado, July 3–9, 1909, pp. 49–70.

Haynes, Benjamin R., and Harry P. Jackson. *A History of Business Education in the United States.* Cincinnati: South-Western Publishing Company, 1935.

Hays, Samuel P. "The Politics of Reform in Municipal Government in the Progressive Era," *Pacific Northwest Quarterly,* Vol. 55, No. 4 (University of Washington, October 1964).

———. *The Response to Industrialism: 1885–1914.* Chicago: U. of Chicago Press, 1957.

Henderson, C. Hanford. *Pay-Day.* Boston: Houghton Mifflin, 1911.

Herzberg, Frederick. *Work and the Nature of Man.* New York: World, 1966.

Hofstadter, Richard. *The Age of Reform.* New York: Knopf, 1955.

Howell, Clarence E. "Commending the N.E.A. Resolution on Vocational Education," *Industrial Arts Magazine,* Vol. 8, No. 10 (October 1919).

Hullfish, H. Gordon. "Looking Backward with Snedden," *Educational Review*, Vol. 57 (1924), pp. 61–73.

Hunt, DeWitt. "The Development of Work Experience as a Part of Secondary Education in American Schools," U.S. Office of Education *Bulletin* No. 5 (1957).

———. "Type 6. Remunerative Vocational Work Experience Programs in High Schools Subsidized from Federal Vocational Educational Funds," *Work Experience Education Programs in American Secondary Schools*. U.S. Office of Health, Education and Welfare Bulletin No. 5 (Washington, D.C.: Government Printing Office, 1957).

Hunter, Robert. *Poverty*. New York: Macmillan, 1909.

James, Edmund J. "Education of Business Men—I and II," address before the Convention of the American Bankers' Association, at Saratoga, Sept. 3, 1890. New York: American Bankers' Association, 1892.

Jernegan, Marcus Wilson. *Laboring and Dependent Classes in Colonial America, 1607–1783*. Chicago: U. of Chicago Press, 1931.

Joncich, Geraldine. *The Sane Positivist: A Biography of Edward L. Thorndike*. Middletown, Conn.:Wesleyan U. Press, 1968.

Johnson, Ben W. "Children Differ in Vocational Aims: Industrial Education in the Elementary School," National Education Association *Proceedings*, 1910, pp. 253–260.

Kandel, I. L. *American Education in the Twentieth Century*. Cambridge: Harvard U. Press, 1957.

Katz, Michael B. *The Irony of Early School Reform*. Cambridge: Harvard U. Press, 1968.

Keppel, Ann. "Country Schools for Country Children: Background of the Reform Movement in Rural Elementary Education, 1890–1914." Unpublished Doctoral Thesis, University of Wisconsin, 1960.

Kingsbury, Susan M. "The Relation of the Children to the Industries," The Report of the Commission on Industrial and Technical Education. New York: Teachers College Press, 1906.

Kipnis, Ira. *The American Socialist Movement, 1897–1912*. New York: Columbia U. Press, 1952.

Kohler, Mary Conway. *Youth and Work in New York City*. New York: Taconic Foundation, March 1962.

Krug, Edward A. (ed.) *Charles W. Eliot and Popular Education*. Classics in Education No. 8. New York: Teachers College Press, 1961.

———. *The Shaping of the American High School*. New York: Harper, Row, 1964.

Lane, Winthrop. *Survey*, November 1912.

Leavitt, Frank M. "How Shall We Study the Industries for the Purposes of Vocation Guidance?" U.S. Bureau of Education *Bulletin* No. 14 (Washington, D.C.: Government Printing Office, 1914).

Leonard, Robert J. *Richmond Survey for Vocational Education.* Indianapolis: Indiana State Board of Education, 1916.

Lewis, W. D. "The High School and the Boy," *Saturday Evening Post,* Apr. 6, 1912.

Lichter, Solomon O., Elsie B. Rapien, Frances M. Seibert, and Morris A. Sklansky *The Drops-Outs.* New York: Free Press, 1962.

Link, Arthur S. "What Happened to the Progressive Movement in the 1920's?" *The American Historical Review,* Vol. 54, No. 4 (July 1959), pp. 833–850.

_____. *Woodrow Wilson and the Progressive Era.* New York: Harper, 1954.

Lorwin, Lewis L. *The American Federation of Labor* (Washington, D.C.: Brookings Institution, 1933).

Lovejoy, Owen R. "Vocational Guidance and Child Labor," U.S. Bureau of Education *Bulletin,* No. 14 (Washington, D.C.: Government Printing Office, 1914), p. 42.

McConnell, Grant. *The Decline of Agrarian Democracy.* Los Angeles: U. of California Press, 1959.

McManis, John T. *Ella Flagg Young and a Half Century of the Chicago Public Schools.* Chicago: McClurg, 1916.

Mann, Arthur. *Yankee Reformers in the Urban Age.* Cambridge: Harvard U. Press, 1954.

Marot, Helen. *Creative Impulse in Industry:* A Proposition for Educators. New York: Dutton, 1918.

Maxwell, William H. "Education for Efficiency." National Education Association *Addresses and Proceedings,* 1905.

_____. *A Quarter Century of Public School Development.* New York: American Book, 1912.

Mayhew, Katherine C., and Anna C., Edwards. *The Dewey School.* New York: Appleton, 1936.

Mays, Arthur Beverly. "The Concept of Vocational Education in the Thinking of the General Educator, 1845 to 1945." *Bulletin* of the Bureau of Educational Research, No. 62. University of Illinois, College of Education, 1946.

Mead, George Herbert. "The Larger Educational Bearings of Vocational Guidance," U.S. Bureau of Education *Bulletin,* No. 14 (Washington, D.C.: Government Printing Office, 1914), 16–26.

_____. *A Report on Vocational Training in Chicago and Other Cities.* Chicago: City Club of Chicago, 1912.

Mearns, W. Hughes. "Our Medieval High Schools," *Saturday Evening Post, Mar. 2, 1912.*

Miller, Herbert Adolphus. *The School and the Immigrant*. Cleveland: Survey Committee of the Cleveland Foundation, 1916.

Morison, Elting E. *Men, Machines, and Modern Times*. Cambridge: Massachusetts Institute of Technology Press, 1966.

Morrison, Henry C. "Vocational Training and Industrial Education," *Educational Review*, October 1907.

Mowry, George E. *The Era of Theodore Roosevelt*. New York: Harper, 1958.

Munroe, James P. *New Demands in Education*. New York: Doubleday, 1912.

_____. "President's Address," National Society for the Promotion of Industrial Education *Proceedings*, 1911.

National Association of Manufacturers. *Proceedings*, 1895–1914.

National Education Association. *Addresses and Proceedings*, 1885–1918.

National Education Association. *Cardinal Principles of Secondary Education:* A Report of the Commission on the Reorganization of Secondary Education. U.S. Bureau of Education *Bulletin*, No. 35 (1918).

National Society for the Promotion of Industrial Education. *Addresses and Proceedings, 1907–1917*.

Neilson, William Allan. *Charles W. Eliot: The Man and His Beliefs*. New York: Harper, 1926.

New York State Federation of Labor. *Proceedings*, 1921.

Ovington, Mary White. *Half a Man: The Status of the Negro in New York*. New York: Longmans, 1911.

Parsons, Frank. *The City for the People*. Philadelphia: Taylor, 1901.

_____. *Choosing a Vocation*. Boston: Houghton Mifflin, 1909.

_____. *Our Country's Need*. Boston: Arena, 1894.

_____. "The Vocation Bureau," *Arena*, Vol. 40 (September 1908), pp. 171–183.

Payne, Arthur F. "The NEA Adopts a So-Called National Policy of Vocational Education," *Industrial Arts Magazine*, Vol. 8, No. 9 (September 1919), pp. 364–365.

Peabody, Selim H. "The Value of Tool Instruction as Related to the Active Pursuits in Which Pupils Subsequently May Engage," National Education Association *Proceedings* (July 1889).

Pease, Otis (ed.) *The Progressive Years: The Spirit and Achievement of American Reform*. New York: Braziller, 1962.

Perkinson, Henry J., *The Imperfect Panacea: American Faith in Education, 1865–1965*. New York: Random House, 1968.

Prosser, Charles A. "Practical Arts and Vocational Guidance," National Education Association *Proceedings*, 1912, pp. 645–661.

_____. *Secondary Education and Life:* The Inglis Lecture, 1939. Cambridge: Harvard U. Press, 1939.

_____. *A Study of the Boston Mechanic Arts High School:* Being a Report to the Boston School Committee. New York: Teachers College, Columbia University, Contributions to Education, No. 74, 1915.

Prosser, Charles A., and Thomas H. Quigley. *Vocational Education in a Democracy.* Rev. Ed. Chicago: American Technical Society, 1950.

Reed, Louis S. *The Labor Philosophy of Samuel Gompers.* New York: Columbia U. Press, 1930.

Resek, Carl. *The Progressives.* Indianapolis: Bobbs-Merrill, 1967.

Reston, James. St. Louis *Post-Dispatch,* June 26, 1969.

Richards, Charles F. "Some Notes on the History of Industrial Education in the United States," National Education Association Report on *The Place of Industries in Public Education,* 1910.

Riis, Jacob A. *The Children of the Poor.* New York: Scribner's, 1892.

_____. *How the Other Half Lives.* New York: Sagamore Press, 1957.

Rippa, S. Alexander. *Education in a Free Society:* An American History. New York: McKay, 1967.

Rockefeller, John D., Jr. *The Personal Relation in Industry.* New York: Boni and Liveright, 1924.

Ross, Earle D. *Democracy's College: The Land-Grant Movement in the Formative Stage.* Ames: Iowa State College Press, 1942.

Ross, Edward Alsworth. *Changing America:* Studies in Contemporary Society. New York: Century, 1912.

_____. *Social Control.* New York: Macmillan, 1912.

Roszak, Theodore. *The Making of a Counter Culture: Reflections on the Technocratic Society and Its Youthful Opposition.* Garden City, N. Y.: Doubleday, 1969.

Russell, James E., and Bonser, Frederick G. *Industrial Education.* New York: Teachers College Press, 1912.

Russell, John D., and associates. *Vocational Education:* Staff Study No. 8. Washington, D.C.: Government Printing Office, 1938.

Saloutos, Theodore, and John D., Hicks. *Agricultural Discontent in the Middle West, 1900–1939.* Madison: U. of Wisconsin Press, 1951.

Schilpp. Paul A. (ed.) *The Philosophy of John Dewey.* New York: Tudor, 1951.

Schlesinger, Arthur M. *The Rise of the City,* Vol. X of *A History of American Life.* New York: Macmillan, 1933, pp. 79–80.

Schoenhals, Louise. "Mexican Experiment in Rural and Primary Education: 1921–1930," *Hispanic American Historical Review,* Vol. 44, No. 1, (1964).

Schon, Donald A. *Technology and Change.* New York: Delacorte, 1967.

Seybolt, R. F. *Apprenticeship and Apprenticeship Education in Colonial New England and New York.* New York: Teachers College Press, 1917.

Simons, Diane. *George Kerschensteiner.* London: Methuen, 1966.

Smith, John E. *The Spirit of American Philosophy.* New York: Oxford U. Press, 1963.

Smith-Hughes Act of 1917, U.S. *Statutes at Large.* Vol. 39. (1917).

Snedden, David. *American High Schools and Vocational Schools in 1960.* New York: Bureau of Publications, Teachers College, Columbia University, 1931.

——. "Differences Among Varying Groups of Children Should Be Recognized," National Education Association *Addresses and Proceedings,* June 29–July 3, 1908.

——. "Discussion and Correspondence," *School and Society,* May 5, 1921.

——. "Education for a World of Teamplayers and Team Workers," *School and Society,* Vol. 20, Nov. 1, 1924.

——. "History Study as an Instrument in the Social Education of Children," *Journal of Pedagogy,* Vol. 19, June, 1907, pp. 259–268.

——. "Fundamental Distinctions Between Liberal and Vocational Education,"National Education Association *Proceedings,* 1914.

——. "Liberty of Teaching in the Social Sciences," *School and Society,* Vol. 13, Feb. 12, 1921.

——. "Teaching History in Secondary Schools," *History Teachers Magazine,* Vol. 5, (November 1914).

——. *The New Republic,* Vol. 3, May 15, 1915.

——. "Progress Towards Sociologically Based Civic Education," *The Journal of Educational Sociology.* Vol. 3, No. 7 (March 1930), pp. 481–496.

——. "The Public School and Juvenile Delinquency," *Educational Review,* Vol. 33 (April 1907), pp. 374–385.

——. *Towards Better Educations.* New York: Bureau of Publications, Teachers College, Columbia University, 1931.

Spaulding, Frank. "The Application of the Principles of Scientific Management," National Education Education Association *Proceedings* (1913).

Spencer, Herbert. *Education: Intellectual, Moral, and Physical.* New York: Appleton, 1860.

Steigerwalt, Albert K. *The National Association of Manufacturers, 1895–1914: A Study in Business Leadership.* Grand Rapids, Michigan: Dean-Hicks Company for the Bureau of Business Research of the Graduate School of Business Administration of the University of Michigan, 1964.

Stephens, W. Richard. *The Junior High School, A Product of Reform Values, 1890–1920.* Terre Haute: Indiana State University, 1968.

——. *Social Reform and the Dawn of Guidance.* Terre Haute: Indiana State University, 1968.

Stimson, Rufus W., and Frank W., Lathrop (eds.). History of Agricultural Education of Less Than College Grade in the United States: A Cooperative Project of Workers in Vocational Education in Agriculture and in Related Fields. Washington, D.C.: Government Printing Office. Vocational Division Bulletin No. 217, Agricultural Series No. 55 of the U.S. Office of Education, Federal Security Agency. 1942.

Struck, F. Theodore. *Vocational Education for a Changing World.* New York: Wiley, 1945.

Tarbell, Ida. "What Industrial Training Should We Give the Average Girl," National Society for the Promotion of Industrial Education *Proceedings,* 1915, pp. 132–135.

Taylor, Albion Guilford. *Labor Policies of the National Association of Manufacturers.* Urbana: U. of Illinois Press, 1928.

Taylor, Frederick. *The Principles of Management.* New York: Harper, 1911.

Thomas, Alan M., Jr. "American Education and the Immigrant," *Teachers College Record,* Vol. 55, No. 5 (February 1954), pp. 253–270.

Thorndike, Edward L. "Disciplinary Values of Studies: A Census of Opinions," *Education,* Vol. 35 (1914–15).

Tilgher, Adriano. *Homo Faber: Work Through The Ages.* Chicago: Regnery, 1958.

U.S. Bureau of Education, *Bulletin,* 1916, No. 21.

U.S. Bureau of Education. *Circulars of Information.* No. 2–1874. Washington, D.C.: Government Printing Office, 1874.

U.S. Commission of Labor. *Seventh Annual Report.* Washington, D.C.: Government Printing Office, 1902.

U.S. Commission of Labor. *Twenty-fifth Annual Report, Industrial Education.* Washington, D.C.: Government Printing Office, 1911.

U.S. Department of Health, Education, and Welfare. "Education for a Changing World of Work," Report of Consultants on Vocational Education, 1963.

U.S. Report of the Commission on National Aid to Vocational Education. Washington, D.C.: Government Printing Office, 1914.

United States Senate, Notes and Working Papers Concerning the Administration of Programs Authorized Under Vocational Education Act of 1963. Prepared for Subcommittee on Education of the Committee on Labor and Public Welfare. Washington, D.C.: Government Printing Office, March 1968.

U.S. *Senate Documents.* No. 936, Vol. XL, 62nd Cong., 2nd Sess., 1911–12.

Van Cleave, James W. "Industrial Education from the Standpoint of the Manufacturer," National Society for the Promotion of Industrial Education *Bulletin,* No. 5 (April 1908).

Van Hise, Charles R. *The Conservation of Natural Resources in the United States,* New York: Macmillan, 1910.

Van Worst, Mrs. John. *The Cry of the Children:* A Study of Child-Labor. New York: Moffat, Yard, 1908.

Venn, Grant. "Learning Beyond the Classroom," *American Vocational Journal,* Vol. 42, No. 6 (September 1967).

_____. *Man, Education, and Work.* Washington D.C.: American Council on Education, 1964.

Veysey, Laurence R. *The Emergence of the American University.* Chicago: U. of Chicago Press, 1965.

"Vocational Education at the N.E.A.," *Industrial Arts Magazine,* Vol. 8, No. 9 (September 1919).

Walling, William English. *The Larger Aspects of Socialism.* New York: Macmillan, 1913.

Ward, Lester F. *Dynamic Sociology.* New York: Appleton, 1897.

Welter, Rush. *Popular Education and Democratic Thought in America.* New York: Columbia U. Press, 1962.

Wesley, Edgar B. *NEA: The First Hundred Years.* New York: Harper, 1957.

White, Dickson Andrew. *Autobiography.* New York: Century, 1905.

Whittemore, Richard. "Nicholas Murray Butler and the Teaching Profession," *History of Education Quarterly,* Vol. 1 (September 1961), pp. 22–37.

Wiebe, Robert H. *The Search for Order.* New York: Hill and Wang, 1967.

Wilson, James W., and Edward H., Lyons. *Work-Study College Programs:* Appraisal and Report of the Study of Cooperative Education. New York: Harper, Brothers, 1961.

Wilson, Woodrow. "A Liberal Education," *The Educator-Journal,* Vol. 8, No. 6 (February 1908), pp. 261–270.

Wirth, Arthur G. *John Dewey As Educator.* New York: Wiley, 1966.

Woelfel, Norman. *Molders of the American Mind.* New York: Columbia U. Press, 1933.

Woods, Robert A., and Albert J., Kennedy. *Handbook of Settlements.* New York: Russell Sage Foundation, 1911.

————. *The Settlement Horizon:* A National Estimate. New York: Russell Sage Foundation, 1922.

Woodward, Calvin M. "Manual, Industrial and Technical Education in the United States," *Report of the U.S. Commissioner of Education.* 1903.

————. *Manual Training in Education.* New York: Scribner, 1890.

————. *The Manual Training School.* Boston: Heath, 1887.

Wyllie, Irving J. *The Self-Made Man in America: The Myth of Rags to Riches.* New York: Free Press, 1954.

Young, Michael. *The Rise of the Meritocracy, 1870–2033: An Essay on Education and Equality.* Baltimore: Penguin Books, 1958.

Index

White, Andrew, 8
Wiebe, Robert H., 67
Williamson Free School of Mechanical Trades (Philadelphia), 17
Wirt, Henry, 71, 200
Wisconsin plan for vocational education, 38, 61
Woods, Robert, 71, 76, 80
Woodward, Calvin M., 10 ff.

Work, changes in nature of, 48–51
Workingmen's Parties, 43–46
Work-study plans, Fitchburg, Massachusetts, 38

Young, Ella Flagg, 76, 202, 212
Young, Michael, *The Rise of the Meritocracy*, 104
Youth discontents, 225